UNIVERSAL DEMOCRACY
(HOLOCRACY):
THE RULE BY ALL PARTIES

UNIVERSAL DEMOCRACY (HOLOCRACY): THE RULE BY ALL PARTIES

Olubadejo Olorunleke Banjoko

Spectrum Books Limited
Ibadan
Abuja • Benin City • Lagos • Owerri
www.spectrumbooksonline.com

Published by
Spectrum Books Limited
Spectrum House
Ring Road
PMB 5612
Ibadan, Nigeria
admin1@spectrumbooksonline.com

in association with
Safari Books (Export) Limited
1st Floor
17 Bond Street
St. Helier
Jersey JE2 3NP
Channel Islands
United Kingdom

Europe and USA Distributor
African Books Collective Ltd.
The Jam Factory
27 Park End Street
Oxford OX1, 1HU, UK

First published, 2004

ISBN: 978-029-417-1

Printed by: Evi-Coleman & Co.

DEDICATION

This book is dedicated to the glory of God.

CONTENTS

viii

PREFACE

Since I was young, happenings in the political arena had always bothered me. Many people tell us that the problem is in the political actors and not in the political systems. They say that politics or election into political office is a game like football or wrestling, where one party fights another and the winner takes all and the loser is expected to give the winner a handshake and congratulate him for his valour. In my spirit, I have always believed that that is not all there is to politics. Politics may indeed be a game to the extent that two or more political organisations compete with themselves for political offices. But that is not all there is to politics. Politics is not for entertainment or amusement or pleasure, as football is. It is not a pastime. It is serious business. The life, welfare and well-being of a whole.lot – may be billions of people – depend on it.

It must be accepted that politics is also about the representation of the people, and a great deal more. Everywhere one goes, especially in multicultural polities, people complain of being marginalised. If politics were merely a game, people would have no business complaining of marginalisation. They will have no business taking up arms against the government of the day. They will not risk their lives as rebels in their own country and live as refugees in other peoples' lands. Politics is indeed the life of the people. It is indeed representation among the people. It is the means for co-operative living among the people. It is indeed inclusive and fair competition among political parties and equitable representation in government of the different and various groups of the people in a country. The list is unending. The problem seems more systemic than otherwise. That is the evidence of history from time immemorial to the present day. It is high time we thought twice about the system by which we govern ourselves. That type of thought is what gave birth to this book.

The book is in four parts. The first part is the preamble and comprises the first three chapters. Chapter one is the introduction that surveys what political thinkers and writers have said about political systems over the centuries. Chapter two discusses the objectives of the book and the methodology to achieve them. Chapter three looks at ramifications of democracy and identifies 'Universal Democracy', nicknamed HOLOCRACY.

Part two establishes or identifies the so-called twenty principles of Universal Democracy and consists of chapters four to twenty-four. Chapters four to fifteen discuss the so-called twelve principles of political liberty while chapters sixteen to twenty discuss the so-called five principles of equality of political rights; and chapters twenty-one to twenty-three, the so-called three principles of political decision-making by consensus or majority will. Chapter twenty-four comprises brief summaries of the so-called twenty principles to facilitate their quick reference by the reader.

Part three deals with the institutions and structures of Universal Democracy. It comprises chapters twenty-five to twenty-nine. Chapter twenty-five discusses Political Parties; chapter twenty-six, the Legislature; chapter twenty-seven, the Executive; chapter twenty-eight, the Judiciary; and chapter twenty-nine, Elections and Electoral Systems.

Part four is the summary of the book. It consists of only chapter thirty, which attempts, as an example, to draw together in a form or system of government the concepts, principles, institutions and structures of Universal Democracy that have been discussed in the book.

Rev. (Dr.) Olubadejo Olorunleke Banjoko, *Ph.D., Dip. Th.*

ACKNOWLEDGEMENTS

First, I thank God Almighty, who enabled me, an engineer and a cleric, to write this book on politics.

Next, I thank all members of my family, from my wife Titi, who patiently and encouragingly bore my absence from her during the writing of the book; to my children, Femi, Toun, Bola, Funke and Ope-Oluwa, all of whom spent hours on end in the typing of the manuscript.

Finally, I am grateful to numerous other people, including Mr. Remi Akinoso, Dr T.A. Ibidapo and Professor Déle Osibanjo, who in one way or another contributed to the production of this book.

PART ONE

Preamble

1

INTRODUCTION

The whole world has long been aware that partial or unequal representation of the citizens in government is incompatible with human
nature. It causes tension in the society and leads to government
instability and therefore authoritarian rule. Representation in government
means one's mandataries – that is, one's representatives or choice
cultural/ethnic/geographical constituency and selected political party
or agents/choices – participate (i.e. hold political office) in government.
Equal representation means one's or a group's representative(s) hold the
same number and types of political offices as do the representative(s)
of any other citizen or group. This may be either within or over
periods of rule or both. For example, Harold J. Laski, in his book, *A
Grammar of Politics* (p.27), stressed the need for a universal share in
government to avoid tension in the society.

> The purpose of the State affects each alike in its working, and its
> performance is therefore of equal interest to each. This has been
> the obvious lesson of history. Classes excluded from a share in
> power have always been classes excluded from a share in benefits.
> The limitation in the number of those upon whom social good is
> conferred, whose personality, that is to say, finds satisfaction in
> the working of political institutions, has always meant, in the
> end, an assault upon the foundations of the State by those
> excluded from its direction. For the identity of men's nature
> makes them need a common minimum of satisfaction for their
> wants. The implication of that common minimum is a share in
> power that they may protect the fulfilment of their desires.

3

The demand has also been well articulated that, to avoid tension, the system of power in the society should be built upon the similarities between men. For example, the Declaration of the Rights of Man drawn up by the French Revolutionaries in 1789 proclaimed the doctrine of political equality with religious fervour: 'Men are born, and always continue, free and equal in respect of their rights.' Also, Appadorai wrote that Aristotle studied the history of 158 constitutions and revolutions before his day. From the study, Aristotle could formulate that 'the most general cause for revolutionary movements was the craving of men for equality; and their best preventive, the principle of the mean.' The *Encyclopaedia of the Social Science Vol. V* also stressed the need for political equality in the following words:

> Of the permanence of this demand there can be no doubt; at the very dawn of political science Aristotle insisted that its denial was the main cause of revolutions. Just as the history of the State can perhaps be most effectively written in terms of the expanding claims of the common man upon the results of its effort; so the development of the realisation of equality is the clue to the problem of democracy.

Furthermore, in the concluding part of an article titled 'Who Gets What in Nigeria? The Root of Inequality and Exploitation', a Nigerian magazine, *The Analyst* (Volume 3 · Number 3, 1988), emphasised the need for universal and equal representation of the citizens in their government to solve the problems of Nigeria's incessant political instability:

> The greatest source of national friction is the issue of controlling state administration and all the benefits it confers. Appointments to various national institutions have tended to be the main source of disharmony and the basis for whipping up communal support. Democratic representation of all Nigerians in the affairs of the federation is the surest path to solving such a problem. The efforts at quota, federal character, etc., are all formulae designed to address this problem. Let it be fully understood that participation in national affairs is the only way for being part of it. The argument against representation is usually based on the

abstraction of merit from its political and social context. The major merit in a federal and democratic set-up is participatory and proportional representation and there is no reason why this cannot be done on the basis of professional competence in Nigeria today. The extensive deepening and entrenchment of democracy in our national affairs means more than the act of voting. It also embodies individual and group rights as well as their participation in national affairs.

However, the two existing forms of democratic representative government, the parliamentary system and the presidential system, are rules of exclusion and inequality because they lack universal and equal representation of the citizens in the rulers. They are based upon majority representation. This, as the name implies, gives power to the majority partisan and/or cultural groups of a country to the exclusion of the minority groups.

To the so-called minority partisan and cultural groups in a culturally heterogeneous country, self-rule does not mean rule by themselves along with others. Rather, it means rule 'by other partisan groups and cultural communities without them. Under majority rule, or the parliamentary and presidential systems, self-rule has a double meaning: it means two different things to two different groups of people in the same country. Its meaning to the majority groups in the country is different from the meaning it has to the minority groups in the country.

To the majority group, it means rule by their kith and kin but to the minority group, it means rule by others – the majority groups – not by themselves. It means rule not by their kith and kin but by the kith and kin of others above and without them, not along with them. In majority rule systems, therefore, the minority groups are second-rate citizens in their own country. They are subject to the rule of others over them. It is little wonder therefore that the Croats in former Yugoslavia wanted to be separated from the Serbs. The Ibos, the Yorubas, the Tivs, etc., in Nigeria also want to have a taste of power.

The destabilising effects of rule of exclusion and inequality are not easily discernible in most of the West European countries. This is perhaps because of their relative cultural homogeneity, geographical isolation and their hereditary monarchs. All these factors, Rhodee *et al* have noted, work in the direction of national identity, common purpose and majority rule. Nevertheless, the destabilising effects are still there and can be seen if carefully observed. For example, many writers erroneously attribute the government instability usually associated with coalition governments to the use of multiple party systems or the proportional representation system. It is in fact due to rule of exclusion and inequality in the executive arm of government.

Italy has an average of about one government every (other) year since the Second World War. This high turnover of government is due to rule of exclusion and inequality and not to the use of proportional representation as wrongly believed. Such governmental instability is unknown in Switzerland where there are many political parties. This is because Switzerland has an arrangement close to universal and equal representation of the citizens in the executive arm of government. In Switzerland, the members of the executive are elected not only from different party groups but from party groups fundamentally opposed to each other (Brooks p.127).

Also, the offices of the President and Vice-President are rotated yearly among the partisan groups or linguistic groups. Authoritarian rule in a mild form is also discernible in the West. For example, in 1978, in its Fifth Republic, France had to revert to 'Bonapartism or strongman rule' to end the threat of a military coup (Jacobsen and Lipman p.143).

Moreover, the lack of separation of legislative, executive and judicial powers that is characteristic of the parliamentary system of government is somehow authoritarian, for as the American Classic, The Federalist (1788), Essay XLVII, said:

> The accumulation of all powers, legislative, executive and judiciary, in the same hands, whether of one, a few, or many, and whether hereditary, self-appointed, or elective, may justly be pronounced the very definition of tyranny.

The parliamentary system concentrates legislative power and executive power in the hands of the majority party or majority coalition. There is majority tyranny in majority rule.

The destabilising effects of rule of exclusion and inequality are pronounced in culturally heterogeneous states, which lack a natural basis for national identity or a common purpose. In such states, rules of exclusion and inequality often reinforce 'those longstanding culture cleavages that had divided the state into many nations', using the words of Rodee *et al*. The political instability and unrest in Lebanon, Sudan, Ghana, Benin Republic, Nigeria, Northern Ireland, Liberia, Mali, Burundi, Congo and in other parts of the world in recent times have their roots in majority representative systems or rules of exclusion and inequality. So also are the authoritarian regimes in USSR, Cuba and China, all culturally heterogeneous countries that could not keep together under the Western form of democracy. They have to maintain their own form of rule of exclusion and inequality by rigid control and forced subservient obedience to authority. It is noteworthy that USSR, Yugoslavia and Czechoslovakia eventually had to break up.

Rodee, Anderson, Christol and Greene (1983) have explained the relative political stability in the USA compared with other states of similar heterogeneity of their people as follows:

> In the critical stages of political and economic development in the United States, politics has been the almost exclusive affair of political elite who are white, protestant, and whose native language was English. This helps to explain a large part of the political stability, in an evolving democratic context, that distinguishes United States politics from the politics of much of the rest of the world. (p. 316)

However, the likes of 'unelectable' Jesse Jackson may cause problems for the USA in future if the rule of exclusion and inequality there continues. Rodee, Anderson, Christol and Greene (1983) (p.316) have also noted that the continued 'failure of the Republicans to capture significant support from Black and Hispanic voters might cause problems in the future, however, rendering United States national politics more a case of culture conflict than it has been in the past'. Some writers have even described the presidential system as a form of authoritarian rule and constitutional monarchy.

Rodee *et al* have aptly summarised the political instability and move to authoritarian rule in Africa, where 'territorial boundaries drawn by European imperialism reflected the economic and political interests, the military and administrative capabilities of the European powers, not the essential tribal characteristics of African society'. They wrote:

> Since the late 1950s, Africa has been devastated by eleven wars, at least a dozen chiefs of state have been assassinated, and there have been more than fifty *coups d'etat*. At least five million Africans today live unsettled and uncertain lives of refugees. There are fourteen one-party dictatorships, while military elite rule in an additional twenty black African states. Political instability, authoritarian politics. (p. 296-7)

The case of Nigeria typifies the general situation of the new states. Chuba Okadigbo in *Power and Leadership in Nigeria* (p.1) wrote:

> In the short span of twenty-five years (1960-1985) since independence (in 1960), Nigeria has experimented with parliamentary, military, presidential and again military governments and systems. There have been eight leaders of Nigerian national governments. Two of them were civilians, while six were soldiers. Three of them were assassinated. Now, Nigeria, with about 250 ethnic groups, is searching once more for a new political order, which will hopefully put a stop to the syndrome of political instability and its attendant economic morass.

In fact, the military regime of General Ibrahim Badamosi Babangida, unable to find a better alternative, decreed a two-party presidential system for Nigeria's Third Republic. However, an imposed two-party system, in which only one party is to rule, is a rule of exclusion and inequality. It is therefore unlikely to cause the much-desired political unity and stability in Nigeria. Even that imposed two-party system was prematurely aborted by its architect. Nigeria has since had to revert to a controlled multi-party presidential system for another trial. Indeed, the Oputa Panel of Enquiry that the ensuing Obasanjo government set up to investigate cases of abuse of the citizens' human rights brought out from the citizens feelings of deep-rooted structural injustice and political inequalities among the various nationalities of Nigeria that need to be genuinely addressed to ensure lasting peace and unity.

In the face of political unrest, *coups d'etat* and military regimes, many people have called for a new political system which would preferably 'be a final state of political equilibrium'. For instance, in a report carried by the *Daily Times* of Nigeria (on 23 April 1983 p.12) on a lecture titled 'Ethnicity, Social Cohesion and National Integration' at the National Institute of Policy and Strategic Studies in Kuru, Plateau State, Nigeria, Alhaji Shehu Musa, the then Secretary to the Nigerian Federal Government, attacked the rule of exclusion in the following words:

> It may, perhaps, be necessary to re-examine the system by which we govern ourselves. We need not sheepishly copy the American, British or any foreign model. We can definitely build our own system which in the light of our peculiar situation, ought to dwell more on consensus rather than the winner-takes-all system we have chosen to adopt from foreign lands whose culture, norms, values, traditions and beliefs are far different from ours.

Professor Peter Harris also called for a greatly modified 'western institutional democracy' for new states:

> In a world which appears to be increasingly unable to solve its political problems, and which so often cheerfully hands political power to soldiers in preference to corrupt or semi-corrupt politicians, there must still remain an ideal to which politics will return, perhaps after crippling economic crises, or after the soldiers retire, or after a particular prince or president-turned-tyrant dies or is removed. What is this ideal? The prospect would appear to be contained in the concept of democracy, however vague. But such an ideal needs no longer be referred to as democracy. It might just as well be liberty, equality, fraternity,

justice or even patriotism ... We are suggesting, therefore, that a great deal of modification is necessary before western institutional democracy can become appropriate for the new states.

A leading article in *The Times* of London of 17 August, 1970 concluded an examination of the many Asians as follows:

> It is time Asia was released from the flat western stereotypes of the last century. The continent is not one, unified by poverty. It is not in accordance with any of the current political-economic categories of western thinking. Every part has its own distinctive past and its own different present, and the parts should be studied and valued and treated for what they are.

Commenting on this conclusion, Professor Peter Harris wrote that these words are so true for Asia (and also for Africa) that they would be regarded by many as truisms. There is a danger, he said, that one might conclude that no general statements at all should be made about democracy in Asia since everything there is so relative. However, it would be wrong for Africans and Asians to refrain from trying to establish in some degree, if not precisely, what democracy is supposed to be.

The author not only agrees with Professor Harris that Africans and Asians need to establish what democracy is supposed to be but also believes that the whole world needs to establish, and precisely too, what democracy is supposed to be. There is much tension in the world today. New states move unsatisfactorily and helplessly from one form of majority rule system to another, with consequent but avoidable untold sufferings to their peoples. There is therefore an urgent need for a form of government that is in consonance with human nature and with the social ideals of individual liberty and equality generally associated with democracy.

However, it appears that this may be a very difficult task, if not an impossible one, for most political scientists to achieve, since they are already subsumed in the existing order of things. For example, Peter Harris (p.229) wrote that:

... there is ... an implied value judgement contained in many American textbooks on history, international relations and law, that the American version of democracy is the epitome of political wisdom and maturity.

Thus, the largely unstated assumption of liberal political development theorists like Almond and Powell seemed to be that political development was a process whereby liberal – democratic political systems on the lines of the United States — one might say an idealised model of the United States — would necessarily emerge. Moreover, the concern of others like Huntington for political order in the developing world is of little help. They appeared to hold that American policy should be directed to the creation within modernising countries of at least one strong non-communist political party, and that if such a party already existed and was in a dominant position, support of that party should be the keystone of policy.

In view of the above and as the author is not aware of any work going on presently on the establishment of a form of government based upon universal representative participation of the citizenry in the government, he has through the grace of God, taken up the challenge. This is in the fervent belief that it will help to alleviate the sufferings of millions of people in the world and contribute to bring peace, love and unity everywhere on the globe, including his own beloved country, Nigeria.

2

THE OBJECTIVES AND THE
METHODOLOGY USED

This chapter describes 'the objectives of the book and the methodology to achieve them.

Objectives

The main objective of this book is to find the form of political rule, a political framework, which will ensure universal and equal representation of the citizens in the rulers, both politically and culturally. The particular objective of the book is four-fold as follows:

1. Establishment of a political paradigm, through a definition of representative political democracy, to harmonise existing doctrines and form the basis of resolving the question of stable political institutions and structures.
2. Development of the principles of representative political democracy as defined in (1) above, and their standards of measurement.
3. Identification or establishment of political institutions or structures that are consistent with the principles in (2) above.
4. Development of a system of representative government that embodies the political institutions or structures in (3) above.

Methodology

What procedures are to be adopted for the achievement of the above objectives? Rodee, Anderson, Christol and Greene (1983), in an attempt to establish the 'characteristics of stable democracy', wrote among other things:

> Ideally, our study of the phenomena of politics would be structured by some conceptual equivalent of the physicist's speed of light, speed of sound, velocity of a falling body, specific density, or absolute zero. These are absolute standards of measurement. They are easily classified. Their characteristics and effects are observable. Their properties are quantifiable. And an infinite variety of physical phenomena have meaning as mathematical functions of these standards. In the study of politics, however, our inability to conceive of absolute standards of measurement requires us to fall back on an alternative strategy for advancing our understanding: *comparison*. Much of what we think we know about politics is the result of systematic comparison of one aspect of the political process with another, of one type of government with another, of one group of countries that typified some political characteristic (such as stability, or democracy) with another group of countries that typify an alternative or opposite characteristic (such as instability or authoritarianism). In the study of politics, there are no parallels to the sudden sweeping insights that marked the scientific contributions of Galileo, Kepler, Newton, or Einstein. (p. 271-2)

I do not agree that the strategy of comparison is a scientific enough approach for this book. This empirical approach, the type of which Sir Karl Popper (1945, 1962) has called the 'bucket' theory of knowledge, attempts to induce a general theory from observations of particular events. I feel that by so doing, we have already constrained ourselves as the particular events may be obeying different theories. Two examples will help to illustrate this point.

First, Rodee, Anderson, Christol and Greene (1983) had concluded from their study of comparative politics that 'it is very difficult to maintain political stability and to build democratic institutions in societies that are marked by major culture cleavage', thereby associating culture cleavage with political instability and authoritarianism. This conclusion is inevitable, within the context of comparative politics, that is, when one considers politics in some European countries, whose people are of high cultural heterogeneity, and in Africa, where the territorial boundaries drawn 'by European imperialism reflected the economic and political interests, the military and administrative capabilities, of the European powers, not the essential tribal characteristics of African society', with politics in some relatively culturally homogeneous and technologically advanced countries.

However, the conclusion is based on some assumptions: that the political institutions in those countries are truly democratic, and that they are suitable for countries with or without major cultural cleavage. But are these assumptions true? Are the political institutions really democratic? Are they suitable for countries with (major) cultural cleavage? Is it not possible that these countries with major cultural cleavage provide an acid test for the suitability of the political institutions in such situations? Is it not probable that the difficulty to maintain political stability in those countries is due to the unsuitability or insufficiency of the political institutions being used rather than to the countries' cultural cleavages per se?

Secondly, comparative politics associates stable democracy with high-levels of literacy, advanced economic development and a large middle class, and associates underdevelopment with authoritarian politics. As a Yorubaman in underdeveloped Nigeria, I find this conclusion difficult to swallow. For a long time, kings have governed many towns in Yorubaland. Each town has about four or five ruling houses to provide the king, and succession to the throne has always been based on rotation among the ruling houses, which, in Athenian direct democracy discussed in chapter 3, is a democratic element.

This system has operated for centuries in these towns and has been greeted with peace among the ruling houses and stability within the towns ever since, even though the societies still remain underdeveloped. This experience continues to ring a bell in me that whether a society is developed or underdeveloped, whether it is cleavage-ridden or not, it must have a government and that that government can be stable if it is democratic, if it is based on the right of all the people – and that includes all the cleavage groups if they exist – to participate in government on equal basis.

These examples make me feel that comparative politics should be rejected for its alternative – politics based on absolute standards of measurement. This uses what Popper has called the 'search light' theory of knowledge. The *Concise Oxford Dictionary* (1982 edition) defines science as 'systematic and formulated knowledge'. As Bernard, M. C. (1865) and later Sir Karl Popper (1945, 1962) supported by Professor Davies (1973) have pointed out:

> Science is much more than a mere 'body of facts'; it is a collection of data from experiments and observations, the collection having been assembled according to collectors' interests and points of view. These are determined by preconceived ideas which, when crystallised in the mind in potentially experimental terms, are called scientific theories. With some theory in mind, we select from the infinite variety of possible observations and experiments those that are relevant to this theory. But we do not select only such facts as are in accord with the theory; we (or our scientific rivals) are prepared to find experimental results which may show a flaw in the theory, so that it must be modified, or abandoned in favour of a better theory. (Davies (1973) p. 2)

If politics is a science, and science is systematic and formulated knowledge based on preconceived ideas, then in the study of politics, there should be 'parallels to the sudden and sweeping insights that marked the scientific contributions of Galileo, Kepler, Newton, or Einstein'. In the study of political science, it should be possible, with God's help, to conceive of absolute standards of measurement which are easily classified, whose characteristics and effects are observable, and whose properties are quantifiable.

Therefore, in achieving the objectives stated above, I prefer to go by the method of finding absolute standards of measurement, using deductive techniques or systems that are based on postulates, accepted concepts or assumptions. For any deductive system, we must begin with certain undefined terms and certain accepted statements or assumptions indicating the properties which we want the undefined concept to have. Such statements are called axioms or postulates. The axioms are statements we assume to be true. Using the undefined terms and the set of axioms concerning them, we can derive further statements about the undefined terms by using the laws of logic.

A distinguishing characteristic of a deductive system is that, if the axioms are accepted and the method of reasoning is valid, then the theorems that are proved must also be accepted, because we can argue soundly from true premises to true conclusions, from false premises to true conclusions, or from false premises to false conclusions, but false conclusions cannot be obtained from true premises.

This book makes extensive use of deductive logic, making deductions and predictions from premises or theories and criteria that are informed by intuition, by rational thinking and by data from observations and from historical and comparative methods of data collection and analysis. It also makes use of simple mathematics and adopts the method of precise definition of terms.

3

WHAT IS DEMOCRACY?

This chapter looks at the ramifications of democracy and identifies 'True Representative Political Democracy', which it calls 'Universal Democracy', nicknamed HOLOCRACY.

Definition of Political Democracy

As Charles Blitzev of the American Council of Learned Societies wrote in *New Age Encyclopedia*, few words on the modern political lexicon are used more often or more confusingly than 'democracy', and so the meaning of the word must be sought in its origins and history rather than in its current usage.

The writings of both Plato and Aristotle show clear evidence that from the very beginning, in the time of Ancient Greece, the term 'democracy' has been used in two quite distinct though related senses: a general sociological meaning and a specific political meaning. In the first sense democracy is a way of life and in the second sense it is a form of government, an ordering of public offices.

As a way of life, democracy is based on the conviction that all people are valuable as individuals, have inalienable rights among which are life, liberty, property, security and the pursuit of happiness, and that these rights must be defended and preserved (United Nations Universal Declaration of Human Rights). Sociological or social democracy is, in the words of *New Age Encyclopedia* (Vol. 5, p.522), a society of free and equal citizens; a society in which the worth of each individual is recognised and cherished irrespective of sex, tribe, ethnic grouping or religion; a society unmarked by special privileges of birth, wealth, status, profession, etc.

Political democracy is the second sense in which democracy is used. This book is primarily concerned with political democracy. As a form of government based upon social democracy in its composition, political democracy has not been precisely defined. Here are some of the definitions that have been given by various writers.

1. 'A form of government in which the citizens exercise the governing power either directly or through their elected representatives who may be changed or re-elected periodically' (Uchenna Nwankwò).

2. 'A system of government under which the people exercise the governing power either directly or through representatives periodically elected by themselves' (A. Appadorai).

3. 'Government by all the people, direct or representative' (*Concise Oxford Dictionary*, 1982 edition).

4. 'A system of government usually involving freedom of the individual in various aspects of political life, equality among citizens, justice in the relations between the people and the government and the participation of the people in choosing those in government' (Okwudiba Nnoli).

5. 'Popular control, or control by the vast majority of the inhabitants of a country' (Peter Harris).

6. 'Government of the people, by the people, for the people' (American President, Abraham Lincoln).

7. 'A regime in which those who govern are chosen by those who are governed by means of free open elections' (Professor Duverger).

8. 'Institutional arrangement(s) for arriving at political decisions in which individuals acquire the power to decide by means of a competitive struggle for the peoples' vote' (Professor Schumpeter).

9. '(Country with principles of) government in which all adult citizens share through their elected representatives' (*Oxford*

Advanced Learner's Dictionary of Current English, 1974 edition, 1980 impression).

10. '(Country with) government which encourages and allows right of citizenship such as freedom of speech, religion, opinion and association, the assertion of the rule of law, majority rule, accompanied by respect for the rights of minorities' (*Oxford Advanced Learner's Dictionary of Current English*, 1979 Edition, 1980 impression).

11. 'A form of government in which political power is regularly exercised by the citizenry' (*New Age Encyclopedia* Vol.1 p.522).

12. 'That form of government in which the ruling power of a state is legally vested not in any particular class or classes but in the members of a community as a whole' (A.Appadorai, p. 187).

13. '(Society in which there is) treatment of each other by citizens as equals and absence of class or feelings'. (*Oxford Advanced Learner's Dictionary of Current English*, 1974 Edition, 1980 impression.)

14. 'The collective determination of law and policy by a people, equal in citizenship rights, who reach decisions after public debate by a procedure of majority rule.' (*Macmillan Students' Encyclopedia of Sociology.*)

It is obvious that a satisfactory definition of political democracy is difficult to obtain from such a list of diverse definitions as this. However, a satisfactory definition will emerge from these definitions if we remember two things. First, that political democracy, as a form of government, is a means to achieve social democracy. And second, that social democracy is concerned with individual freedom or liberty and equality (Article 1 of Universal Declaration of Human Rights). Laski, in *A Grammar of Politics* (Chapters III & IV), classifies the content of necessary individual liberty under three headings: private or civil liberty, political liberty and economic liberty. Private or civil liberty consists of the rights and privileges that the State creates and protects for its subjects (R.G. Gettell, Political Science, p.148). It is 'the opportunity to exercise freedom of choice in those areas of life where the results of one's efforts are mainly personal to oneself ' e.g. freedom of religion, personal safety, right to life, property etc., (Appadorai p.69). Political liberty is the right of an individual (a citizen) to take part in the affairs of the state, i.e. the right of a citizen to a share in the government of the state. Economic liberty is the 'security and the opportunity to find reasonable significance in the earning of one's daily bread' (Appadorai p.69).

Equality has also been classified into civil equality, political equality and economic equality (Appadorai, p.87-89). Civil equality is 'equality before the law'. Political equality is equality, identity, or sameness in the share that the citizens of the state have in their government. Economic equality is the provision of adequate opportunities for all, 'an organisation of opportunities that no man's (or woman's) personality suffers frustration to the private benefits of others'. (Appadorai p.89).

Thus, social democracy is concerned with civil liberty and civil equality, political liberty and political equality, economic liberty and economic equality. It follows therefore that to achieve social democracy, political liberty and political equality must be achieved, among others. Therefore, a government that is to achieve social democracy must achieve political liberty and political equality among others. But political liberty and political equality are concerned with the constitution or composition of the government itself. Therefore, the starting point of the achievement of social democracy is the achievement of political liberty and political equality in the composition or organisation of the government that is to achieve the remaining elements of social democracy. It follows from this deduction that the government of the state must be based upon political liberty and political equality to achieve a social democratic state.

Political democracy can now be thought of as a form of government based upon individual political liberty and the political equality of the citizens. We can recap and move forward. Political liberty is the right of a citizen to a share in the government of the state. Moreover, political equality or equality of political right is the equality or sameness of the share which the citizens have in their government. Therefore, political democracy means a form of government in which all citizens have not only a share but also equal shares in the government of the state.

In other words, political democracy is the form of government in which all citizens are entitled not only to participation but also to equal participation. It is a government by *all* the citizens and on the basis of their (political) equality. It can be concluded therefore that the definition given by *Concise Oxford Dictionary* 1982 edition that political democracy is 'government by *all* the people, direct or representative' is along the correct path, although inadequate or not full. It must be quickly added that political democracy is based also on a third factor: collective decision-making by consensus or by at least majority vote. It is clear that in a situation where many people will have to arrive at a decision, a decision-making method is necessary. Decision-making through discussion and consensus or at least majority vote of all persons concerned provides the answer.

As Jacobsen and Lipman (p.69) wrote, 'The decisions of the majority, though not infallible, should govern because they provide the only practical way of deciding what is just and for the best interest of society'. And according to Laski (p.35), the will of the state is 'the will which is adopted out of the conflict of myriad wills which contend with each other for the mastery of social forces. It is never deliberate in the sense that it is always determined by rational considerations. It is never single, in the sense that it derives from a unanimous agreement of those to whom it applies'. History shows that rational men through the ages have accepted this doctrine.

Political democracy is thus based upon three core concepts: political liberty, political equality and political consensus or collective decision-making by the will of the majority of all concerned. It may be defined as *government in which the citizens are universally entitled to equal participation and in which public policies are made on the basis of the will of at least a majority of the participating citizens.*

Political democracy can be direct or representative as discussed below.

Direct Political Democracy

This is a government in which all the citizens have a right to equal direct shares and in which public policies are made as the will of the majority of the participating citizens. The individual states of Ancient Greece, especially Athens, typified direct political democracy and dramatised its meaning. For the Athenians, political democracy meant the direct participation of the mass of the citizenry in the processes of government: all adult male citizens of Athens were expected to participate in person in government. Laws were made by vast popular assemblies, officials were chosen by lot and served for short periods on a rotating basis, even lawsuits were decided by direct vote after a theatrical trial. (*New Age Encyclopedia*, Volume 5, page 522).

It is clear from this short account that political democracy means the participation of all the people, without exception and on equal basis, in all the processes of government. The processes of government include the making and administering of public policy as well as the adjudication of law. Participation in all the processes of government including the executive, on equal basis is dramatised by the choosing of officials by lot, and their serving for short periods on rotating basis and by the participation of all citizens in law making, in law execution and in law adjudication. Decision making by the majority vote of all the participants was also the practice. It is the government of each man by all the society including himself, not by the rest or the majority of society without him.

The Athenian "Assembly, in which every citizen could take part, was the sovereign body in the state to decide national affairs, great and small. The opportunity for the citizen to take part in the executive and judicial administration of the state was considerable. Unlike in modern times, there was no permanent bureaucracy or judiciary who looked to the executive and the judicial work; these were undertaken for short periods by ordinary citizens." (Appadorai p. 187-8). The systems of lot and election, payment and short tenure of office ensured equal opportunity for all. On the authority of Aristotle, it has been reckoned, as written by A.J. Grant and by Aristotle that, excluding those employed on military duties, there were ten thousand officials in a state whose total number of citizens certainly did not amount to much more than twice that number. (However, W.W. Fowler arrived at a total of 1,900 officials out of an adult male population of about 30,000, i.e. not less than six per cent. But Fowler did not take into account the jurymen and others included by Aristotle in arriving at his total number). It is thus believed, as Appadorai (p. 188) wrote, that in practice 'every Athenian citizen probably held an official post of some sort once in his life;' and that 'very many must have held such posts many times; depending on how often they were available.

Modern Political Situation

The direct participation of the citizens in politics that is the hallmark of direct Athenian democracy was possible for three main reasons. Firstly, the territory and the number of citizens of a state were small. For example, it is reported that in describing the 'best possible' state, Plato fixed the proper number of citizens at exactly 5,040; and it was argued that the territory of a state should never be so large that a man could not walk across it between dawn and dusk. Secondly, the citizens' leisure was bought by the labour of tens of thousands of slaves. It has been estimated that in Athens a citizen population of roughly 30,000 was supported by the labour of some 100,000 slaves. Athenian democracy was a slave-owning democracy. Thirdly, individual life was less complex than in the modern time. Thus there was no need for specialisation then and so executive and judicial works could be undertaken for short periods by ordinary citizens.

However, in the modern world, the number of citizens in the country is so large (and composed of many social groups with overlapping membership) that it is practically impossible for all citizens to be in government. Also the territory is so big and the citizens' leisure so small (as most of the citizens have to engage directly in economic activities for sustenance of life) that it is impracticable for all citizens to effectively participate directly in government processes. Moreover, the need for specialisation has changed the nature of government. Whereas there was no bureaucracy in the Greek-States, there is nowadays a bureaucracy, which is filled on merit, and the (political) Executive, which is filled primarily on the basis of citizens' interests, caters for very much fewer posts. Thus government or public posts are classifiable into two main categories: political or elective posts and non-political or non-elective or bureaucratic posts.

A political office or post is taken to be a public office or post held primarily (i.e. before merit considerations) on the basis of the citizens' will and interests and the appointments to which is therefore necessarily based upon citizens' votes. Elective/political posts/offices are held for a fixed period of time, called a period of rule in this book. In this book, elective/political posts themselves are classified further into two types: partisan elective (or political) posts, which are those that are based upon both partisan and cultural considerations of the people, and non-partisan elective (or political) posts, which are those based upon only cultural considerations without partisan considerations. The non-partisan posts are therefore so called because their occupiers are supposed to be people who have not been involved in party politics.

By contrast, a non-political or bureaucratic post or office is defined as a public office held purely on personal merit, i.e. on the basis of the training, capacity, and the knowledge of the work to be done; the appointment to which is made by political or non-political officeholders following an open competition (supplemented by interviews when necessary) in order to reduce to a minimum the chances of personal favouritism. The tenure of office of a non-political officeholder is permanent and dissociated from the changes of government, as he holds office until the age of retirement, subject only to efficiency and good behaviour.

There is also the need for some minimum academic and professional qualifications for those individuals that will govern, i.e. those that will hold political posts. Moreover, men are endowed with different talents so that some persons have more ability or capability to govern or occupy certain political posts than others. Therefore, there is the need to have the best or most outstanding of the aspirants to govern.

In short, the modern society may rightly be described as a large number of citizens, each politically free or independent and equal to the other in political right. The citizens are in multifarious groups, with diverse and overlapping interests and goals that may be partisan (i.e. social, economic, ideological), ethnic (i.e. racial, linguistic, or tribal) and religious. They possess different governing capabilities related to age, sex, professional experience and natural endowments, and must govern themselves as a political entity (i.e. a polity) through a relatively few partisan and non-partisan political posts of different types and numbers; the types and the number of each of post or office also being capable of varying over the years.

Representative Government

Under such circumstances where direct participation of all citizens in government is either impossible or undesirable because of their large number and because of the need to have the best or most outstanding of the aspiring citizens to govern, the idea of a representative government, a government run by the representatives of the people, emerged. Instead of every citizen having a right to participate in person in the government of the land, every citizen now has a right to participate in the government through representative(s), who can represent him, i.e. speak or act in government for or on behalf of him, as well as for many other citizens for the protection of their interests.

In other words, instead of every citizen having a right to a direct share in government, he now has a right to a representative share or a representation in government because he delegates his direct share in government to his representative(s). In this way, it is possible for those in government to be few because a representative can (be made to) represent as many citizens as necessary. It is also possible with this arrangement and under the appropriate conditions described elsewhere in this book, for those in government, i.e. the individual political officeholders, to be the best of the aspirants for the political posts because they can be selected based on their personal merits for the elective or political posts to be held.

In order to ensure that the electorate does not abandon its sovereignty to its representatives, such democratic devices or institutions like the *recall*, the *initiative* and the *referendum* are used (e.g. in some European states and several states of the United States of America) in conjunction with a representative government. The recall means the "calling back" of political officeholders before the end of their term, followed by the election of others to replace them. The initiative is the right of free private citizens to bring forward a proposal of a constitutional or legislative nature on any matter for the decision of the representative government and, if necessary, of the whole people. The referendum consists of the submission to the people, for approval or rejection, of a law passed by the government but against which an acceptable number or percentage of the people petition. These democratic institutions help to ensure that the fundamental human rights of the people, such as freedom, equality, justice, etc., are not subverted by a representative government and so are considered in this book as part and parcel of the concept of representative government.

True Representative Political Democracy (T.R.P.D.)

With the idea of a representative government goes the idea of representative political democracy in place of direct political democracy. Direct political democracy has been defined above as 'government in which all the citizens have a right to equal direct shares and in which public policies are made as the will of the majority of the participating citizens.'

The definition of representative political democracy will be derived from this definition by making the following substitutions. First, *'direct shares'* is replaced by 'representation' or 'representative shares'. Secondly, the *'will of the majority of the participating citizens'* is replaced by the 'will of the representatives of the majority of the participating citizens', since it is the representatives of the people, and not the people directly, who rule in a representative government and since what matters is the will of the participating citizens and not merely that of the representatives irrespective of the number of participating citizens represented. Thirdly '*the participating citizens*' is replaced by 'the voters in a general election to choose the political representatives'. Then the definition of representative political democracy is obtained from the definition of direct political democracy as:

> a representative government – government by the political representatives of the people – in which all the citizens have a right to equal representation or equal representative shares and in which public policies are made as the will of the representatives of the majority of the voters in a general election to choose the representatives.

It should be particularly noted that the 'will of the majority of the participating citizens' has been replaced by the 'will of the representatives of the majority of the voters' and not merely by the 'will of the majority of the representatives of the voters' because the '*will of the majority of the voters*' and not merely the 'will of the majority of the representatives' is what matters. This is so because analysis and historical evidence (see the Principle of Group or Corporate Representatives for Voters) have shown that, depending on the definition and method of selection of the political representatives, the 'majority of the representatives of the participating citizens' can actually be the 'representatives of the minority of the voters'.

That means that the second phrase, i.e. 'the will of the majority of the representatives of the voters' can actually turn out to be the 'will of the minority of the voters, which is in conflict with the concept of public policy being the '*will of the majority of the participating citizens (i.e. voters)*'. Therefore, since public policy will always be made by the will of the majority of the decision-makers, for example, the legislators, the use of the 'will of the representatives of the majority of the voters' means that true representative political democracy obtains only where the definition and method of selection of the political representatives are such that a majority of the decision-makers are actually the representatives of a majority of the participating citizens, who are the actual voters at a general election to choose the political representatives.

It should be remembered that the above definition rests on the four concepts of political liberty of the citizen, political equality of all citizens, decision-making by majority will (or political consensus) and the representation of the citizens in government, i.e. representative government.

It should also be remembered that, as earlier noted, the concept of a representative government does not and should not subvert the sovereignty or authority of the people, if the government is truly the people's government. Thus, the concept of democratic representation includes the right of the people to *recall*, if and when necessary, and replace the individual representatives or agents that they have chosen, the right of *initiative* of private citizen(s) outside government to bring forward for legislation by the representative government any proposal on *any* matter of public interest, and the necessity or compulsion for such a proposal that is not passed by the representative government to be submitted to the people, the general electorate, in a *referendum*, for approval or rejection.

This book will identify and develop, using rational thinking, logic and historical experience, the political principles and political institutions that are *simultaneously* consistent with all the four concepts of political democracy. In particular, the principles and institutions will be those that are consistent with the four concepts simultaneously and not those that are consistent with some of the four concepts while being inconsistent with the rest. This is the 'True Democratic' situation. It is the 'Rule by All Parties' situation. It is 'Universal Democracy'. It is here nicknamed **HOLOCRACY**.

PART TWO

The Principles of Universal Democracy (i.e. True Representative Political Democracy)

The next twenty chapters (four to twenty-three) discuss the principles that together define True Representative Political Democracy, as given above. The first twelve of the principles (chapters four to fifteen) are derivable from the democratic concepts of political liberty and representative government; the next five principles (chapters sixteen to twenty) rest squarely on the democratic concepts of equality of political rights and representative government, and the last three principles (chapters twenty-one to twenty-three) revolve round the democratic concepts of political consensus or decision-making by majority will and representative government. Chapter twenty-four gives a summary of each of the twenty principles or pillars of Universal Democracy for ease of reference.

It should be noted that some of the principles have been known in the political arena for a long time, even though the rest are the author's new development. Moreover, the concept of representation underlies all the twenty principles.

4

THE PRINCIPLE OF
SEPARATION OF POWERS

This is the principle that the three governmental powers, namely legislative, executive and judicial powers, should be exercised by separate branches or arms of government, with no overlapping membership. A branch or arm of government is here defined as any unit or department of government solely exercising the whole or a part of one of the three governmental powers – namely legislative or executive or judicial powers – and having no member holding political office in any other department of government.

This principle is arrived at from the following considerations which concern the political liberty of the citizenry. Governmental power expresses itself in three forms: legislation, administration and judicial decision. It is of prime importance to the theory of the organisation of (representative) government to determine whether, and to what extent, these powers should be combined in the same persons or body of persons, or should be entrusted to three separate agencies which are co-ordinate and mutually independent.

Bodin, a French writer, was the first to point out in *The Republic* (1576) that:

> To be at once legislator and judge is to mingle together justice and the prerogative of mercy, adherence to the law and arbitrary departure from it: If justice is not well administered, the litigating parties are not free enough, they are crushed by the authority of the sovereign.

Then Montesquieu clearly formulated the need for the separation of the three political powers:

> When the legislative and executive powers are united in the same person, or in the same body of magistrates, there can be no liberty; because apprehension may arise, lest the same monarch or senate should enact laws, to execute them in a tyrannical manner. (The Spirit of Laws (1748))

He continued:

> Again, there is no liberty, if the judicial power be not separated from the legislative and executive. Were it joined with the legislative, the life and liberty of the subject would be exposed to arbitrary control; for the judge will be then the legislator. Were it joined to the executive power, the judge might behave with violence and oppression. There would be an end of everything, were the same man or the same body, whether of the nobles or of the people, to exercise those three powers, that of enacting laws, that of executing the public resolutions, and of trying the causes of individuals.

Then in 1765, Blackstone, an English jurist, expressed similar views:

> In all tyrannical governments the supreme magistracy, or the right both of making and of enforcing the laws, is vested in one and the same man, or one and the same body of men; and wherever these two powers are united, there can be no public liberty. The magistrate may enact tyrannical laws, and execute them in a tyrannical manner, since he is possessed in quality of dispenser of justice with all the power which he as a legislator thinks proper to give himself.

> Were it (the judicial power) joined with the legislative, the life, liberty, and property of the subject would be in the hands of arbitrary judges, whose decisions would be then regulated only by their own opinions and not by any fundamental principles of law; which, though legislators may depart from, yet the judges are bound to observe. Were it joined with the executive, this union might soon be an overbalance for the legislature.

Finally, The Federalist (1788), an American classic, is another authoritative exposition of the theory of separation of power:

> The accumulation of all powers, legislative, executive, and judiciary, in the same hands, whether of one, a few, or many, and whether hereditary, self-appointed, or elective, may justly be pronounced the very definition of tyranny.

There has been much controversy among students of political science whether Montesquieu, the author of the theory (and others who followed him), contemplated an absolute or only a limited separation of the three powers. It has been argued that the sound opinion, as the Federalist pointed out, is that he did not mean that the three departments ought to have no partial agency in, or no control over, the act of each other. However, it appears to me from the quotations above that the only logical meaning of the theory is that the control of any two or more of the three departments should not be in the same hands, whether of one, a few, or many, and whether hereditary, self-appointed, or elective.

Those who make laws should not participate in their execution nor in their adjudication; those who execute laws should neither participate in their making nor in their adjudication; and those who adjudicate laws should not participate in their making or in their execution. It follows also that the same person should not hold political office in more than one branch/arm or sub-arm of government, as otherwise two or more governmental powers would be accumulated in the same hands and so havoc might be wrecked.

An important implication of this principle is that each branch of government should derive its powers direct from the mandates of the electorate and therefore not be under the control of any other branch by appointment, funds control or otherwise. It should be noted that any one of the three powers may be exercised by more than one branch or arm of government but no two of the three powers should be exercised by the same branch or arm of government and no two branches or arms of government must have overlapping political membership. Thus, for example, the legislature may have two arms: Lower House and Upper House, and the executive may have two sub-arms: the executive council and the general executive; but the legislature may not perform executive functions nor the executive, legislative functions.

In the parliamentary system of government, the cabinet (i.e. the executive) is part of the legislature as it sits in Parliament and takes full part in its deliberations. This seems to me to be a violation of this principle. However, in the presidential system, the executive power is separated from the legislative power. But in both the parliamentary and presidential systems the judicial power is often joined with the executive or legislative power or with both, as judges are appointed by nomination by the executive (e.g. Britain, the U.S.A., Australia) or election by the legislature (e.g. Switzerland) or nomination by the executive and confirmation by the legislature (e.g. Nigeria).

. Insinuations that many Nigerians do not believe that the judicial power is separated from the executive power can be seen in the following two passages. First, *The Guardian* of Nigeria (Friday 23 May 2003, page 2) reported that the Patriot, a group of renowned Nigerians led by Chief F.R.A. Williams, a legal luminary of international repute, opined on the tension that followed the Nigerian 2003 elections that it was not "a satisfactory solution to the crisis to say that anyone .ot satisfied with the conduct of the elections should go to the tribunal. Anyone who is knowledgeable about procedure before the tribunals will readily agree that there is a limit to which the machinery of the tribunals can cope with massive riggings at gubernatorial or presidential elections. . . ". Secondly, the *Sunday Tribune* of Nigeria (8 June 2003, page 2) reported that Arewa Youth Consultative Forum (AYCF), a vocal interest group from the Northern part of Nigeria, wrote to President Obasanjo on 2 June 2003 as follows (among other things): "While Otunba Iyiola Omisore was charged for murder of Chief Bola Ige, Lt. Gen. Bamaiyi, Al-Mustapha and others were charged for the murder of Kudirat Abiola and attempted murder of Chief Alex Ibru, we state in clear terms that it would amount to a great injustice to grant bail to Otunba Iyiola Omisore and refuse that of

Gen. Bamaiyi and others since all were charged for a similar offence. . . We hold that Nigeria is a country founded on the principle of justice, equity and fair play and having applied these principles to Otunba Iyiola Omisore's case, the federal government should extend the same principle to bear on the case of Lt. Gen. Bamaiyi and others as strict continued incarceration of these men will aggravate the greater part of the Northern psyche to be negative in their thinking considering the bail granted to Otunba Iyiola Omisore for his alleged involvement in the assassination of the former Minister of Justice, Chief Bola Ige while in office". (Otunba Iyiola Omisore, like Chief Bola Ige, Mrs Kudirat Abiola and President Obasanjo, is Yoruba from South-Western Nigeria but Lt. Gen. Ishaya Bamaiyi and Al-Mustapha are from Northern Nigeria).

In true representative political democracy (T.R.P.D.), justice must be seen to be well-administered. The decisions of the judges must be (seen to be) regulated only by fundamental principles of law that they are bound to observe and not by the arbitrary opinions or wishes of either themselves or any officers of government however highly-placed. Otherwise, the litigating parties are not free enough and would be crushed by the authority of those in power. The decisions of the judges cannot be seen to be always regulated only by fundamental principles of law where the executive or the legislature or both in one way or another appoint the judges.

The author believes that the insinuations in all the above are caused mainly because the judicial power is not (seen to be) truly separated from the executive power in Nigeria, making the judiciary to look like an arm of government that President Obasanjo and his PDP (or any other persons and parties in power) can manipulate as they wish. The earlier the country and others like it reverse the situation (along the lines given in this book) the better, as otherwise the life and liberty of the people, high and low, would be (thought to be) exposed to arbitrary control, fairness and justice could (be thought to) elude the populace, politics might reinforce culture cleavages, and disunity and instability may ensue or thrive.

5

THE PRINCIPLE OF UNIVERSAL REPRESENTATION OF VOTERS

This is the principle that *every* citizen has a right to (cultural and partisan) representation in government through his/her personal choice made by voting. The principle stems from the definition of representative political democracy that is given in chapter 3, as the following analysis shows.

First, that every citizen has a right to a share in government through representative(s) follows directly from the definition of representative political democracy as 'a representative government in which *all* the citizens have a right to ... representation or ... representative shares...' If *all* the citizens have a right to representation or representative shares in a representative government – i.e. a government run by the representatives of the people – then *every* citizen has a right to a share in government through representative(s). A representative in government is a person chosen to act or speak or be a symbol of belonging in government for those outside it. The representative may be an individual or a corporate body. It is shown by the principle of Group Representatives for Voters that the political representative(s) of a citizen is/(are) a corporate person or persons and not an individual person. The representation in government of those to be represented takes place when their representatives actually participate in government, i.e. hold political office in government, since government is run through political posts or offices. A citizen is therefore represented

36

in government when his/her representative(s) participate(s) (i.e. hold(s) political office) in government.

Next, there is a need for clarification about who chooses a citizen's political representative(s). It is not enough for a citizen to be just one of those to be acted or spoken for by a representative in government for that representative to qualify as the citizen's representative. Rather, it is essential for a citizen's political representative – the (corporate) person who participates in government on his/her behalf – to be the citizen's choice.

This fact is established by the democratic concepts of political liberty and political equality as the following analysis shows. A citizen's representative in government must be chosen by someone – either himself or another person. If a citizen's representative in government is to be chosen by another person, then the citizen has no political freedom, i.e. is not free from the control of others, and so the concept of the political liberty of the citizenry, the very basis for the citizen's right to participation in government through representative(s), is negated. Moreover, no citizen would have the right to have a representative in government who is appointed or elected by himself, since the concept of the political equality of the citizens implies that if a citizen has no right to appoint his representative in government, then all the other citizens also must have no right to appoint theirs and vice versa.

Therefore, it is also inconsistent with the concept of the political equality for some citizens to be represented in government by representatives appointed by themselves while the other citizens are purportedly represented in government by representatives appointed by others. This is in addition to the violation of the political liberty of the citizens who do not choose their representatives in government by themselves.

On the other hand, a system whereby every citizen has representative(s) in government who is/(are) selected by the citizen himself means that every citizen has political freedom. It also means that all the citizens have an equal right in the selection of their representatives in government. Thus, a system whereby every citizen's representative in government is his personal choice is consistent with both the concepts of the political liberty and political equality of all citizens and hence with Universal Democracy. Therefore, the concepts of the political liberty and political equality of all citizens imply that a citizen is entitled to representative(s) in government who is/(are) his personal choice.

If voting at a general election, as is globally the practice nowadays, is taken to be the means for a citizen who has a share in government through his representative(s) to choose such political representative(s), then it follows that by voting at a general election to choose his political representative(s), the citizen confers on his chosen representative(s) the right for the representative, if partisan, to represent, i.e. act or speak for, him in government or, if non-partisan, at least to serve as his symbol of belonging.

Without the vote or consent of the citizen to be represented so conferred, no one has the right or the obligation in government, either expressly or implicitly, to be the political representative of the citizen. Therefore, the representation of a citizen in government means that the representative(s) whom the citizen has chosen, elected or voted for, is/(are) in government. In other words, a citizen has a representative share in government when his chosen representative(s), for whom he has personally voted, for the purpose, participate(s) in government.

Therefore, the definition of representative political democracy as 'a representative government in which all the citizens have a right to ... representation or ... representative shares...' implies that all the citizens have a right to have their individually or personally chosen representatives participate in government. In other words, every citizen has a right to have his chosen representative(s) – the (corporate) person(s) whom he has personally appointed or voted for – to participate in government.

This conclusion means that *every* citizen who votes in an election so as to be represented should actually be represented by having his/her chosen representative(s) literally participating in government. In other words, representative political democracy implies *universal representation* of the voters. This means that, subject to consistency with the requirements of the other democratic principles, all the political posts/offices in the branch or branches or arms of government where the people are supposed to be represented by a general representation election should be shared among or allocated to *all* the prospective representatives who receive votes, because they are all the choices of the people. That is to say, that there should be inclusive, not eliminative, competition among the prospective representatives in a general representation election.

There is a competition among the prospective representatives because they will receive political posts, in quantity and in quality, according to the number of votes they win, as discussed under the principles of equality of political rights. The competition is inclusive because all the prospective representatives, not just one or few or majority of them, may receive political posts. It should be noted that the general election under reference is the one meant for the representation of the voters (i.e. the participating citizens in the definition of political democracy). And this should be distinguished from the merit elections, which are meant for electing individuals by a majority vote into political posts on their personal merits for the posts to be occupied and which are not meant for the representation of voters. The election under reference is the one in which voting is on the basis of the voters' own (cultural and partisan) interests and not just on the personal merits of the individual candidates for political office. And this is called the General Universal Representation Election (GURE) as discussed under the principle of Separation of Elections.

According to the principle of Homogeneity of Candidates, partisan and cultural differences are factors that should be represented and not left to competition. Moreover, according to the principle of Limited Separation of Representation, there must be representation only on the basis of cultural/geographical constituencies and political parties for any branch or arm of government at any level of government. The implication of all this with respect to the present principle is that there should be universal representation of the voters in terms of their partisan and cultural cleavages, i.e. there should be universal partisan and universal cultural representation of the voters.

This means that there should be no eliminative competition between cultural constituencies or between political parties for political posts. Rather, there should be the sharing of the political posts among all the cultural constituencies and among all the political parties, such that each cultural constituency and each political party will hold political office in every branch of government in every period of rule if possible, or at regular intervals of a reasonable number of periods of rule if the totality of the political posts is scarce (because the posts are few or because the alternative groups are too many) and if representation in rotation over periods of rule is feasible among the alternative groups. A period of rule is taken to be the optimum length of time for a representative to hold political office and is the fixed life of a government.

Now, according to the principle of Rotation of a Scarce Political Post Type, representation of voters by a scarce political post type in rotation over periods of rule is feasible among alternative cultural/geographical groups but not among alternative partisan groups.

Thus, whatever the number of alternative cultural/ethnic groups, the alternative groups' universal participation in government or in a particular branch or arm of government through the available number of political posts, however few, (i.e. the sharing of the posts among all of them), can still be achieved satisfactorily - over periods of rule if not within a period of rule, so long as the cycle of rotation is not such that would give the impression of permanent exclusion from (a branch of) government or of inequitable representation of the alternative groups in government. On the other hand, all political associations that receive votes in the General Universal Representation Election for a period of rule must receive political posts in that period of rule, if possible, to become political parties. If some of the political organisations would have been unable to receive political posts because their votes are insufficient, they must combine with themselves and/or with those that have sufficient votes, so that all the resulting political parties will receive political posts in the period of rule.

One very important implication of this principle is that the majority concept is not involved in the selection of the political representatives of the people because all voting citizens and not merely some of them should be represented. This is in line with the observation that a citizen is an individual and not a multitude, and so there is no reason why the majority concept should be involved in the selection of his/her political representative(s).

Therefore, the single-member electoral systems, – i.e. the simple plurality (or first–to–pass–the–post) system, the majority system and their variants such as the double-ballot system – all of which are based upon the majority representation system, are undemocratic for representing the voters because they represent not all voters but only those who vote for the single winners. Rather, universal representation of all voters should be effected by allocating the political posts concerned to all the political representatives whom the people have voted for, the method of allocation being in accordance with the appropriate principles of political equality, discussed elsewhere in this book. In true or universal democracy, political representation is not the right of only the majority voters but rather the right of all voters.

As noted in the first chapter, the main problem with the existing forms of government is that the composition of government is based upon eliminative competition among alternative sub-interest groups of a country instead of upon the universal participation of the alternative sub-interest groups, resulting in the installation in government of some sub-interest groups to the exclusion of others.

The principle of Universal Representation of Voters shows that the practice is against true democracy. Historical experience has confirmed that such a rule of exclusion of sub-interest groups either from government as a whole or from particular branches or arms of government or political offices, is unacceptable to the people and is the greatest cause of the tension and turmoil in many parts of the world today, e.g. Sudan, Lebanon, Liberia, Nigeria, Northern Ireland, Togo, Cote d'Ivoire, Burundi, Somalia etc. The saying of the Lord and Saviour, Jesus Christ in St. Luke's Gospel, chapter 11 verse 17 that: 'Any country that divides itself into groups which fight each other will not last very long; a family divided against itself falls apart' (Good News Bible 1976 edition) is very appropriate in this matter. It shows that God is against the system. Perhaps the Koran has a similar injunction.

Most European countries have discarded the Single-Member (S.M.) electoral system for the Proportional Representation (P.R.) electoral system for legislative elections. This is in consonance with the Declaration of the Rights of Man: 'The law is an expression of the will of the community; all citizens have the right to concur, either personally or by their representatives, in its formation'. However, many countries of the world today, e.g. Great Britain and Nigeria, still deny many of their voters representation in the making of laws by sticking to the S.M. system and not using the P.R. system in the election of their legislators. For example, in Nigeria's just concluded 2003 elections, most of the incoming legislative houses would have 90 - 100% of their members from the so-called majority parties, whereas in such polities (or states) the opposition parties had not less than 30 - 40% of the votes. Thus in Nigeria, up to 30 - 40% (or perhaps more) of the voters may not be represented in the legislative houses. This is undemocratic and should change without further delay for a better future. A change is effected by discarding the S.M. electoral system and its variants for the P.R. electoral system, as discussed in this book. The unfounded fears that have been expressed about the P.R. system have been debunked in this book in the chapter on Elections and Electoral Systems.

It must be accepted that every voter in a general representation election has appropriated his right of participation in the democratic processes and so is entitled to actual representative participation through actual representation not only in the legislature but also in every arm of government. It is satisfying that the new South Africa (after apartheid) has an all-party cabinet in which representation is made proportional to the overall percentage performance of each party, i.e. based upon the P.R. system.

6

THE PRINCIPLE OF UNIVERSAL SUFFRAGE

This is the principle that every free citizen has a right to elect personally his or her own representative(s) in government. It stems from the political liberty concept of the definition of representative political democracy that has been given in this book.

As stated under Representative Government in chapter three, the concept of political liberty of the citizens means that all persons with political liberty have a right to a share in government through their representatives. A person's representative is his/her personal choice made by voting, as shown under the principle of Universal Representation of Voters. Therefore, all persons with political liberty have a right to vote to select personally their representatives in government.

Most countries of the world now practise universal adult suffrage, meaning in this context that all free adults, both male and female, have a right to vote to choose their political representatives. However, children, usually persons under the age of eighteen years, have no such rights, being considered still under their parents. Therefore, the measure for this principle is universal adult suffrage.

The age at which a free citizen is considered to be an adult of voting age varies from country to country. In U.S.A., Nigeria and Great Britain, it is 18 years; in Germany, 20 years; in India, 21 years, and in Japan, 25 years. Each country should be free to fix its minimum voting age. However, as social democracy is against special privileges of sex, birth, wealth, status, profession, etc., Universal Democracy is against the right to vote or to be represented being restricted to citizens who possess specified qualifications in respect of race, property, sex or education as it was in apartheid South Africa; but persons of unsound mind, criminals (in detention, condemned or on trial) and aliens (or foreigners) are usually left out.

The importance of this principle of Universal Suffrage lies in the fact that it is a necessary step towards the representative participation in government of every person with political liberty. It is the right through which a citizen chooses his prospective representative in government. It is like the right to participate in the democratic processes in direct political democracy. Therefore without this principle, the possibility or opportunity of the representative participation of every citizen in government, which representative political democracy requires, does not exist. The right to vote is neither voting nor representation; it does not even guarantee voting or political representation for a free citizen but it is a necessary step for voting and political representation. Without it there cannot be democratic political representation.

The election under reference here is the General Universal Representation Election (GURE), as described under the principle of Separation of Elections. As stated under the principle of Group or Corporate Representatives for Voters, the candidates will be expressly political parties and implicitly cultural constituencies.

The people will vote expressly for the alternative political organisations that freely come up, for the purpose of holding the people's partisan political posts, which will be allocated to the political parties in proportion of the polity's total votes that they receive at the election.

The people will vote as distinct cultural constituencies whose votes will be separately aggregated for the purpose of their cultural representation through the partisan and non-partisan political posts, which will be allocated to the cultural constituencies in proportion of the polity's total votes that they cast at the election. Then, non-partisan posts will be held by members of the appropriate cultural constituencies' relevant professional body or bodies that have the requisite knowledge for the posts.

The implication of voting as distinct cultural constituencies is that a voter is entitled to representation as a member of his/her cultural constituency irrespective and independently of the political party that he/she has expressly voted for, i.e. irrespective of the political opinion that he/she holds. This gives only the members of a cultural constituency in a political party the sole right to hold the cultural constituency's political posts that are also allocated to the political party.

Therefore, voting as distinct cultural constituencies means the spelling out by the people themselves of how the partisan political posts allocated to a political party are to be shared among its cultural/ ethnic components and how the non-political posts are to be shared among the polity's cultural/ethnic constituencies and among members of their relevant professional and learned components. Each region, state/province/canton, local government area, or ward of a country (see the principle of Free Grouping of Citizens) is an example of a cultural constituency.

Voting as distinct constituencies encourages a voter to choose where he/she wants to vote and may involve some movement of voters to their areas of origin to vote if they so wish, but such a movement is unnecessary because people should be identified with their places of abode and because the net difference is usually negligible, so that the end does not justify the means.

In sophisticated societies, voters can be identified with constituencies other than those in which they reside in the following way. Cultural constituencies will be identified with codes. Voters will enter the code of their constituency on the ballot paper. The computer will pick these codes and sort the ballot papers by constituencies. In this way, movement of interested voters to their areas of origin in order to vote for these constituencies will be avoided. However, this method is not much recommended because people should be encouraged to remain and vote in the constituency where they normally reside and derive their benefits.

7

THE PRINCIPLE OF
APPROPRIATION OF POLITICAL
RIGHT

This is the principle that a citizen has to vote in a general representation election in order to be represented in government, i.e., have representative participation in government. The principle stems from the definition of representative political democracy as follows.

In representative political democracy, the citizen has a right to representative participation in government, i.e. a share in government through his representative(s). He has to choose a representative in order to have a representative, since his representative is his personal choice, by the principle of Universal Representation of Voters. He really has no representative if he does not choose one. In other words, a citizen has to claim or appropriate his right to a share in government through his representative by choosing his representative; otherwise, he forfeits a share in government for the period of time that he chooses no representative. Now, voting at the General Universal Representation Election (GURE) will be the means for a citizen who has a share in government through his representative(s) to choose such political representative(s). It follows therefore that a citizen must vote in the election in order to be represented in government, and in order to participate in government through his representative(s); otherwise, his share in government for the period(s) of rule concerned is forfeited.

The principle is in consonance with what obtains in direct political democracy where the right to a share in government is claimed or appropriated by actual physical participation in government. Even though all citizens in direct political democracy have a right to participate in government directly i.e. in person, nevertheless only those who actually present themselves and physically participate in governmental processes claim or appropriate and really enjoy their shares in government. Those who do not actually present themselves to participate in governmental processes forfeit their shares in government for the periods of time that they do not participate.

The implication of all the above is that, contrary to current practice in many parts of the world, political posts must be shared, allocated, zoned or apportioned on the basis of votes and not on any other basis such as population or land area, and after, not before, the General Universal Representation Election (GURE) for the current period of rule. Otherwise, the allocation is undemocratic. It must be remembered that a population includes people of non-voting age, criminals, the destitute and aliens, all of whom are not entitled to the franchise, as well as others who, though qualified to vote, nevertheless by commission or omission do not vote and therefore cannot be and are really not represented. Moreover, political liberty and hence participation in government through a representative belongs to the citizens, the human beings, and not to the land mass or territory per se.

The use of any basis unrelated to the current voting strength may satisfy convenience but misses the real democratic points here, which are two-fold. First, that public policy should be the will of at least the majority of the voters. Secondly, that the votes of the citizens in one constituency or section of a country/polity should not have a different value from the votes of the citizens in another constituency.

This second point is the same as saying that in the partisan and/or cultural allocation of political posts for the universal representation of the citizens, a number of votes from one constituency should not win or be entitled to win a greater or smaller number, or a better or worse type, of parliamentary seats or legislative/

executive political posts than the same number of votes from an alternative constituency.

To be otherwise would imply that some voters are more important than others and hence that some subgroups/constituencies or sets of interests are at a disadvantage vis-à-vis the others. These points, which ensure consistency with the concepts of political liberty and political equality of the citizens, are considered part of the bedrock of unity in a country/polity, as the lack of them is undemocratic and chiefly responsible for the political turmoil, disunity, and instability in many countries of the world today.

The distribution of seats in the Nigerian House of Representatives (October 1979 to September 1983) among the then nineteen states is an eloquent historical example of the inequitable nature of the allocation of political posts on the basis of population. It is shown under the principle of Proportional Representation of Voters, that if all voters are equally represented numerically, then in a branch of government, the value of the ratio of the proportion (or percentage) of total political posts held to the proportion (or percentage) of total votes received or cast should be one (that is, unity) for all alternative political groups. This ratio is referred to in this book as the Proportional Representation Ratio · (P.R.R.). Any difference between the P.R.R. and one, (positive or negative), is a distortion and is expressed in percentages in the last column of Table 1, showing inequalities in the representation of the voters in the government of their country.

It can be seen, for example, that a voter in Kano State (P.R.R. = 1.46) was worth in terms of political rights about one and a half times a voter in Sokoto State (P.R.R.= 0.98) or Rivers State (P.R.R.= 0.95), about twice a voter in Bendel State (P.R.R.= 0.74) and almost two and a half times a voter in Ogun State (P.R.R.=0.65). In fact, Kano State was over-represented by as many as fifteen seats (46% distortion) in the Nigerian Federal House of Representatives, a figure more than the total number of seats by which a state such as Kwara (14 seats), Lagos (12 seats), Niger (10 seats), Ogun (12 seats), or Rivers (14 seats) was represented.

On equitable basis, Kano State should have had 31 seats instead of forty-six seats it was allocated on population basis. This type of undemocratic practice should no longer continue in today's world.

Table 1: The Distribution of Seats in the Nigerian House of Representatives (October 1979-September 1983)

STATE	NUMBER OF SEATS ALLOCATED (y)	TOTAL VOTES CAST (x)	NUMBER OF VOTERS PER SEAT $\frac{(x)}{(y)}$	P.R. RATIO $\frac{(y/M)}{(x/N)}$	EQUITABLE NUMBER OF SEATS $\frac{(x)}{(N/M)}$	DISTOR-TION 100 *(P.R. Ratio -1)
ANAMBRA	29	1,108,771	38,233	0.87	33	-13
BAUCHI	20	807,210	40,361	0.82	24	-18
BENDEL	20	903,140	45,157	0.74	27	-26
BENUE	19	513,359	27,019	1.23	16	23
BORNO	24	736,327	30,690	1.08	22	8
CROSS RIVER	28	729,667	26,060	1.28	22	28
GONGOLA	21	668,381	31,828	1.05	20	5
IMO	30	1,162,689	38,756	0.86	35	-14
KADUNA	33	1,256,780	38,087	0.87	38	-13
KANO	46	1,045,154	22,721	1.46	31	46
KWARA	14	340,692	24,335	1.37	10	37
LAGOS	12	595,149	49,596	0.67	18	-33
NIGER	10	299,712	29,971	1.11	9	11
OGUN	12	612,454	51,038	0.65	18	-35
ONDO	22	824,759	37,489	0.89	25	-11
OYO	42	1,011,233	24,077	1.38	30	38
PLATEAU	16	584,167	36,510	0.91	18	-9
RIVERS	14	491,264	35,090	0.95	15	-5
SOKOTO	37	1,250,647	33,801	0.98	38	-2
TOTAL	449 (M)	14,941,555 (N)	33,277 $\frac{(N)}{(M)}$	1.00	449	0

8

THE PRINCIPLE OF FREE AND
FAIR ELECTIONS

This is the principle that the candidates for elections should freely come up, that every voter is free to choose as he or she likes/wishes, and that the election results are neither suppressed nor interfered with in any way.

This principle stems from the need to ensure that the political liberty and political equality of the citizens are not subverted by cheating, fraud, finance, intimidation or fear. The criterion, therefore, implies that every interested aspirant, corporate or individual, is able to participate in any appropriate election without hindrances or frustration; that the bodies responsible for elections should use the best available methods to ensure that every citizen is able to cast his or her vote without molestation or intimidation or dictation or instruction from anyone; and that the counting and recording of votes and the announcement of results are neither fraudulent nor susceptible to fraud but correctly done.

Therefore there should be accreditation, voting in the presence of all, secret balloting, counting in the presence of all and collation and announcement of results in the presence of all immediately after counting of votes.

It should be ensured that no hindrance is placed in the way of the representation of any interest or of the participation of any prospective candidate. Electioneering should be inexpensive and hardly arduous so that no prospective aspirants for political office will be discouraged for reasons of finance or health, and so that political offices would not be mortgaged for money at the expense of merit and good government.

The body that is responsible for conducting elections in a polity is very important to the success of any election. For example in 1993, the Nigerian Electoral Commission failed to announce the result of the presidential election. This singular action led to the cancellation of the whole election and the abortion of the Nigeria's third republic, which the election would have ushered in. This was despite the fact that all the other elections had been successfully conducted earlier and the results announced and accepted by the public. The popular opinion about the presidential election itself is that it was the best conducted presidential election in the country so far. However, its result was allegedly unfavourable to the people in power at that time, and so it was cancelled.

The failure to announce the result of the election and its eventual cancellation made the election not to be free and thwarted the political liberty of the voters. To facilitate the avoidance of such infringement of the political freedom of the citizenry, it is essential to ensure that members of the electoral commission are men and women of high integrity and reputation who have never been directly or indirectly involved in partisan politics. That is to say that the political posts they hold should be non-partisan, i.e. allocated only to cultural/geographical constituencies. There should be non-partisan allocation of electoral commission posts, for which all interested qualified persons will apply upon advertisement as independent candidates. The candidates will then be nominated/ elected by the general electorate of the cultural/geographical constituencies to which the posts to be filled are allocated, as discussed in the appropriate section of this book.

Another factor that is crucial to free and fair elections is the organization of the elections. Who conducts the party merit elections - the political parties themselves or the electoral commission? In Universal Democracy, all elections should be conducted by the electoral commission. This should be so because all elections in true representative political democracy are of vital importance. That the General Universal Representation Election

(GURE) should be conducted by the electoral commission cannot be controversial because the election is obviously of national concern. That the General Merit Elections (GME) should be handled by the electoral commission should also not be controversial since the elections involve independent non-partisan candidates that may not be in any organized body that can conduct such elections. However, that the electoral commission should handle the Party Merit Elections (PME) may be controversial because political parties are organized bodies and because they have been conducting primary elections in the existing majority rule systems.

Nevertheless, in Universal Democracy, the electoral commission should conduct the party merit elections because the party merit elections are more important than the party primaries in the existing majority rule systems. In Universal Democracy, the party merit elections come after the general representation election and result directly in the election of the partisan political officeholders – from the president downwards. This is in contrast with the existing majority rule systems where the party primaries precede the actual elections into the political offices and so any aspirant that is wrongly treated by his/her party leadership at the party primaries can pull out of the political party and try his/her electoral fortunes in other political organisations/parties before it is too late for the in-coming period of rule. For example, at the just concluded Nigeria's 2003 general elections, some persons who failed at the primaries to get their party's candidature for political office immediately pulled out of their parties and joined other political parties where they eventually became candidates to contest the elections.

Therefore, the party merit elections should not be left in the ambit of political party leadership who can toy with them to suit their whims and caprices and so thwart the political liberties of the prospective candidates, thereby unfairly influencing the choices of the voters.

One way the political party leadership uses to frustrate prospective aspirants for political offices is to use all dubious devices/means to prevent or limit opposition to their choice or favoured candidates. Yet another way is to impose such a heavy electoral fee on the prospective aspirants that most of them except perhaps the party leadership's choice or favoured candidates would be unable to afford. In the existing majority rule systems, electioneering funding is often through very expensive fund-raising dinners/luncheons, at which entry tickets cost over twenty-five to a hundred times the usual or normal rates and at which friends and party "faithfuls" alike donate "very generously" in anticipation of eventual party/government patronage in respect of contracts and/or political appointments. In this way, government contracts and appointments are mortgaged for electioneering finance and so corruption thrives. Little wonder then that many political actors prefer a system whereby they will be able to make political appointments at will, so that they can compensate their benefactors.

Therefore, for free and fair elections, the electoral commission should handle all the elections, including the party merit elections. Moreover, neither the political parties nor any candidates should pay any fee for the elections, which should be funded from public coffers. If public office is to be occupied for public service and public good and is not to be mortgaged for electioneering money at the expense of merit and good government, then public funds should be used for conducting the election into it. Furthermore, all candidates for public office, partisan or non-partisan, should apply directly to the electoral commission at the appropriate level of government, which body should process the applications and conduct the elections for all the candidates that apply and are qualified in accordance with the constitutional requirements for the political office(s) to be occupied.

One more factor that stands in the way of free and fair elections is the manipulation of the political party membership list by the party leadership to satisfy their whims and caprices. Therefore, fool proof devices should be used to ensure that the membership lists used for the party merit elections are correct and authentic.

9

THE PRINCIPLE OF GROUP OR CORPORATE REPRESENTATIVES FOR VOTERS

This is the principle that the political representative of a voter (in true representative political democracy) is not an individual but rather a corporate body or a group. Each of the four concepts of representative political democracy – namely political representation, political liberty of the citizens, political equality of the citizens, and collective decision-making by majority vote – leads separately to this principle.

By the concept of all voters participating in government through their own chosen representatives, the choices of all voters in a. general election to choose their partisan political representatives must be included in government. This is the essence of the principle of Universal Representation of Voters. However, the total number of the choices of all the citizens participating in the election, if the choices are individuals, may be more than the desirable number of members of government – i.e. the number of available political posts that the prospective representatives will occupy in a period of rule.

This means either that some of the choices would be dropped or alternatively that the choices would combine to form a fewer number of corporate representatives. The first option means that some voters in the society would not have partisan representation in government in a period of rule, which is inconsistent with true representative political democracy as government by the representatives of all the voters as expressed by the principle of Universal Representation of Voters (or Universal Rule), which requires universal partisan representation to be achieved in every period of rule; and so it is unsatisfactory.

The second option is satisfactory in that all the political representatives may have political posts – i.e. all the voters would be represented by their choices – in every period of rule but it also means that the representative holding a political post is a group of people – i.e. a corporate body and not just an individual, as required to be shown.

The political equality of all voters also implies that a partisan political representative should be a group of citizens. In general, the number of voters that select each political representative will differ, so that the various representatives would be representing different numbers of voters.

Now for consistency with the political equality of all voters, all the voters must be represented at the same rate. This means for example, that there must be the same number of voters per legislative seat or that each political representative must have the same type of political posts in proportion to the number of votes received.

This in turn implies that the political representatives may have different numbers of political posts, since, as mentioned above, the political representatives may receive different numbers of votes. This . 1eans that a representative may have more than one political post and hence, a representative must comprise more than one individual person, i.e. must be a group of individuals capable of holding several political posts, since an individual is supposed to hold not more than one political post, e.g. a legislative seat, and since an individual may not make political appointments outside himself (principle of Non-Transferability of Delegated Mandates).

Thus for consistency with the concept of the political equality of all voters and the principle of Non-Transferability of Delegated

Mandates, the partisan political representatives of the people should each be a group of persons, as required to be shown.

The democratic concept of collective decision-making by at least a majority vote is yet another factor that makes it essential for the partisan political representatives of the citizens to be corporate bodies instead of individuals. By the concept of collective decision-making by majority vote as applied to political democracy, the general will or public policy is the will of at least a majority of the participating citizens, who are the voters.

In representative political democracy, this means the will of the partisan political representatives of the majority of the voters (in the general election to choose the political representatives). Now if the people's choices are individuals, they would have been elected on the basis of the simple plurality or majority electoral system.

Then for the purpose of public policy making, a majority of them would be taken to be the representatives of a majority of the voters and hence of the (participating) people, since public policy should be the will of a majority of the (participating) people. However, analysis, confirmed by historical evidence, shows that this assumption is faulty, as in reality a majority of individuals elected by the simple plurality or majority electoral system is not necessarily the choices of a majority of the voters.

Analytically, each of such individuals is the choice of the majority of the voters in a single-member constituency. The fact that public policy will be made by a majority vote of such elected individuals means that public policy-making under this situation involves the product of two majorities: a majority of voters in electing a decision-maker and a majority of decision-makers in making a public policy. Therefore, unless the majority in electing any decision-maker (i.e. legislator or partisan executive member) and making any public policy are either not less than about 71% or are such other similar combination of percentages whose product is over 50% (e.g. 60% and 85%), public policy will be the will of the minority of the participating citizens. That would be inconsistent with the concept of public policy being the will of at least the majority of the participating citizens.

But this necessary condition is clearly impossible or most difficult to achieve often in practice as it is outside the usual range of majorities. For example, suppose each individual (political representative) is elected by a conservative two-thirds majority of all the voters in the constituency concerned and that a public policy is also made by a conservative two-thirds majority of the votes of all the individually-elected decision-makers. Then the public policy would be the will of four-ninths $(2/3 \times 2/3 = 4/9)$ of all the participating citizens concerned, which is a minority of the participating citizens from all the constituencies. Thus the notion of a citizen's partisan political choice in government being an individual will often result in public policy being the will of the minority of all the participating citizens and so is inconsistent with the democratic concept of public policy being the will of at least the majority of the voting (or participating) citizens.

Granted that those who govern are a small proportion of the voting citizens, nevertheless public policy emanating from the rulers should, as required by true political democracy, be the will of a majority of the voting citizens. That is possible only if any majority of all the decision-makers (i.e. the rulers) are the partisan political representatives of a majority of the voting citizens, since public policy will in practice be made by the will of a majority of all the decision-makers.

Two historical examples will be given to show that a majority of individuals elected by the simple plurality or majority electoral system is not necessarily the political representatives of a majority of the voting public. The first example is Great Britain, where the members of the House of Commons, the only representative legislative chamber in the country, are chosen as the appointees of the majorities of the voting citizens of multiple single-member constituencies. Moreover, it is a system where the political party or coalition of political parties having a majority of the members of the House of Commons forms the executive. The electing majorities are sometimes plural and sometimes absolute, as more than two political parties are sometimes involved. The records of the percentage vote and of the percentage seat of the party in power in the country from 1945 to 1979, over three decades,

(Table 2(a)), shows clearly that the successive governments in that country since 1945 (to 1979) have been minority governments. This is so because the 'majority' parties forming the governments represented the minority of the voting public and so the general will was the will of the minority of the voting public. This example shows clearly that in reality, a majority of individuals elected by the single-member electoral system more often than not represents a minority of the voting public in a country.

The second example is the often quoted results of the South African general election of 1948, as a result of which the policy of apartheid was entrenched in that country. Again, the election was based upon choosing members of Parliament (MP's) as the appointees of the majorities of the voting citizens from multiple single-member constituencies. In that election, only two parties – the National Party (Melan) and the United Party (Smuts) – were involved and so no MP was returned on a minority vote, i.e. all the electing majorities were absolute majorities.

Table 2 (a): Percentage Vote and Percentage Seat of the Party in Power in Great Britain (1945-1979)

YEAR	% VOTE	% SEAT	P.R. RATIO	% DISTORTION**
1945	48.0 (34.9)*	61.4	1.28	28
1950	46.1 (38.7)	50.4	1.09	09
1951	48.0 (39.6)	51.3	1.07	07
1955	49.7 (38.2)	54.8	1.10	10
1959	49.3 (38.8)	57.9	1.17	17
1964	44.1 (34.0)	50.3	1.14	14
1966	48.1 (36.5)	57.8	1.20	20
1970	46.4 (33.4)	52.4	1.13	13
1974 FEB	37.2 (29.3)	47.4	1.27	27
1974 OCT	39.3 (28.6)	50.2	1.28	28
1979	43.9 (33.4)	53.4	1.22	22

*Figures in brackets are % votes discounted by 20% to allow for ineffective votes scored by unselected candidates of the party or parties in power, as such voters are not in reality represented in government under majority rule systems.
** See the principle of Proportional Representation of Voters for "Distortion" and "P.R. Ratio"

It is however clear from the results (Table 2(b)) that the National Party (Melan), which represented the minority (only 44.7%) of the voting public, got the majority (56.5%) of the seats and so 'won' the elections whereas the United Party (Smuts), which represented the majority (55.3%) of the voting public, got the minority (43.5%) of the seats and was declared the loser. Thus, as Professor Peter Harris wrote, the policy of apartheid received its letters of credit on a minority vote, with immensely important consequences for both South Africa and international politics. How indeed true is the Biblical saying: 'My people are destroyed for lack of knowledge ...' (Hosea 4:6, Holy Bible, King James Version).

Table 2(b):   Results of the South African general election of 1948

| POLITICAL PARTIES | VOTES WON | | SEATS WON | | P.R. | % |
	NO.	%	NO.	%	RATIO	DISTOR-TION
United Party (Smuts)	547,437	55.3	60	43.5	0.79	-21
National Party (Melan)	442,338	44.7	78	56.5	1.26	26

It can be safely concluded from the foregoing theoretical analysis and historical examples that, if the partisan political representatives are individuals, the will of a majority of them is not necessarily the will of the political representatives of a majority of the voting public and hence not necessarily the will of a majority of the voting public (or the participating citizens). It follows that the partisan political representatives being individuals is inconsistent with the democratic concept of public policy being the decision or policy or will of the majority of the participating citizens. So it is undemocratic. On the other hand, if the people's choices as partisan political representatives are corporate bodies, which can hold political posts in direct proportion to the number of voters that choose them, so that not only does each legislator or executive post occupier selected from them represent the same number of voters but also all the voters are represented, then any majority of the legislators or executive post occupiers in government will represent a majority of the voting public.

Moreover, the will of such a majority of legislators or executive post occupiers at any point in time and on any issue will always be the will of the political representatives of the majority of the voting public, which is the will of the majority of the voting public or the will of the participating citizens. Therefore, the choice of corporate bodies by the citizens as their partisan political representatives is consistent with the democratic concept of public policy or general will, being the will or policy of at least a majority of the participating citizens whereas the choice of individuals is not. It is therefore concluded from all the above that representative political democracy implies corporate bodies and not individuals to be the partisan political representative of a (voting) citizen.

The implication of this principle is the election by the voting public of political associations or parties rather than individuals for purposes of their partisan representation in government. The people will vote as distinct cultural constituencies whose votes will be separately aggregated for purposes of their cultural representation in government, i.e. for determining the partisan and non-partisan political posts through which the cultural constituencies will be represented in government. The partisan political posts will be equitably allocated to the political parties, as the cultural constituencies' partisan political representatives, to hold on behalf of the cultural constituencies.

Thus, each partisan political post has dual allocation, being allocated to both a cultural constituency and a political party. A political party later fills each partisan political post allocated to it by a party merit election, or by lot, from among its qualified aspirants from the cultural constituency to which the post is also allocated. On the other hand, each non-partisan political post has a single allocation, being allocated only to a cultural constituency. The cultural constituency (or an appropriate learned/professional component of it) later fills such non-partisan political post allocated to it by a general merit election, or by lot, from among its interested and qualified members.

Examples of group representative systems exist in practice in Switzerland, Germany, Israel, etc. In these countries, citizens vote for political parties and not individuals as their political representatives.

The importance of this principle, and hence its necessity to representative political democracy, is that, it is essential to the realisation of true political democracy, as most of the other principles of representative political democracy cannot be attained without it. Such other democratic principles as universal representation (i.e. representative participation) of voters in government, proportional representation of voters, realisation of public policy as the will of the majority of the voters, and the like would otherwise be pre-empted and therefore outside the realm of realisation. For example, America's presidential system selects as the people's representatives individuals rather than groups and so excludes or pre-empts the principle of Non-Transferability of Delegated Mandates since the American President, for instance, chooses his own ministers and advisers. Moreover, Nigeria, like Great Britain, elects individuals as political representatives (e.g. legislators, senators) and so cannot represent all its voters; public policies are often the will of the minority of its voters.

The inescapable conclusion from all the above is that it is undemocratic for the general public to elect individuals rather than political parties as their political representatives. Doing so leads to undemocratic practices and inconsistencies in the democratic processes. Democratic countries should therefore elect political parties rather than individuals as the voters' political representatives in government.

10

THE PRINCIPLE OF FREE GROUPING OF CITIZENS

This is the principle that the grouping of the people into political units such as political associations and cultural constituencies for the purpose of their political representation should be free. This principle stems from the following premises.

By the principles of Homogeneity of Candidates and Limited Separation of Representation, representation should be in terms of political parties and cultural/ethnic groups. The concept of the individual liberty and the equality of political rights of the citizens both imply that the citizens are entitled to an unrestricted choice of political parties and cultural/ethnic groups, as can be seen in the following analysis.

By the concept of the private or civil liberty of the citizens, every citizen is entitled to freedom to hold opinion and freedom of association including freedom to belong to a political party or to an ethnic or cultural group. Therefore, a restriction on the choice/ number of alternative partisan associations – each of which is by definition, a body of opinions or policies on the controversial issues in the society – or on the number of cultural/ethnic groups to which people may belong for purposes of political representation means a denial of some citizens' right of freedom to hold opinions or freedom to belong to an ethnic or cultural group and is therefore undemocratic. Moreover, restriction on the choice or number of alternative political associations or cultural/ethnic groups that may be represented is a violation of the concept of equality of the political rights of the citizens. This is because it means that some citizens would be represented by the political associations of their choice, and by members of their cultural/ethnic groups while other citizens would be denied the same rights, as their real choices would not be among the representatives.

With regards to the partisan representation of the people, the conclusion from all the above is that there should be no limit to the number of alternative political parties, except as required by the necessity to hold political office in every period of rule in each branch of government, in consistency with the principle of All-Branch Representation of Voters. This principle requires all voters to have partisan representation in all partisan branches or arms of government in every period of rule. A branch or arm of government is defined as a unit of government exercising the whole or a part of one of the three governmental powers – legislative, executive and judicial – and having no overlapping membership with any other department of government as far as the occupiers of the political posts are concerned.

If the political posts in all branches of government are allocated on the basis of the results of one general election, and bearing in mind that universal partisan political representation must be achieved within a period of rule as opposed to over a number of periods of rule, the above requirement is satisfied if a political organisation wins sufficient votes to hold at least a partisan political post in the branch of government with the smallest number of partisan political posts. This is because it is the branch or arm of government that requires the largest number of votes per partisan political post according to the principle of Proportional Representation of Voters. Thus, a political organisation must in a period of rule win enough votes to hold a political post in the branch or arm of government with the smallest number of political posts, before it can exist as a political party in that period of rule.

In order that no voter will be without a partisan political representative in the period of rule, a political organisation that does not meet this requirement must team up with another political organisation that has sufficient votes to exist separately or with other similar small political organisations to form a political party if their total (pooled) votes are sufficient to do so. Such a political organisation shall have the right to team up with any political party or other such political organisation(s) of its choice. Thus, the only constraint on the number of political parties in a period of rule should be the number of voters required for a political post, which factor depends only upon the total number of posts in the arm or branch or sub-branch of government with the smallest number of partisan political posts and the total number of voters. It also means that the standard of universal democracy is not met where there are two or more political parties but the total number of political parties allowed is restricted in some other way. It also means that the requirement is not met if there is only one political party, or a no-party system is used.

One aim in the cultural/ethnic representation of the citizens is to divide the people into groups that are viable to provide suitable candidates for a post and are culturally/ethnically homogeneous such that each of the groups may satisfactorily make a selection of a political post occupier from among its members by a majority vote of its members without cultural/ethnic bias, in accordance with the principle of Homogeneity of Candidates. The best judge of whether a group is culturally/ethnically homogeneous or not is the people themselves.

Therefore, all the tribes or sub-tribes that want to be separately represented in a country qualify as cultural/ethnic groups whose votes at a General Universal Representation Election (GURE) may be separately aggregated for purposes of political representation. However, if there are too many cultural/ethnic groups, the universal cultural/ethnic representation of voters in (a branch or arm of) government within every period of rule may be impossible, as the available number of all political posts in (a branch of) government may become scarce for the alternative groups.

Since universal cultural/ethnic representation of voters is not limited to within a period of rule but rather is achievable over periods of rule, in accordance with the principles of rotation of scarce political posts, no problem is envisaged in such a case, as long as the number of periods of rule for a complete rotation is reasonable, say two to four. The cultural/ethnic groups will be represented in turn over the periods of rule. This means that some cultural/ethnic groups may not be represented in some periods of rule in any arm or branch of government or in some arms or branches of government while others will be, but equity in the cultural representation of the voters will be achieved over the periods of rule.

However, if the universal cultural/ethnic representation of voters is desired within every period of rule or within a much smaller number of periods of rule for all or some of the branches of government, then a much fewer number of cultural/ethnic constituencies is required, unless the number of relevant political posts is appropriately increased, which is not always reasonable to do. In that case a number of tribes and/or sub-tribes are combined by language or a set of customs or traits common to them into a much fewer number of secondary or ·even tertiary cultural/ethnic constituencies for the purpose of achieving a universal cultural/ ethnic representation of the people within every period of rule in every branch or in the branches of government desired.

This second option is facilitated by the fact that each tribe or sub-tribe inhabits or predominates in a specific geographical area of the territory of a country. The tribes or sub-tribes that are combined to form a secondary or tertiary cultural/ethnic constituency would be those that are contiguous geographically and are able to vote together as a monolithic constituency and make a selection on merit among any members of the secondary or tertiary constituency without cultural/ethnic bias.

Both options may be used at the same time for a level of government. For example, tertiary constituencies may be used for the elective executive posts of the central (or national) government to ensure full cultural/ethnic executive representation within every period of rule whereas primary or secondary constituencies are used for the elective legislative posts, for which universal cultural/ethnic representation may span more than one period of rule.

This process of grouping primary constituencies into secondary constituencies or even tertiary constituencies leads to a very interesting development, giving rise to intermediate levels of government in addition to the central or national government, in order to reduce the span of management of the central government. The government of the country as a whole is referred to as the central or national government. In this book, clans, villages and wards of a town or city are taken as the lowest level or primary cultural/ethnic groups, which can be compounded into a fewer number of secondary cultural/ethnic constituencies, known as local government areas.

These secondary cultural/ethnic constituencies will give rise to the lowest level of governments, known as local governments. The number of local governments is the number of secondary constituencies into which the primary constituencies are grouped. With secondary constituencies compounded into tertiary constituencies, another level of governments the state or canton or provincial government level is created between the local and central/national government levels to allow for separate representation for the constituent secondary ethnic groups.

The number of provincial, state or canton governments is the number of tertiary constituencies into which the secondary constituencies are compounded. Where the tertiary constituencies are themselves compounded into a smaller number of fourth-level constituencies, another level of governments, the regional government level, is interposed between the provincial, state or the canton government level and the central government level.

The number of regional governments is the number of fourth-level constituencies into which the tertiary constituencies are compounded. With this arrangement, the structure of a country is as follows. It comprises a number of regional (i.e. fourth-level) constituencies, each of which is composed of a number of provincial, state or canton (i.e. tertiary) constituencies, each of which is in turn made up of a number of local (i.e. secondary) constituencies, each of which comprises a number of villages, clans or wards of a town or city, which are the primary, i.e. lowest-level cultural/ethnic constituencies. Any intermediate level may be omitted.

It should be noted that alternative cultural/ethnic constituencies need not be equal in population or in the land area of the polity they occupy and need not contain the same number of lower-level groupings because the unit of reckoning for equality of political rights (e.g. the allocation of political posts) is the citizen voter. The number of votes cast by each group at the General Universal Representation Election (GURE) determines the group's strength for the allocation of political posts at any level of government.

The summary of the import of this principle is as follows: all political organisations that score enough votes for at least a partisan political post in every arm or branch/sub-branch of government in a period of rule must have legislative and executive participation in government as political parties and all freely-formed cultural groupings or suitable combinations of them should have legislative, executive and judicial participation in government as often as their respective cumulative voting strengths will allow.

One very important implication of this principle is that the political party system should be free, meaning a multiparty system. Therefore, it is undemocratic to impose only two parties or political organisations on a country. In the arena of decision-making or public policy making, analysis shows that a multiparty setting produces a better, more virile and more nationalistic public policy than a two-party setting because the concurrence of a larger number of separate social groups is required for a policy. For example, if T1 and T2, two parties in a two-party system, represent 51% and 49% of the people respectively and M1, M2 and M3, three parties in a multiparty setting, represent 39%, 36% and 25% of the people respectively, then under party voting and discountenancing situations of 100% concurrence of the parties, public policy will result from the will of the representatives of 51% of the people in the two-party system, whereas in the three-party system, public policy may result from the will of the representatives of either 61% (M2 and M3) or 64% (M1 and M3) or 75% (M1 and M2) of the people.

Therefore, not only may public policy in the three-party system derive from the will of a larger number of citizens (as any of the three combinations produces a percentage higher than 51%) but the public policies will also be more representative of the will of the society, as any of the three combinations of parties may be operative for an issue and as the operative combination may shift from issue to issue e.g. M2 and M3 on one issue, M1 and M2 on another issue and M1 and M3 on yet another.

Moreover, as no single party represents the majority of the people and so at least two of the parties have to combine to make a public policy, no one party can afford to maintain a hard-line all the time. In other words, the three-party system allows for compromises and negotiations between parties.

There is incentive for parties to take into consideration the views or wills of other parties and so to modify their views or opinions and produce a policy that is acceptable to a large number of the parties concerned. By contrast, in the two-party system (which includes a multiparty system where a single party has over 50% majority), public policy derives from the will of the majority party only and there is little or no incentive for it to take into consideration the views of the minority party or parties because it has the majority that is required in public policy making.

Therefore, the people should vehemently oppose anyone or any group that tries, either by rigging elections or otherwise, to impose a two-party or a one-party system on them.

With a free political party system, many social types will find political expression and the political party system will be a realistic reflection or model of the society. In direct political democracy, the general will results from the consensus of all or from shifting majority vote as issues change. It follows that representative political democracy would work best if it is a system which comprises enough groups or parties to enable the general will to result from shifting majority vote as issues change. This implies at least a three-party system where every party has less than 50% of the total vote. This is consistent with the principle of Shifting Majority Will.

Two parties imply either of two situations in order to effect a swing or a shifting majority. Either there is a mass movement of people from their support for one party to another. This is unnatural and causes disaffection among the people. Or else there is no swing or shifting majority and so there is the perpetual feeling of domination of one section of the community by another, leading to disaffection and possibly, instability. What is better or best is temporary alignment and realignment of groups for purposes of public policy, which will not cause inter-group animosity and will be without permanent acrimony or animosity. This implies a multiparty system and a multiparty government.

Moreover, a free political party system will enhance political responsibility. In theory there may be as many political parties as there are seats in the Parliament. In practice, however, this will not be so. For example, the fact that the relative strengths of the political parties in Parliament and in the Executive will depend on the partisan distribution of the popular vote will discourage a proliferation of parties and encourage political parties to bargain with their closest ideological and socio-economic competitors in order to occupy some important posts or to get their programmes through in government.

In this way, a free political party system may simplify party competition by polarising public opinion between a few major parties. It should be recognised, however, that the complexity of the culture cleavages in a country will to a large extent determine the number of political parties in the country. The more complex the cleavages, the more the number of political parties likely, even though consistency of this principle with the principle of All Branch Representation of Voters will prune down the number, as earlier indicated.

It should also be recognised that the number of political parties should not and cannot have an adverse effect on representative democracy, if rule by all – i.e. all-party rule is practised in the executive as required by True Representative Political Democracy (T.R.P.D.). Whether there are as many political parties as there are legislators or members of the executive, a consensus or majority can always be obtained whenever a vote is taken in Parliament or in the Executive. And a stable Executive can also always be formed based on the principle of distributing executive power to all the political parties on the basis of the method of Co-ordinated Proportional Representation by Multiple Unequal Scarce Posts (COPREMUSPO) and not tying its existence to the whims and caprices of the Parliament.

Admittedly, the more political parties there are, the more fragmented the Parliament and the Executive will be. But this is good for the society, which itself is fragmented into millions of citizens or families. The government is a micro-model of the society at large and the more characteristic of the prototype the model is, the more correctly it will represent the prototype and the happier the citizens will be. For instance, the more fragmented the parliament is, the less perfunctory and the more stimulating parliamentary debates are likely to be, and consequently the more nationalistic and acceptable public policies are likely to be.

Therefore fragmentation of the Parliament resulting from a large number of political parties should be a blessing and not a curse. A government with many political parties and party voting is not worse than a government with three or even two parties with each member of government voting separately, i.e. with several voting or without party voting that some countries practise.

It is noted that what makes a small number of political parties to appear to be a strong factor for the stability of contemporary governments is the absence in those governments of the upholding of the right of all people to participate equally in their government, as such governments are based on rule by the majority party or majority coalition but never on rule by all, i.e. there is no universal partisan representation in the Executive.

Such a system institutionalises permanent majorities and permanent minorities and is an unrealistic model or representation of a strong plural society. This accounts for the political chaos presently in most African and other countries with major and strong cultural/ethnic cleavages. By contrast, Switzerland is a living example of a plural but very stable country, in spite of having several political parties, because it practises what is akin to rule by all.

On the other hand, a restricted number of political parties may have adverse effects on a country by reinforcing culture cleavages. For example in Nigeria where the problem of north-south dichotomy is reinforced by religious and population cleavages – the north has been predominantly Muslim and more populous than the south, which is predominantly Christian – an imposition of a two-party system may cause politics to reinforce the north-south dichotomy further and therefore increases the potentials for political instability.

In conclusion, it must be reiterated that this principle requires that the number of political parties in a country, as well as the number of regions, provinces, states, cantons, or local government areas should not be undemocratically restricted. For instance, the situation whereby different ethnic groups, tribes or sub-tribes are forced together into the same region, province, state, canton or local government area against their wishes, but purportedly to keep a country together, is undemocratic and should be avoided. It leads to incessant clashes among the citizens and is a potential cause for disunity and instability. On the other hand, it must be accepted that a country/polity, where truly democratic principles like those described in this book are operative, need not fear dismemberment, as the people would be happy and united.

11

THE PRINCIPLE OF NON-TRANSFERABILITY OF DELEGATED MANDATES

This is the principle that political representatives may not by virtue of their mandates create political representatives out of non-political representatives i.e. a political representative may not make political appointments outside himself or itself.

This principle is obtained as follows. By definition, a truly democratic representative government is a government run by the people's political representatives, i.e. a government in which those who hold political posts in government are the people's political representatives. They are those selected by the people themselves to represent them. They are the ones people directly give their votes to at a general election for the purpose and for the period of rule in question.

It follows from logical reasoning that only political representatives may occupy political posts and that political representatives are made only by the people in the General Universal Representation Election (GURE) for a period of rule. Now those appointed by the people's political representatives outside themselves are their representatives' representatives and not their chosen political representatives. Therefore, it is inconsistent with the definition of a truly democratic representative government for the people's political representatives'

representatives, unless they are a part of the people's political representatives, to hold political posts. Therefore, it is inconsistent with true representative political democracy for the people's political representatives to make political appointments outside themselves.

Political appointments by the people's political representatives outside themselves are also inconsistent with the concept of the political liberty of the people, which makes the people's political representatives to be the people's trustees, the nominal owners of the mandate given them by the people to participate in government on their behalf. The real owners of the mandate are the people.

The transfer by a people's representative of part of his delegated mandate to another person by appointing the other person into a political post/office (of the people) means a change, a transfer of the representative's status from that of a trustee, a delegate, a representative, i.e. a nominal owner of the mandate, which he actually is, into that of a real owner, which he is not. He has thereby shifted the focus from the real owner – the people, to himself. This is immoral because it arrogates to the people's political representative the right that he does not have: the right to solely appoint another person into political office.

It also erodes the authority (even if only in part) of the citizen, as the second-degree political representative will be more concerned with the protection of the interests of the first degree political representative that appointed him, to the detriment or even the total neglect of the interests of the citizens that appointed the first-degree political representative. Therefore, where the interests of the first-degree representative differ from (even some of) those of his selectors – the citizens – his own interests or personal agenda, and not those of the citizens he is supposed to protect, get the attention from the second-degree political representative.

Realising as it were the nature of man that a representative may not give one hundred percent attention to the protection of the citizens' interests, one would then see that there is a better chance for the citizens' interests to be protected by their direct representatives than by their representatives' representatives, who owe no direct responsibilities (or allegiance) to the citizens but rather to the citizens' representatives.

Thus, the principle has the following implications. The mandate given to an individual political representative is delegated to a particular person, who and who alone may utilise it: he may not rightly re-delegate it, in whole or in part, to other persons, by appointing them into political posts. On the other hand, the mandate delegated to a corporate political representative of the people, for example a political party, is given to a number of persons as a body and without particularising, except in so far as cultural representation is concerned. The mandate is given to all the members or persons that may constitute the corporate representative, subject only to cultural representation.

Therefore, all the members of a corporate political representative may, as far as possible within the limits of cultural representation, occupy political posts on its behalf and, decide, as and when necessary, which one or more (as appropriate) of them should utilise their joint (i.e. the corporate representative's) mandate on its behalf.

Thus, any accredited member (male or female) of a current corporate political representative of the people may occupy a political post or office for which he has the requisite qualifications, including cultural qualifications, since all the members of the corporate representative are integral parts of the (corporate) person to whom the people themselves directly give their votes at a general election for the current period of rule. However, a non-member of the corporate representative is not entitled to any of its allocated political posts since he (or she) is not logically a part of the corporate representative and since he may not in practice actually share or uphold the corporate representative's policy or interests for which the people (who voted for it) have appointed it.

Moreover, it is the corporate body that has the right to appoint its members into its allocated political posts. By so doing, the corporate representative is not transferring the mandate delegated to it because it is making the appointment by itself and from within itself and not from outside itself. It may be wished for the general electorate to elect a member of a political party to which a political post has been allocated to fill the post, as the political party is a part of, i.e. within, the general electorate. However, since the general electorate has given the mandate to the political party, the latter should have the sole right to make the appointment for which it is responsible.

Thus, for example, a political party to which some political posts have been allocated has the sole right to fill them by itself and from among its members. Similarly, the ethnic constituency/group to which some of the political posts have also been allocated has the right to fill the posts by itself and from among its members.

It must be added here that, in accordance with the principle of Political Party Dominance, political parties should take precedence over cultural/ ethnic groups in the matter of the right to elect or nominate individual partisan political office occupiers for the partisan political posts that have been allocated to the political parties. This implies that a partisan political post allocated to a political party and to an ethnic constituency is allocated to the political party and its members from the cultural/ethnic constituency concerned. This means that either the entire political party or its cultural/ethnic component can make an appointment from within the cultural/ethnic component, and that the entire cultural/ethnic constituency may not make a political appointment from among its members from the political party concerned. This also implies that the general electorate should not make an appointment from within a political party once the political posts have been allocated to the political parties and the cultural/ethnic constituencies.

However, appointments into non-partisan political posts, whose occupants should be persons who have not been involved in party politics, and which therefore may not be allocated to political parties but only to cultural/ethnic constituencies, may not be made by political parties as the appointees may not come from within them. The appointments should be made by the entire cultural/ ethnic constituencies concerned, or the professional bodies (if applicable) and their cultural/ethnic components from among which the appointees would come.

Finally, a member whom a corporate representative, e.g. a political party, appoints to occupy one of its political posts has no right to make by himself a political appointment even from within the corporate representative, as that would amount to a transfer of the mandate delegated to him because he is a part of the corporate representative but the corporate representative is not a part of him. He may not make a political appointment outside himself.

The further implications of all the above are as follows. A corporate political representative of the people may re-delegate its mandate in part or in whole to only a part of itself and no other, for a political party rightly holds political office through its members appointed by itself from among itself. However, an individual political post occupier must hold political office by himself or herself alone and may not appoint others, whether within or outside a political party or a cultural/ethnic group, as agents to hold political office either on his behalf or to assist him because that would amount to a transfer of the mandate delegated to him, since such agents are not part of him and so are not part of the person to whom the mandate is given and who is directly responsible to the original giver. This means that there may be a re-delegation of the whole or part of a mandate but that at every stage of the delegation or re-delegation of mandate, the delegate in whole must be a part of the delegator – i.e. the person or body making the delegation – otherwise the delegation amounts to a transfer of mandate and so is undemocratic.

Therefore, instead of a political system allowing the people's "political representatives" to make political appointments outside themselves, the system should allow the people either to choose as their representatives corporate bodies, which can make political appointments within themselves, or to choose enough individual political representatives that would not warrant the representatives making political appointments outside themselves.

Thus political parties elected at the current General Universal Representation Election (GURE) as the partisan political representatives of the people or the general electorate voting as separate cultural/ethnic constituencies may make political appointments from among their members and only on merit. (In very special circumstances the members of all the elected political parties-in-government may replace the general electorate and a party-in-government may replace the party electorate as long as the appointees come from among the electors).

It should be pointed out that a violation of this principle is a violation of rational thinking and an erosion of the foundation of political democracy. This is so because the principle is derived rationally from the definitions of representative government and the political representative of the people, both of which themselves derive from the concepts of the political liberty and the political equality of the citizens, the very foundations on which political democracy rests.

For instance, there is no political freedom or political equality for the citizens in the selection of their government if they select one or few members of government who will then exclusively select a much greater number of other political members of the same government and from among the people for that matter. Those members of government who have to appoint their 'lesser' counterparts are clearly politically superior to any other person, in or out of government, in the selection of the government. Moreover, the allegiance of such a government will be more to those who appoint their counterparts than to the general electorate it is supposed to represent and serve.

Furthermore, why should a people elect an individual to shoulder the responsibilities of several persons, knowing fully well that the individual will afterwards turn back upon them and subjectively pick some of them to share the responsibilities with him? Where is rationality in such an arrangement? Where is the political liberty of all the citizens in the arrangement? Where is the political equality of all the citizens in it? And where is objectivity in it? Definitely nowhere.

For example, in the United States of America, the president (with his vice) is popularly elected and he may appoint his ministers, advisers and other members of the executive, which he may choose from among his friends, relations, close associates etc.

Again, in Japan the prime minister is himself a member of the Diet, the Japanese bicameral parliament fully directly elected by the citizens. However, he or she may choose up to 50% of his or her cabinet from outside the Diet.

This means that in such a situation, some (or may be the majority) of those who occupy political office would not be the representatives of the people, i.e., those elected by the people; nor will they necessarily be people appointed on merit.

The practice is therefore inconsistent with the principle of Non-Transferability of Delegated Mandates and so to that extent undemocratic. No wonder then that such governments are usually neck-deep in corruption. This situation is unacceptable firstly because it offends against rational thinking for a person to turn back and arbitrarily appoint some of the citizens whose representative he is as his own representative to share part of the burden that has been unwittingly imposed upon him.

Secondly, it means that the will or interests of the voters may be replaced by the will of some of the elected members who have to appoint the other political office occupiers. Thirdly, it goes that the appointment of political officers may be arbitrarily done at the discretion of a few individuals instead of being based upon the personal merits of the occupiers of the posts decided in competition with other qualified and interested citizens.

Lastly and most importantly, many of those handling the affairs of the polity would have no direct responsibility to the people but rather to the president or prime minister who appoints them. Therefore, the people's interests may suffer. All these anomalies are undemocratic and could seriously affect the people's welfare, and so generate discontent and disaffection among the citizens.

It is however democratic for the already elected political appointees to elect by majority vote from among themselves those to occupy new political responsibilities. This procedure ensures that elected political office occupiers do not by themselves create other political office occupiers – that is, there is no transfer of delegated mandates. It also ensures that the appointee has some responsibility to the appointing body.

12

THE PRINCIPLE OF PERIODIC REPRESENTATION OF VOTERS

This is the principle that every citizen has the right to renew periodically his or her choice of political representation in government. This principle stems from five premises.

First, government is based upon citizens' will, interests and demands. But a citizen's will, interests and demands may change over time, in terms of the policies or personnel by which he or she is represented in government. Therefore, he or she should be able to effect a change, as he or she deems necessary.

Secondly, individual liberty implies that the destiny of any group of people is in their own hands. It should therefore be possible for any subgroup within a political party that feels its interests can be better looked after outside the party to join another party or form itself into a new political party. The realisation of the objective of such a change of one's political party demands an opportunity for citizens to be able to renew or change their choice of representation in government.

Thirdly, as Lord Acton, a high political authority, has rightly observed, power tends to corrupt those who wield it and absolute power tends to corrupt absolutely. Therefore, the freedom of each citizen demands that he or she should not grant power to be ruled unconditionally to his or her political representative. This means that a citizen must have opportunities to review, renew or change his or her political representative in government. As the *New Age*

Encyclopaedia has put it, those who rule must be regularly subjected to the control of those over whom they rule to check abuse of power.

Fourthly, the composition of a nation is dynamic. As people die and new ones are born and attain adulthood or voting age, the composition of the (adult) citizens of a state or society changes and there is therefore the need for new people to be represented in government as well as to have the opportunity of being rulers.

Fifthly and lastly, the periodic renewal of a citizen's choice of political representation in government is essential. It is a necessary framework for the realisation of the objective of equal representation over time of the various interest or culture groups within the society.

The implication of this principle is that a government must have a fixed life, i.e. political representation must be for a limited period of time.

This fixed life is termed a period of rule in this book. It is the optimum length of time for a political representative or an agent in government to hold political office continuously at a time.

The period of rule is an important parameter in this book. It is taken as one of the absolute standards of measurement of the phenomenon of politics. For instance, it plays a significant role in the definition of the post-period or cumulative quantity of a political post over several periods of rule, as described under the principle of Rotation of a Scarce Political Post Type.

Each country fixes the life of its government as it pleases. For example, in Nigeria the president is elected for four years. So also are the state governors and the federal and state legislators. But the local government chairmen and councillors are elected for three years. Discussions are currently going on in the country to change the tenure of office for the president, governors and legislators to five years. In the U.S.A., the president is elected for four years, the members of the Lower House for two years, and the members of the Upper House for six years. These examples show that differentiation does often exist in the tenure of office of political officeholders in different branches or arms of government and at the various levels of government.

However, differentiation in the tenure of office cannot change the character of the affected officeholders and so is considered unnecessary. On the other hand, it introduces complications into the political system as more than one set of periods of rule will become applicable and the same General Universal Representation Election (GURE) cannot apply to the various branches/sub-branches and levels of government. Therefore, differentiation in the tenure of office of political officeholders is disadvantageous and so should not be used.

Rather, the same fixed life should apply to all the arms or branches and levels of government in a country. Moreover, the principles of political equality show that equitable distribution of political posts among alternative groups from one period of rule to another is enhanced if the value of the period of rule does not vary for a country over time.

13

THE PRINCIPLE OF SEPARATION OF ELECTIONS

This is the principle that the general election for the universal representation of the citizens should be separate from and precede the election(s) for the selection of the individual political office occupiers (on merit). The premises for this principle are as follows.

Normally, there are several aspirants to a political post and the aspirants are differently qualified and endowed for the political post. Since qualification and endowment are personal attributes, it is therefore desirable and generally accepted that the best of the candidates on their personal merits for the political post should occupy it. The post being a political one, the choice is to be made by a majority vote of the people concerned (selectors). Now by the principle of Homogeneity of Candidates, a selection by lot, or on merit by majority vote, is possible or realistic only when there is partisan and/or cultural homogeneity among the candidates for the political post. But, in general, the candidates for a political post may be of diverse partisan and/or cultural origin, unless there is a prior partisan and/or cultural allocation of the position.

Therefore, a partisan and/or cultural homogeneity of the candidates for a political post presumes a prior allocation of the political post to a specific partisan and/or cultural group. But such an allocation is democratic only if it results from a prior universal representation of the voters in terms of their partisan and/or culture cleavages, if it is based upon the partisan and/or cultural distributions of popular votes, and after a general election for the purpose for the current period of rule.

Therefore, there must be a general election for the universal representation of the people that must precede the election(s) for the merit selection of the individual political post occupiers. Thus the election for the partisan and cultural representation of the citizens should precede the election(s) to choose the individual political post occupiers.

This principle therefore implies that there must be a general election, termed in this book as the General Universal Representation Election (GURE), in which the candidates will be expressly political parties and implicitly cultural constituencies, as the voters will belong to distinct cultural groups or constituencies (e.g. geopolitical zones, states, local ` government areas, etc). The partisan and cultural votes' distributions of this election will be the basis of the partisan and/or cultural allocations of partisan and non-partisan political posts. The election will precede (and be separate from) any other general, partisan or cultural elections, termed in this book as the Merit Elections (ME), whose purpose is to select the individual political post occupiers.

Without this principle, there will be no partisan and cultural allocations of political posts, or such allocations will be undemocratically based upon population figures as is presently the case with geographical constituencies for legislative seats in majority representation systems, or will be done arbitrarily as has been the case with various spurious zoning formulae sporadically adopted by some political parties in many countries e.g. Nigeria.

It is noteworthy that in the existing majority rule systems, the election for the representation of the citizens and the elections for the selection of the individual political officeholders are not separated. In both the parliamentary and the presidential systems of government, there is no election that is purposely set aside solely for the representation of the citizenry. For example, in the parliamentary system, the parliamentary elections result in the selection of the members of the Parliament. In the presidential system, e.g. in Nigeria, the legislative elections result in the selection of the legislators and the presidential election in the selection of the president and the vice president. Thus, the election to represent the voters and the election to select the political officeholders are joined: they are one and the same. Now, the need to select the political officeholders is more obvious than the need to represent the voters and so overshadows the need to represent the voters. Consequently, the elections are generally regarded as elections for the selection of the individual political officeholders, to the detriment of the political representation of the people that vote for the losers.

This principle shows clearly that such a practice is undemocratic. Representative political democracy demands that first and foremost all the voters in a general election must be represented, and then the political office occupiers are selected either by lot or by merit elections in an atmosphere of partisan and/or cultural homogeneity. The earlier a country/polity adopts this system, the better for its people.

It must be accepted that the voters are short-changed or cheated when they are not represented. Instincts sometimes make some such voters and their "losing" candidates to react violently against the system. Some people call them bad losers; they are most likely not, under the right system. It must be accepted that political representation is the right of every voting citizen. It is undemocratic to deny it to any voter, who has, by voting, appropriated his inalienable right to representative participation in a representative government. It is like a qualified citizen in direct political democracy physically presenting himself for participation in governmental processes and yet being denied participation for no reason. Every country of the world should stop such an undemocratic practice by separating the two types of elections and representing all voters.

14

THE PRINCIPLE OF LIMITED SEPARATION OF REPRESENTATION

This is the principle that factors of representation should be separated only as far as representation of voters in terms of each of them is desirable and feasible. This principle has arisen because of the need for self-rule and because of voting complexities as follows.

According to the principle of Homogeneity of Candidates, factors such as religious, ethnic and political differences, which have little or no relevance to the competence of individuals for political office but border on the voters' interests and hold a very strong appeal on the voters, should be eliminated from, or emasculated in, the process of selection of individual political officeholders by majority vote, in order to base the process solely on merit and so make it fair and hence sociably democratic.

This implies that matters such as religious, ethnic and political differences should be separate subjects of representation of voters, because they are so important that they cannot be wished off.

However, a three-dimensional representation system involving political parties, ethnicity and religion is very difficult for the following reasons, among others.

First, it can result in unsatisfactorily small constituencies that produce mediocres as candidates for political offices. Secondly, the level of complexity in a three-dimensional voting pattern, in the attendant sorting and counting of votes, and in the subsequent allocations of political posts is considered too much for present-day electorate in most parts of the world.

Moreover, experience shows that ethnicity and religion are often interwoven, as an ethnic group may be virtually or wholly people of the same religion, so that ethnicity and religion may be considered together under a general heading of cultural groups.

Therefore, in general, ethnicity and religion would be considered inseparable and only a two-dimensional representation system involving political parties and cultural/ethnic/geographical constituencies will be considered in this book as feasible.

Thus, this principle requires that at every level of government there must be representation only on the basis of political parties as well as on the basis of cultural/ethnic/geographical constituencies for any branch or arm of government at any level of government.

The purpose of cultural/ethnic representation is to ensure that the government (i.e. the legislature, judiciary or executive) will be the same sort of people, i.e. typical of or having the same personnel characteristics, as the citizenry. It entrenches self-rule or participatory/inclusive democracy.

Cultural/ethnic representation means that each voter in voting is entitled to representation, i.e. has shares, in government purely as a member of his/her cultural constituency irrespective and independently of his/her partisan affiliations, i.e. irrespective of the political opinion he/she holds or the political party that he/she has voted for. This gives only the members of a cultural constituency in a political party the sole right to hold the cultural constituency's political posts that are also allocated to the political party. As his chosen cultural group or constituency may necessarily be policy-heterogeneous, this principle implies that a voter's cultural representative includes all political officeholders from his/her chosen cultural group, whether or not they are from his chosen political party. After all, even in the existing majority rule systems, every one expects to see members of his/her cultural constituency in the government in power even when that government is not the one for which he/she or the majority of his/her cultural group has voted.

Otherwise, the shouts of cultural marginality would not have been so loud and vigorous in such systems.

Partisan representation of the citizens means that each voter delegates his partisan share in government to the political party of his/her choice to utilise on his/her behalf.

Therefore, a separation of cultural representation from partisan representation means that the voters delegate their policy in government to the respective political parties that they have voted for while expecting any members of their (chosen) cultural constituency in whatever political party to which is allocated the political post for their constituency to be their brothers' keepers and speak for them on cultural matters. This breeds nationalism. Therefore, separate partisan representation with separate cultural representation ensures that the government will protect the interests of the whole citizenry. As a result, the government will have the same complexion in personnel and in policy, as the citizenry.

Cultural representation and partisan representation will be achieved by the people voting as distinct cultural constituencies and for the political organisations/parties of their choice at the General Universal Representation Election (GURE), which the principle of Separation of Elections provides for. Then the polity's political posts are separately allocated to the cultural constituencies and to the political parties independently of each other, using respectively the cultural and partisan distributions of the polity's total votes at the election at the level of government concerned.

This principle implies that no voter should be denied cultural representation on account of his/her political opinion, i.e. on account of the political party that he/she has voted for. This implies that cultural allocation of partisan political posts may not be done on the basis of the partisan distribution of cultural votes as some voters may thereby be denied cultural/geographical representation. Similarly, the principle implies that no voter should be denied partisan representation on account of the cultural constituency to which he/she belongs or has chosen to belong. This implies that partisan allocation of (partisan) political posts should not be done on the basis of the cultural distribution of partisan votes as some voters may thereby be denied partisan representation. Cultural representation of the voters is correctly realised in the following 3-step procedure. First, the people vote in the General Universal Representation Election as distinct cultural constituencies. Secondly, the polity's partisan and non-partisan political posts are shared equitably among the cultural constituencies according to their respective performances for the polity at the election. Thirdly, members of each respective cultural constituency (competitively selected by merit elections) occupy the constituency's allocated partisan and non-partisan political posts. Partisan representation of the voters is also correctly realised in the following 3-step procedure. First, the people vote in the General Universal Representation Election (GURE) for the political organizations (or parties) of their choice. Secondly, the polity's partisan political posts are shared equitably among the emerging political parties according to their respective performances for the polity at the election. Thirdly, each respective political party fills its allocated partisan political posts with its members (competitively selected by party merit elections) from the cultural constituencies to which the posts are also allocated.

It is common knowledge that people of the same opinions on controversial socio-economic issues in the society cut across cultural/ethnic/geographical boundaries. Therefore, the partisan factor of representation is separable from the cultural factor of representation. It is very unlikely that only partisan representation can be satisfactory to the people, because it ignores self-rule for the different cultural groups. The attempt in the existing majority representation systems to elect members of the legislature on constituency basis, using single-member or multi-member constituencies based upon population is an example of the use of cultural or geographical constituencies, showing that partisan and cultural factors of representation are not only separable but also desirable.

That explains why many people in Israel (where the members of Knesset (the Parliament) are elected by the Proportional Representation (P.R.) electoral system *with lists* and with the whole country treated as a constituency) are displeased with the P.R. system and are agitating for its traditional alternative, the single-member (S.M.) system.

However, Israel should not adopt the traditional S.M. system but should rather replace the lists with cultural (e.g. geographical) allocation of Knesset seats after the General Universal Representation Election and then elect the legislators by party merit elections, as discussed under Elections and Electoral Systems in this book.

The lack of universal partisan representation or cultural representation or both in the Executive in the majority representation systems has contributed much to the emergence of culturally-based (i.e. ethnic and/or religious) political parties in majority rule systems, in spite of some cultural representation in the legislature.

If there is partisan allocation and cultural rotation of political posts in all branches or arms of government, then any political office, be it legislative or executive, may be allocated to any political party and/or any cultural group. Under such a situation, a proliferation of culturally-based political parties will be an aberration, because it would then be proper for electoral commissions to insist that, to exist, a political party must not only comprise the members of all the cultural groups but also contain them in sufficient number and quality to enable every cultural group to hold any political post within any political party. Thus the separation of partisan representation from cultural representation will not only result in a small number of political parties but also make the political parties nationalistic in outlook and composition and make the political system more satisfactory and stable.

One very important implication of the separation of partisan and cultural representation of the voters that must be borne in mind is the separate allocations of the political posts (through which representation of voters is effected) to cultural constituencies and to political parties independently of each other. In other words, each of the two types of allocation is independently based upon the polity's total vote at the General Universal Representation Election (GURE). This means that neither the Cultural-cum-Partisan Method nor the Partisan-cum-Cultural Method but the Parallel

Method (described under the chapter on Elections and Electoral Systems) is applicable for the allocation of political posts to the cultural constituencies and to the political parties in Universal Democracy.

President Olusegun Obasanjo of Nigeria (1999 – 2003) is a good example of the separability of partisan representation and cultural representation. He became the president of Nigeria under the majority rule system. He is a Yoruba man from the south-western part of Nigeria. He did not have up to a quarter of the votes of his people, the Yorubas. He became the president of the country on the platform of the Peoples Democratic Party (P.D.P.) while the Yorubas massively supported another political party, the Alliance for Democracy (A.D.). So he was not the partisan representative of the Yorubas. But the Yorubas were pleased that for once, a Yoruba man became the elected president of Nigeria.

They saw him as their cultural representative in the Nigerian polity and accepted him as such. Thus even though he was not their partisan representative, they accepted him as their cultural representative. This is a significant illustration that partisan representation and cultural representation are separable and can be accepted as such by the people without difficulty.

Even in Nigeria's 2003 elections, the A.D. political party refused to field a presidential candidate. This strategy would undoubtedly enable the Yorubas, a very large majority of whom were supporters of A.D., to vote massively for the incumbent President Olusegun Obasanjo (of the P.D.P.) against several other presidential candidates of various ethnic groups (there are presently thirty registered political parties) in an attempt to retain him as Nigeria's president for the next period of rule (29 May 2003 - 2007). It is noteworthy that this strategy would have been out of place if separable cultural/ethnic representation rather than cultural/ethnic competition had been in operation in the country. It should be added that the strategy worked very well for President Obasanjo as the Yorubas voted for him and his party, causing the A.D. political party to lose out massively on Yoruba support.

15

THE PRINCIPLE OF POLITICAL PARTY DOMINANCE

This is the principle that the political party rather than the cultural constituency should predominate in the matter of the right to elect or remove individual partisan political office occupiers and decide upon public policy.

The premises for this principle are as follows. Since the voting public must have both cultural/ethnic and partisan representation in government and since the dual political representation requirement can sometimes lead to alternative methods of election of political officeholders, among other things, it has to be decided which takes precedence over the other, after the dual cultural/ethnic and partisan representation.

The very idea of a representative government, i.e. government by the people's representatives, implies that the people surrender or delegate governance to their political representatives. Now, at the General Universal Representation Election (GURE), the cultural constituencies elect the political parties as their partisan political representatives. Therefore the political representatives, not the people or cultural constituencies, should predominate in governance, even though on behalf of the people.

This means that the political parties, as the people's partisan political representatives, should predominate over the cultural constituencies in governance, i.e. in selecting or removing their members in government and in determining public policy, since they are each a body of homogeneous policies on the controversial issues in the society. However, this excludes the allocation of political posts, which process deals with the representation of the people and the installation of the political parties as political representatives and so is beyond the political parties to handle. The selection and removal of non-partisan political officeholders are also beyond the political parties and must be handled by the cultural constituencies and/or their suitable and appropriate professional, learned or other components.

One implication of this principle is that all partisan posts must be filled via party merit elections (or casting lots), as discussed fully under the chapter on Elections and Electoral Systems. Thus, the partisan political posts allocated to a cultural/ethnic constituency are indeed allocated to its members in the political parties to which the posts are also allocated. This means, for example, that either the entire political party or its cultural/ethnic component can make an appointment from within the partisan cultural/ethnic component and that the entire cultural/ethnic constituency may not make a political appointment from among its members in a political party once the political posts have been allocated to the political parties. It means also that there cannot be carpet-crossing by political office-holders from one political party to another because the political post(s) they hold belong not to them individually but to their political party corporately. It also means that the general electorate should not make an appointment from within a political party once the political posts have been allocated to the political parties. However, appointments into non-partisan political posts, whose occupants should be persons who have not been involved in party politics, and which therefore may not be allocated to political parties but only to cultural/ethnic constituencies, may not be made by political parties as the appointees may not come from within them.

The appointments should be made (by lots or) by the appropriate cultural/ethnic constituencies and/or their suitable and appropriate professional, learned or other components, from among which the appointees would come.

Also, the principle implies that there must be party voting by a political party's members in the legislature and in the executive, to show that the political party, as a corporate political representative, is indeed a policy-homogeneous body. It is clear that if the political representative of a citizen in government for purposes of public policy making is a political party, it will have a definite opinion on any controversial issue in the society, since by definition a political party is a policy-homogeneous body, because people of different opinions can easily form themselves into alternative political organisations. However, a cultural/ethnic constituency is a policy-heterogeneous group, without one voice on a controversial issue in the society, and therefore it will be a weak and non-cohesive representative of the citizen in public-policy making in government.

Finally, the principle implies that any individual member of the legislature or of the executive, including the president, may be removed by an absolute or two-thirds majority vote of his/her political party members in the legislature and executive. This will enable a political party to enforce party voting on its members in the legislature and in the executive.

Nothing in all the above should be construed to mean that the people abandon their sovereignty to their representatives — the political parties. To this end, citizen(s) outside legislature shall have the right (of initiative) to introduce in the legislature private bills on any matter of public interest. It should be compulsory for any such bill that is not passed by the legislature to be submitted to the people, the general electorate, (in a referendum) for approval or rejection. This right should be entrenched in the polity's constitution.

16

THE PRINCIPLE OF ALL-BRANCH REPRESENTATION OF VOTERS

This is the principle that every voter should be represented – that is, have his/her chosen political representative(s) – in every one of the different branches into which governmental powers are divided.

This derives from the following premises. The universal and equal representation of voters which true representative political democracy requires implies that all voters are entitled to be represented in each of the branches or arms of government. For, if a voter is represented in only one branch of government while another is represented in a different branch or in more than one branch, then both voters are not being equally represented in government even when both are represented by the same number of political posts, each of which is held for the same number of voters, because the branches are different and so both voters are not being represented through the same type or quality of political posts, rotation of political posts being assumed only within and not across branches of government.

Therefore, the equal representation of all voters in government includes every voter being represented in all the branches or arms of government, i.e. universal representation of the voters in every branch or arm of government.

This principle, combined with the principle of Universal Representation of Voters, implies that there should be universal partisan and cultural representation of voters in all arms or branches of government, either in every period of rule or over periods of rule through rotation. But universal partisan representation of voters should be in every period of rule and not merely over a number of periods of rule because partisan rotation of political posts is not feasible. Therefore this principle and the principle of Universal Representation of Voters imply that there should be universal partisan representation of voters in all arms or branches of government in every period of rule.

This means that each of the partisan branches or arms into which governmental powers are divided should be run by the partisan political representatives of all the voters in every period of rule. That is, each arm of the legislature, as well as the executive, must be manned by members of all the political parties in every period of rule.

Also the non-partisan executive bodies and the Judicial Council must be manned by members of all the cultural constituencies concerned at every period of rule if possible or, if impossible, within a cycle of a reasonable number of periods of rule, through rotation. Moreover, political party members in the legislature and executive must come from all the cultural constituencies if possible at every period of rule but if impossible, within cycles of a reasonable number of periods of rule, through rotation.

This implies an all-party, all-culture or multi-culture legislature as well as an all-party, all-culture political executive. For example, U.S.A., Nigeria etc., elect members directly into the Senate, House of Representatives and the Presidency, showing that some (not all) voters are represented directly in each branch of government. However, the political posts or offices in each of the branches of government should in any period of rule be (qualitatively and proportionally) shared among all the political parties and among as many alternative cultural constituencies as possible.

The practice in most parts of the world is to represent or attempt to represent all the voters in the legislature (when the Proportional Representation Electoral System is used) but only the majority of the voters in the executive. This is what the presidential system or the parliamentary system does. A notable exception is

Switzerland, which has a multiparty, multi-culture executive. The principle of All-Branch Representation of Voters shows that the practice of representing only the cultural or partisan majority in the executive is against the democratic concept of the equality of political right of all voters and therefore is undemocratic.

The experience of many new states, especially those that are culturally heterogeneous, has confirmed the unacceptability of the exclusion of the political or cultural minority from the executive branch of government. For example, Mr. Jonas Savimbi, the leader of U.N.I.T.A. movement, one of the political organisations in Angola that scored 40.07% of the popular vote, was quoted as saying on Monday 30th November, 1992, "the P.M.L.A. (People's Movement for the Liberation of Angola, another political organisation that won 49.57% of the popular vote in the same election) cannot rule the country alone if we are to have a stable country. Those who have fought for sixteen years will not accept to get nothing." *(Daily Times* of Nigeria, Wednesday 2nd December, 1992 page 5).

Switzerland, as has been mentioned above, has a multiparty and multi-culture executive; and so also must many countries of the world in order to make the world a better place to live in.

For example, *TELL* Magazine of Nigeria (23rd May, 1994 page 21) said this about the new South Africa then headed by President Nelson Mandela:

> In all, the twenty-seven member cabinet is made up of sixteen ANC members, six National Party members and three IFP members. This is in accordance with the constitutional arrangement that representation in the cabinet be made proportional to the overall percentage performance of each party.

Even President Olusegun Obasanjo of Nigeria (1999-2003) appointed his ministers not only from his political party but also from each of the two other political parties existing in the country in 1999. He did not have to do so because he was operating under the majority rule system. However, he did, and the country was the better for it. True democracy does not demand less.

17

THE PRINCIPLE OF PROPORTIONAL REPRESENTATION OF VOTERS

This is the principle that the number of non-scarce political posts that may be held by any group – partisan, or cultural/ethnic – in a period of rule is directly proportional to the number of votes cast or won by the group during the period of rule. The principle follows from the following reasoning.

Governments are run through political posts. Therefore, the people's political representatives must hold political posts to be in government and all the political posts compose the government. Let there be during a period of rule a total of N voters at a government level (local government, state, regional, or national) and M non-scarce political posts (in a branch or arm of government) at the level.

By the concept of the political liberty of all citizens and the principle of Appropriation of Political Right by voting, the N voters have a share in and are solely entitled to the M political posts. Also, by the concept of the political equality of all citizens, all the N voters are each entitled to equal shares of the M political posts.

Therefore, any one vote is equivalent or entitled to M/N political posts. Thus if y denotes the number of political posts corresponding to x votes, then $y = (M/N) *(x)$. Hence, a functional relation exists between the number of political posts and the number of votes of the citizens. Since M and N are constants and hence M/N is a constant for a period of rule, the relationship is a linear one, using the mathematical language. This means in the ordinary language that the number of political posts (y) that may be held is directly proportional to the number of votes (x) cast or won.

This principle can be expressed in three different forms as follows. A re-arrangement of the above relation gives the following three relations: (1) $x/y = N/M$, (2) $y/M = x/N$, and (3) $(y/M)/(x/N)$ = 1. Relation (1) means that in a branch or arm of government, the number of voters per political post, x/y, is constant, since the ratio of total voters to total political posts (i.e. N/M) is a constant. Thus, for example, in a country with two houses of Parliament, all the legislators in one house should, within the limits of arithmetical rounding-off errors, each represent the same number, n, of voters and all the legislators in the other house should also each represent the same number, m, of voters, where the two numbers n and m are not necessarily equal unless the two houses have the same number of members. However, if there is only one house of Parliament, then all the legislators must each represent the same number of voters.

Relation (2) means that the proportion or percentage of the total number of political posts, y/M, to which any interest group is entitled (in a branch of government) should equal the proportion or percentage of total votes cast, x/N, which the group has. This means, in a short form, that the percentage of total posts held equals the percentage of total votes possessed. It also means that, since political posts are discrete, the distribution of a number of political posts among a number of alternative political parties or cultural groups is the best integer distribution of the political posts in accordance with the distribution of the total votes among the groups.

The best integer distribution of the posts among the groups is obtained by the rounding up of each group's share in the actual posts distribution, if it is not a whole number or zero, up or down to the nearest whole number (i.e. integer, including zero), with the share having the highest decimal part being rounded up first, such that the sum of the resulting whole numbers and zeros (if any) for all the groups equals the number of the posts being allocated. For example, the best integer distribution of the distribution (1.32, 1.28, 0.40) is (1, 1, 1) whereas that of (1.40, 1.28, 0.32) is (2, 1, 0) because the highest decimal part is 0.40 and the figure containing it is rounded up to the next higher whole number while the other two figures are rounded down to their whole number (or zero) to make the sum of the elements of the integer distribution to remain at 3, which is the sum of the elements of the original distribution.

Relation (3) means that if all voters are equally represented numerically, then in a branch or arm of government, the value of the ratio of the proportion (or percentage) of total political posts held to the proportion (or percentage) of total votes received or cast should be one (that is, unity) for all alternative political groups. This ratio is henceforth referred to as the Proportional Representation Ratio, P.R. Ratio, or P.R.R.

The following points about the three forms of expression are worthy of note. Firstly, the relations represent the equitable conditions. Secondly, if for any group the proportion (or percentage) of the total posts held (y/M) is smaller than the proportion of total votes scored (x/N) or if the P.R. Ratio is smaller than one, then the group or the voters concerned are being represented below the equitable level and so are being cheated, but if otherwise then the group or the voters concerned are being represented above the equitable level and so are cheating some other group(s) or voters. As for the first relation, the group or the voters represented are being represented below the equitable level and so are being cheated if the number of voters per political post (i.e. x/y) is bigger than the ratio of total votes to total political posts (i.e. N/M) but above the equitable level, and so cheating others if smaller.

Tables 3(a) and (b) show the application of the three alternative expressions of the principle to the distribution of parliamentary seats (i.e. non-scarce political posts) among the five political parties shown. It should be noted that the principle is satisfied in Table 3(b) but not in Table 3(a). Table 3(a) shows distortions ranging from -34% (under-representation) to +18% (over-representation). The distortion is the difference between the P.R. Ratio and 1, expressed in percentages. The small discrepancies noticeable in Table 3(b) are due to rounding-off errors caused by the discrete nature of political posts. Table 3(a) was the actual situation under a majority rule system. Table 3(b) is what it should be under Universal Democracy.

TABLE 3

Measurement of Proportional Representation of Voters

(a) Actual Results, using Single-Member (S.M.) Electoral System

Political Party	Votes Received (x)	% Vote 100 * (x/N)	No. of Seats (y)	No. of Voters per Seat (x/y)	% Seat 100* (y/M)	P.R. Ratio (y/M)/(x/N)	%Distortion 100*(P.R. Ratio - 1)
A	2,170,054	14.524	43	50,466	9.58	0.66	-34
B	5,325,684	35.644	168	31,701	37.42	1.05	+5
C	2,391,279	16.005	78	30,657	17.37	1.09	+9
D	1,382,712	9.254	49	28,219	10.91	1.18	+18
E	3,671,553	24.573	111	33,077	24.72	1.01	+1
ALL	14,941,282 (N)	100	449 (M)	33,277 (N/M)	100	1.00	0

(b) Expected Results, using Proportional Representation (P.R.) Electoral System

Political Party	Votes Received (x)	% Vote 100*(x/N)	No. of Seats (y)	No. of Voters Per Seat (x/y)	% Seat 100* (y/M)	P.R. Ratio (y/M)/(x/N)	%Distortion 100*(P.R. Ratio - 1)
A	2,170,054	14.524	65	33,385	14.48	1.00	0
B	5,325,684	35.644	160	33,286	35.63	1.00	0
C	2,391,279	16.005	72	33,212	16.04	1.00	0
D	1,382,712	9.254	42	32,922	9.35	1.01	+1
E	3,671,553	24.573	110	33,378	24.50	1.00	0
ALL	14,941,282 (N)	100	449 (M)	33,277 (N/M)	100	1.00	0

One important implication of this principle is that the popular notion of equality of the units or groups in a federation is undemocratic. According to the principle of Appropriation of

Political Rights (by voting), the constituent units of a country/polity are entitled to political rights (e.g. political posts) in proportion to the number of votes they cast or win. ('Voters' instead of 'citizens' has been used since the citizens have to vote to appropriate any political right).

Now different constituencies or groups of a country/state may comprise different numbers of voters and therefore are entitled to different numbers of political posts e.g. legislative seats. However, the notion of equality of constituencies or groups, if accepted, would mean that the different groups or constituencies are entitled to the same number of political posts (e.g. senate seats), implying that the voters of the different constituencies or groups are not, as individuals, entitled to equal political rights. This result conflicts with the democratic concept of the political equality of all the voters of a country/state. The notion is therefore undemocratic.

Thus, as this principle requires, the citizens of a country must vote as various constituencies and all the political posts concerned are shared proportionally among the constituencies according to the votes that they cast, if the concept of the political equality of all voters is to hold. The notion of equality of constituencies or groups is a palliative used in Parliamentary and Presidential systems purportedly to reduce the undesirable effects of majority representation on minority groups. The minorities are better off with the principle of Universal Representation of Voters and therefore no longer need the undemocratic notion.

The new South Africa's constitutional arrangement, referred to in the last chapter, that "representation in the cabinet be made proportional to the overall percentage performance of each party", dramatises this principle in practice and is worthy of emulation by all democratic nations the world over, not only for their cabinets but also for all the other arms (or branches) of their governments, and not only for their political parties but also for their cultural/ethnic/geographical constituencies.

18

THE PRINCIPLE OF ROTATION OF A SCARCE POLITICAL POST-TYPE

This is the principle that all voters are entitled to be represented by a scarce political post-type in rotation or in turn. A type of political post is taken to be scarce when the available number of the political post-type cannot go round all the alternative partisan or cultural groups to be represented by it when numerically shared among them in proportion to their (current) voting strengths. The rationale for this principle is as follows.

By the concept of the political equality of all voters, all voters are entitled to equal quantitative as well as qualitative representation through political posts. Where all political posts in a branch of government are non-scarce and qualitatively equal, i.e. are of the same type, or where the political posts are not all of the same type but no type is scarce, then there is no problem, as the distribution of every political post-type that satisfies the political equality concept in the numerical or quantitative sense will also satisfy the concept in the qualitative sense.

However, this is not so if some of the political post-types are scarce (e.g. prime minister, finance minister, etc.) even though all the post-types combined are not scarce, because as the political posts are qualitatively unequal, equal shares of them in the numerical sense will be unequal shares in the qualitative sense. Therefore, since each post-type is distinct and unique (i.e. unequal to any other type), and may be desired by all the alternative groups of citizens in the long run, the equal qualitative shares of scarce types of political posts among the citizens implies, among other things, a rotation of such political post-type among all the alternative groups over time, so that all the voting citizens may periodically be represented through every type of political post.

The principle can be realised as follows. The rotation of a scarce political post or post-type among alternative groups can be achieved in at least two ways. One method is to share the holding of a post in a period of rule among the alternative political representatives or groups (in proportion to their voting strengths).

Switzerland is currently using a similar method to rotate its president and vice-president among members of its Federal Executive Council every year.

Israel also used a similar method between 1984 and 1988, when Likud and Labour parties shared the prime ministership for a four-year period of rule, two years each.

However, the method has two drawbacks. Firstly, a period of rule may be considered the optimum length of time mandatory to hold political post and a shorter period may therefore be objectionable. (This is not so for individuals.)

Secondly, depending on the number of the alternative groups involved, the duration of the small intervals of time into which the period of rule is divided to cover all the groups may be ridiculously short and therefore objectionable.

Thus the sharing of a political post by many alternative groups within a period of rule is not considered feasible, as the method is incapable of accommodating the several alternative groups which may come up. The second method is the sharing of a scarce post over and not within periods of rule. Since a post is available for filling every period of rule, then the post becomes available, as many times as there are periods of rule. Thus if there have been n periods of rule since a post has been in existence in a polity, then there have been n instances of the post.

This phenomenon is in this book referred to as n post-period(s) or cumulative quantity of the post to date. What this means is that the consideration of more than one period of rule introduces numerical reckoning (i.e. post-period) into a scarce political post and makes possible its sharing among any number of alternative groups in the same way as many political posts can be shared. This method does not tamper with the established duration of a period of rule and is capable of accommodating as many alternative groups as possible.

It is therefore considered feasible and recommended for adoption. Therefore the principle of the rotation of a scarce post-type is achieved by the sharing of the cumulative quantity (i.e. post-period) of the scarce political post-type among all the alternative groups concerned.

For the method to be feasible is one thing; it also has to be satisfactory to the people as well as being logical or reasonable in its application. These two questions are now considered.

Chuba Okadigbo (1987) has pointed out the non-acceptability of rule of exclusion in the Executive in Nigeria. He wrote:

> The idea of hegemony, of the permanent production of national leadership from the North or any other section alone, is neither desirable nor acceptable and ... the pittance of having a national leader from the South by accident, (i.e. only when an incumbent dies in office or is abruptly removed from office and is replaced by someone from the South by permission of his colleagues from the North as were the cases with Aguiyi-Ironsi and Obasanjo) is equally insulting and reprehensible.

The only equitable solution to this problem is the rotation of the scarce political post in respect of national leadership among the alternative cultural/ethnic/geographical constituencies.

It is desirable that all of a polity's alternative groups should have a share of each of the polity's political post-types in a period of rule; or, if that is impossible because they are each scarce, then over a definite number of periods of rule if representation by a scarce political post in turn is feasible among the alternative groups. Now alternative cultural/ethnic groups can be satisfactorily represented in turn by a scarce political post over a number of periods of rule.

This view is borne out of the fact that cultural/ethnic groups do not complain when their members are temporarily out of government or out of a particular branch or arm of government or political post-type. They complain only when they perceive that they are permanently or for a long time out of government or out of a particular branch of government or out of a particular political post-type.

Thus whatever the number of alternative cultural/ethnic groups, the alternative groups' universal representation in a particular branch or arm of government by the available number of a political post type, however few, can still be achieved satisfactorily over periods of rule if not within a period of rule – so long as the cycle of rotation is not such that would give the impression of permanent exclusion from (the branch of) government or of inequitable representation of the alternative groups.

On the other hand, alternative partisan groups' universal participation in (a branch of) government cannot be satisfactorily achieved by the groups' participation in turn over periods of rule. The reason is that alternative partisan groups represent alternative bodies of policies on the issues of controversy in the society (see chapter on political parties) and alternative policies on an issue cannot be represented in turn either within a period of rule or over periods of rule because one of them either in its pure or modified form has to be adopted as public policy at a particular point in time and all the others jettisoned and perhaps for ever or at least for a very long time, which may approximate to eternity, unless the need arises to change or modify a policy in the light of experience.

Therefore, the participation of alternative partisan groups in (an arm of) government in turn over periods of rule means in effect the total exclusion from (the arm of) government of some of the alternative policies that may compete for the polity's public policy at any particular time. Thus, unlike alternative cultural/ethnic groups, the universal partisan representation of voters in (an arm of) government must be achieved within every period of rule and not merely over periods of rule.

It is thus clear that whereas the universal cultural/ethnic representation of the voters in (an arm of) government may be achieved within or over periods of rule, the universal partisan representation of the voters in (an arm of) government must be achieved within every period of rule. In other words, there should be no rotation of a scarce partisan post-type among political parties over periods of rule. Thus, for example, every partisan group or political organisation that qualifies as a political party in a polity in a period of rule must be in the cabinet (or Executive Council) as well as in each arm of a bicameral Legislature in the period of rule, whereas some cultural/ethnic/geographical groups may be satisfactorily and temporarily left out of any of the arms of government in a period of rule — all because rotational participation in government is feasible and acceptable for alternative cultural/ethnic groups but not for political parties.

The simple conclusion from the above analysis is that a scarce political post-type should be rotated among alternative cultural/ethnic/geographical constituencies so that all of them may, over time, be represented through it; but not so among alternative political parties. A scarce political post-type should not be rotated among political parties.

Now in a polity's arm of government, e.g. the executive, there may be several unequal scarce post-types to be shared/allocated to alternative cultural/ethnic constituencies as well as to alternative political parties. The implication of this principle for political parties in such circumstances is that the totality of the diverse political post-types should be shared equitably both numerically and qualitatively among the political parties *without* rotating the post-types among them, and if the totality of the unequal post-types is also scarce for the political parties, then a limitation is thereby imposed on the number of feasible political parties in the polity. Those political organizations that would not have had a share must combine with themselves and/or with others that would have had a share so that all of them (and hence all of their voters) would now be able to have a share. Such an allocation process will be achieved by the method of Coordinated Proportional

Representation by Multiple Unequal Scarce Posts (COPREMUSPO) described later elsewhere in this book. On the other hand, the implication of the principle for alternative cultural/ethnic/ geographical constituencies in such a situation is that whether the totality of the diverse unequal scarce post-types is scarce for all the constituencies or not, it should be shared equitably both numerically and qualitatively among the cultural groups by proportional rotation of the post-types among them over periods of rule, so that each of the groups may come to be represented by each of the post-types over time. Such an allocation process will be achieved by the method of Coordinated Proportional Rotation of Multiple Unequal Scarce Political Posts (COPROMUSPO), also described later elsewhere in this book.

It should be noted that the political post-types through which the political parties participate in an arm of government may each be scarce for the political parties, as is usually the situation in the executive arm of government - e.g. Prime Minister, President, Vice-President, Minister of Finance, Minister of Agriculture, etc. In such a situation, what matters is the total number of the unequal scarce political post-types, which must not be scarce for the political parties, so that each of them would hold one post-type or another and hence all the voters would have partisan representation in the arm of government. This is because whatever post-type(s) each political party holds in an arm of government does not lead to the total exclusion from the branch of government of the alternative policies that compete for the polity's public policy at a particular point in time, as policy decisions would be taken by the majority vote of the members irrespective of the post-types they hold, in accordance with the principle of Shifting Majority Will. Moreover, the principle of Coordinated Proportional Allocation of Multiple Unequal Scarce Posts ensures that the scarce unequal post-types in the arm of government are equitably allocated to the political parties by the method of Coordinated Proportional Representation by Multiple Unequal Scarce Posts (COPREMUSPO), referred to above. Furthermore, the principle of Limited Separation of Representation, in conjunction with the method of COPROMUSPO (also referred to above), ensures that the need for voters to be culturally represented by every type of political posts through rotation can be equitably met and independently achieved without rotating such posts among alternative political parties.

It should also be noted that every political post-type through which all voters must have partisan representation in an arm of government, e.g. legislative seats, must not be scarce for all the qualified political parties in the polity in the period of rule. Thus, in practice, the number of such a political post-type must be made large enough to accommodate all the political organizations that win the votes of the people in the General Universal Representation Election (GURE) or else the acceptable number of the political post-type will impose an upper limit on the number of political parties that can exist in the polity in the period of rule, as earlier discussed. Both strategies may be used in combination.

It should be noted that the method of Coordinated Proportional Representation by Multiple Unequal Scarce Posts (COPREMUSPO), which this book has used for political parties, leaves the *qualitative* sharing of multiple unequal scarce posts *among alternative political parties* to competition, giving the highest post to the party with the highest number of votes, etc. Strictly speaking, however, the *quality* of the political posts held by each political party may be democratically based on the political equality of the voters, rather than being based on competition. Therefore, multiple unequal scarce posts may (if desired) be shared *equitably both* numerically and qualitatively among alternative political parties by the method of Coordinated Proportional Rotation of Multiple Unequal Scarce Political Posts (COPROMUSPO), like for cultural constituencies, but *after* ensuring (as earlier explained) that the *total* number of the unequal scarce political posts is *not scarce* for the political parties, so that *all* the voters would have partisan representation in the arm of government concerned in every period of rule.

Tables 4 and 7 in this book show political posts rotated among cultural/ethnic constituencies. The necessary calculations can be done manually or by computer. It should be noted that P1, P2, P3 etc., in those tables could be President, Vice President, Minister of Finance, etc.

19

THE PRINCIPLE OF PROPORTIONAL ROTATION OF SCARCE POLITICAL POST-TYPES

This is the principle that the share of the cumulative quantity (i.e. post-period) of a scarce political post-type or post-types that may be allocated to a cultural group is directly proportional to the number of cumulative votes cast or won by the group over the periods of rule concerned. The principle follows from the following reasoning.

Governments are run through political offices. Therefore, the people's political representatives must hold political offices to be in government and all the political offices compose the government. Let there be during a length of time spanning one or more periods of rule a cumulative total of N' voters at a government level (local government, state, regional, or national/central) and M' cumulative quantity (i.e. post-periods) of one or more scarce political post-types (in a branch of government) at the level. So M' may be the product of the number of a type of political post and the number of equal periods of rule for which the post has existed in the length of time under consideration, or the sum of such products for a scarce post-type or for several scarce post-types as necessary.

By the concept of the political liberty of all citizens, the cumulative N' voters have a share in or are solely entitled to the cumulative quantity M' (i.e. post-periods) of the scarce political posts. Also, by the principle of the political equality of all citizens, all the cumulative N' voters are each entitled to equal shares of the cumulative quantity M' (i.e. post-periods) of the scarce political post(s), ignoring for the sake of simplicity the differences in the number of voters or in the number(s) of the post(s) from period of rule to period of rule. Therefore, any one vote is entitled to M'/N' cumulative quantity (or post-period) of the scarce political post(s). Thus if y' denotes the cumulative quantity (i.e. post-periods) of the scarce political posts corresponding to x' cumulative votes, then $y' = (M'/N') * x'$. Hence, a functional relation exists between the quantity of cumulative total post-periods of scarce political posts and the number of cumulative votes of the citizens. Since M'/N' is constant, the relationship is a linear one, meaning in the ordinary language that the post-periods of a scarce political post or of some scarce political posts that may be held is directly proportional to the number of the cumulative votes cast or won over the number of periods of rule concerned, as required to be proved. Still in simpler language, it means that the number of times a group holds a scarce post or scarce posts is directly proportional to the number of cumulative votes it has cast or won.

This principle can be expressed in three forms as follows. A re-arrangement of the above relation gives the following three relations: (1) $x'/y' = N'/M'$, (2) $y'/M' = x'/N'$, and (3) $(y'/M')/(x'/N') = 1$. With respect to the sharing of the post-periods of a scarce political post-type or of multiple scarce post-types among alternative groups, relation (1) means that if all voters from period of rule to period of rule are entitled to equal shares of the post-periods of a scarce political post(s), then in a branch of government the number of voters per post-period, x'/y', is a constant, since N'/M' is a constant. (This means that the rotational rate of voter representation by a scarce type of political post is constant). This means that within the limits of rounding off errors, the number of cumulative voters per post-period of a scarce political post or of a number of scarce political posts should not vary from one cultural, ethnic, or geographical group to another.

Relation (2) means that if all voters are entitled to equal qualitative shares of a scarce political post or of some scarce political post-types, then in a branch of government the proportion of total post-periods, y'/M', to which any group is entitled with respect to scarce political post(s) in any number of periods of rule should equal the proportion of the cumulative total votes, x'/N', which the group has over the periods of rule concerned. This means, in a short form, that the percentage of total post-periods held equals the percentage of cumulative total votes possessed. It also means that, since post-periods are discrete, the distribution of the post-periods of a scarce political post or of some scarce political posts among a number of alternative geographical or cultural groups is the best integer distribution of the post-periods (of the scarce political post(s)) given by the distribution of the cumulative total votes among the groups over the periods of rule concerned. (The proportion or percentage of cumulative total votes possessed or constituted by an interest group is in this book referred to as its cumulative voting strength).

Relation (3) means that if all voters are equally qualitatively represented then (in a branch of government) the value of the ratio of the proportion of the post-periods of a scarce political post-type or of some scarce political post-types held (y'/M') to the proportion of the cumulative total votes cast or won (x'/N') during the same number of periods of rule should be unity (that is, one) for all alternative groups. This ratio will be referred to henceforth as the Proportional Rotational Representation, P.R.R., Ratio (or P.R.R.R.).

The following points about the three relations are worthy of note. Firstly, the relations represent the equitable conditions. Secondly, if for any group the proportion or percentage of the left hand side of the last two relations is smaller than the right hand side, then the group or its voters are being represented below the equitable level and so are being cheated, but if higher then the group or its voters are being represented above the equitable level and so are cheating some other voters. As for the first relation, the group or its voters are being represented below the equitable level and so are being cheated if the left hand side is bigger than the right hand side. The reverse is also correct.

Table 4 in this book shows the proportional rotation of political posts among cultural constituencies.

20

THE PRINCIPLE OF CO-ORDINATED PROPORTIONAL ALLOCATION OF MULTIPLE UNEQUAL SCARCE POSTS

This is the principle that multiple unequal scarce post-types should be allocated to alternative groups by the progressive combined proportional rotation of, or representation by, each post-type with all its superiors.

The premises for this principle are as follows. The rotation of such multiple post-types among alternative cultural groups over periods of rule will be considered first and then their allocation to alternative political parties in a period of rule considered next. The separate or unco-ordinated proportional rotation of individually scarce political posts or post-types can often result in controversial or disproportionate sharing of the multiple scarce political posts among the alternative groups concerned from one period of rule to another, making one group to have most or all of the political posts in a period of rule to the exclusion of the others. This is a violation of the principle of Proportional Representation of Voters and hence inconsistent with the concept of the political equality of the citizens and therefore with true representative political democracy.

Also, the haphazard sequence of rotation of multiple unequal scarce political posts from one period of rule to another can result in unbalanced or inequitable representation of voters by such political posts, as the unsystematic way of spreading out the unequal scarce posts among the alternative groups concerned makes it possible through manipulation for a preponderance of the more important posts to be in the hands of particular groups during any period of rule.

The proportional rotation of multiple unequal scarce political post-types should, in order to achieve equal qualitative and proportional representation of voters, which the concept of political equality of voters also implies, be co-ordinated by considering the totality of the unequal scarce political posts and systematically too in a given order from one period of rule to another.

Consideration of the totality of the unequal scarce political posts implies that the combined updated cumulative quantities (post-periods) of the post-types rather than their individual cumulative quantities (post-periods) should be proportionally shared. However, since the political posts are discrete and the post-types are unique and unequal, the combined updated cumulative quantities (post-periods) of all the post-types may not be shared in one fell swoop, because it will be unclear which post-types should go to which group and consequently discretion or arbitrariness and hence inequality can creep into the allocation process. This implies that the post-types should be allocated in stages, each type at a stage, by proportionally sharing at every stage the combined updated cumulative quantities (post-periods) of a post-type and of all the post-types already considered at the earlier stages.

In that way the recipient(s) of each post-type can be uniquely determined by a consideration of the cumulative quantities (post-periods) of this post-type held by any group in the previous periods of rule as well as the group's share of combined updated cumulative quantities (post-periods) of all the post-types that have been earlier allocated, both categories of information being readily available at each stage. Moreover, the consideration of the totality of the scarce political posts systematically in a given order from period of rule to period of rule implies, among other things, that, in the stage-wise allocation of the post-types, the post-types should be ranked, so that they may be considered in the same sequence from one period of rule to another.

This ranking may be either in the descending order or in the ascending order of importance of the post-types. However, since in the proportional rotational representation of voters the group with the highest proportion of votes will receive a post first, followed by the group with the next highest proportion of votes and so on, it follows from rational thinking that the first group to receive a post should receive the first or 'best' post. This implies that the unequal scarce political post-types should be ranked in the descending rather than the ascending order of importance. In that case at any stage, all post-types that have been earlier allocated will be the entire post-types superior to the post-type under consideration. Therefore, the co-ordination of rotational representation of voters by multiple unequal scarce political posts as a connected whole implies the allocation or distribution of any of the scarce post-types by sharing the combined updated post-periods of the particular post-type and of all the other scarce post-types superior to it. This is the stage-wise or progressive proportional rotation of each post-type with all its superiors, as required to be shown.

This principle implies the following main steps in allocating multiple unequal scarce political posts. The procedure is abbreviated as COPROMUSPO for ease of reference.

(a) Ranking of the scarce unequal post-types in the descending order of importance.

(b) Allocating the post-types in turn, one post-type at a time, and starting from the most important post-type.

(c) Allocating a post-type by the following procedure.

(i) Integer sharing the combined post-periods of the post-type and of all its superiors, among the cultural groups concerned in direct proportion to the groups' shares of the cumulative popular vote over the periods of rule concerned, subject only to rounding-off errors.

(ii) Considering for each group, its actual combined share to date and stage (i.e. past and present periods of rule) of the combined post-periods of the post-type and of its superiors.

(iii)   Finding the difference between the integer part of (i) and (ii) above for each group and ensuring that it is not negative i.e. either zero or a positive number – reviewing (i) if necessary.

To facilitate the best integer distribution process, each group's share of the total post-periods to the post under consideration will be separated into its integer part and its decimal/negative part. Then the rounding off process is done by adding the values of the integer parts for all the groups and if their sum is less than the total post-periods to the post under consideration, then the integer part of the group with the highest value of the decimal/negative part is increased by one to the next higher integer, while the corresponding decimal/negative part is decreased by one to maintain equilibrium.

The process is repeated until the sum of the resulting integer parts equals the total post-periods to the post under consideration. The sum of the decimal/negative parts would also equal zero.

For example, consider the calculations for the allocation to the cultural constituencies of the post-type P3, the previous total post-period of which is 1, the current quantity of which is 1, and the current total post-period of which is 2. The current (cumulative) total post-periods of all posts to the post-type P3 is 6 (Table 4). Bauchi's share of the total post-periods to the post-type P3 is 6*0.065755759 = 0.39453. Kaduna's share is 6*0.083237589 = 0.49943, but written as 1 - 0.50057 because Kaduna has been allocated the superior post-type P2 in the previous period of rule. Ondo's share is 6*0.075625419 = 0.45375, written as 2 - 1.54625 because Ondo has been allocated the superior post-type P2 in this period of rule and the post-type P3 itself in the previous period of rule. Oyo's share is 6*0.088615634 = 0.53169, written as 1 - 0.46831 because Oyo has been allocated the superior post-type P1 in the previous period of rule. Sokoto's share is 6*0.098994848 = 0.59397, written as 1 - 0.0603 because Sokoto has been allocated the superior post-type P1 in this period of rule. The calculated shares of the other constituencies (except Bauchi) to the post-type P3 are as shown in Table 4. The integer parts in the post-type P3 column (with Bauchi's share at 0.39453 as calculated above) sum up to 5, which is less than 6 by 1, the current quantity of the post-type P3. Now Bauchi's calculated share of 0.39453 has the largest decimal/negative part of all the constituencies' shares in the post-type P3 column. Therefore it is written as 1 - 0.60547 in Table 4, thereby allocating the single post P3 to Bauchi for the current period of rule.

Any group's share (previous and current) of the total quantity of the post under consideration is obtained as the group's integer part of the total post-period to the post under consideration less the group's integer part of the total post-period to the post-type immediately preceding (or superior to) the post under consideration.

It should be noted that there is no need for inter-branch multiple proportional rotation of political posts if there is all-branch representation of voters and there is intra-branch multiple rotation of the political posts in each branch of government. If for any reason inter-branch multiple rotation of scarce political posts is to replace all-branch representation of voters, then all the scarce political posts concerned from all the branches of government should be mixed and ranked in their precedent order; otherwise the multiple proportional rotation process might be inequitable.

This method, which uses cumulative votes to date, ensures that political posts (including legislative seats and offices) which are scarce and so unable to go round the appropriate ethnic constituencies in a period of rule will necessarily and proportionally do so over the periods of rule. The method ensures that the members of the executive, including the president and the other top administrators or ministers, who constitute the Executive Council or even legislators and Judicial Council members, are drawn, not from just any cultural group or section of the polity as may happen in the parliamentary and presidential systems, but rather (and proportionally too) from the different cultural/ethnic constituencies. The chief executive may come from any cultural group or section of the polity, minority or majority. So also can any of the ministers and other political office occupiers, whether in the legislature, judiciary or executive. In fact, no cultural constituency or section of the polity has a monopoly of any office, as all the scarce political offices, be they judicial, legislative or executive, will, over periods of rule, proportionally go round all the cultural constituencies.

The order of rotation of political posts among the cultural constituencies is not arbitrary but mathematically proportional to the cumulative voting strengths of the cultural constituencies.

The frequency with which a cultural constituency or section of the polity holds any scarce office relative to another cultural constituency or section of the polity is also not arbitrary but mathematically and so equitably according to their relative cumulative voting strengths to date in the General Universal Representation Election (GURE).

Thus, the equality of legislative, judicial and executive representation of all voters, irrespective of their cultural or partisan affiliations, minority or majority, is guaranteed and no special protection is required for any group, for all groups are equally treated, the individual voter being used as the unit of reckoning.

It should be remembered that there is no partisan allocation of scarce political posts over periods of rule, i.e., using post-periods and partisan distribution of cumulative voters over periods of rule. However, the steps of the method of co-ordinated proportional rotation of multiple scarce political posts may be used for the partisan allocation of different scarce political posts within a period of rule when the current (not cumulative) quantities of the post-types and the partisan distribution of current votes rather than cumulative votes are used. The method is then referred to as the method of co-ordinated proportional representation by multiple unequal scarce posts, abbreviated as COPREMUSPO.

For instance, consider the calculations for the allocation to the political parties of the post-type P5A for the 1983 Election (Table 6). The current quantity of the post-type P5A is 2, and the current total quantity of all post-types to the post-type P5A is 9. NPN's share of this current total quantity is $9*0.474839 = 4.27355$; NPP's share is $9*0.139806 = 1.25825$; PRP-GNPP-NAP's share is $9*0.074577 = 0.67119$, written as $1 - 0.32881$ because PRP-GNPP-NAP has been previously allocated the superior post-type P5; and UPN's share is $9*0.310778 = 2.79700$. NPN definitely has a share of the post-type P5A because the integer part of its calculated total current quantity to this post-type is 4, which is one greater than the integer part of the party's calculated total current quantity to the immediately preceding (or superior) post-type P5, which is 3. With UPN's share still standing at 2.79700, all the integer parts in the P5A column sum to 8, which is less than 9 by 1. Now 0.79700, which is the decimal/negative part of UPN's share, is greater in value than any of the decimal/negative parts of the calculated shares in the P5A column for the other political parties. Therefore, UPN's share is written as 3 - 0.20300, thus allocating the remaining one post of the post-type P5A to UPN for the current period of rule.

Table 4 shows the application (with calculations) of this principle (as COPROMUSPO) to the sharing of political posts among some ethnic/cultural constituencies over two consecutive periods of rule. The calculations for the previous (i.e. 1979) allocations (underlined) are not shown, but these can be estimated off-hand by looking at the previous cumulative vote (1979 Elections) column and giving the cultural constituencies the posts in the descending order of their votes. Table 7 is a summary of the sharing exercise for the cultural constituencies for the two periods of rule.

Table 5 and Table 6 show the application (with calculations) of this principle (as COPREMUSPO) to the sharing of political posts among some political organisations/parties for two consecutive periods of rule (i.e. 1979 and 1983). It should be noted that the calculations are carried out for each period of rule separately, the current votes for each period of rule are used, there is no carry-over of political posts from one period of rule to another, and the first or 'best' post always goes to the political party with the highest number of votes and so on. All political posts are currently allocated in each table. It should also be noted that no votes are ignored: political organisations that did not score enough votes to exist separately as political parties (i.e. GNPP and NAP in 1983) are combined with PRP as PRP - GNPP - NAP to have a good share of the political posts.

TABLE 4

The method of Co-ordinated Proportional Rotation of Multiple Unequal Scarce Posts (COPROMUSPO) applied to the hypothetical sharing of the (Federal) Executive Council positions among the ethnic/cultural constituencies in Universal Democracy, using the results of the Nigeria's 1979 and 1983 Presidential Elections.

IDENTIFICATION CODE OF POST-TYPE	P1	P2	P3	P3A	P4	P5	P5A
PREVIOUS TOTAL POST-PERIODS OF POST	1	1	1	0	1	1	0
CURRENT QUANTITY OF POST-TYPE	1	1	1	1	1	2	2
CURRENT TOTAL POST-PERIODS OF POST-TYPE	2	2	2	1	2	3	2
CURRENT (CUMULATIVE) TOTAL POST-PERIODS TO THE POST-TYPE UNDER CONSIDERATION	2	4	6	7	9	12	14

ETHNIC/ CULTURAL CONSTITUENCY	PREVIOUS CUMULATIVE VOTE (1975 Election)	CURRENT VOTE (1983 Election)	CURRENT CUMULATIVE VOTE (1979 & 1983 Election)	PROPORTION OF CURRENT CUMULATIVE TOTAL VOTE	CONSTITUENCY'S SHARE OF THE CURRENT (CUMULATIVE) TOTAL POST-PERIOD TO THE POST-TYPE UNDER CONSIDERATION (EXPRESSED IN INTEGER AND DECIMAL / NEGATIVE PARTS)						
					P1	P2	P3	P3A	P4	P5	P5A
ANAMBRA	1209033	1158283	2367321	0.055978391	0.111957	0.223914	0.33587	0.391849	0.50381	*1 - 0.32826*	1 - 0.2163
BAUCHI	998683	1782122	2780805	0.065755759	0.131512	0.263023	*1 - 0.60547*	1 - 0.53571	1 - 0.4082	1 - 0.21093	1 - 0.07942
BENDEL	669511	1099851	1769362	0.041838871	0.083678	0.167355	0.251033	0.0292872	0.37655	0.502066	0.585743
BENUE	538879	652795	1191674	0.028178685	0.056357	0.112715	0.169072	0.197251	0.253608	0.338144	0.394502
BORNO	710968	718043	1429011	0.033790828	0.067582	0.135163	0.202745	0.236336	0.304117	0.40549	0.47307
CROSS RIVER	661103	1285710	1946813	0.046034931	0.09207	0.18414	0.27621	0.322245	0.414314	0.55242	*1 - 0.35551*
GONGOLA	639138	723956	1363094	0.032232134	0.064464	0.128929	0.193393	0.225625	0.290089	0.386786	0.45125
IMO	1153355	1588975	2742330	0.064845968	0.129692	0.259384	0.38908	**1 - 0.54608**	1 - 0.42639	1 - 0.22185	1 - 0.09216
KADUNA	1382712	2137398	3520110	0.083217589	0.166475	1 - 0.66705	1 - 0.50057	1 - 0.41734	1 - 0.25086	1 - 0.00115	1.165326
KANO	1220763	1193050	2413813	0.057077755	0.114156	0.228311	0.342467	0.399544	0.5137	1 - 0.31507	1 - 0.20091
KWARA	354605	608422	963027	0.022772029	0.045544	0.091088	0.136632	0.159404	0.204948	0.273264	0.318808
LAGOS	828414	1640381	2468795	0.058377876	0.116756	0.233512	0.350267	0.408645	*1 - 0.4746*	1 - 0.2947	1 - 0.18271
NIGER	383347	430731	814078	0.019249935	0.0385	0.077	0.1155	0.13475	0.173249	0.230999	0.269499
OGUN	744668	1261061	2005729	0.047429077	0.094856	0.189712	0.284568	0.331997	0.426853	0.56014	0.664007
ONDO	1369849	1828343	3198192	0.075625419	0.151251	*1 - 0.6975*	2 - 1.54625	2 - 1.47062	2 - 1.31937	2 - 1.09249	2 - 0.94125
OYO	1396547	2351000	3747547	0.088615634	1 - 0.82277	1 - 0.64554	1 - 0.46831	1 - 0.37969	1 - 0.20246	1.063388	1.240619
PLATEAU	548405	652302	1200707	0.028392282	0.056785	0.113569	0.170354	0.198746	0.255531	0.340707	0.397492
RIVERS	687951	1357715	2045666	0.048372439	0.096745	0.19349	0.290235	0.338607	0.435352	*1 - 0.41953*	1 - 0.32279
SOKOTO	1348697	2837786	4186483	0.098994848	*1 - 0.80201*	1 - 0.60402	1 - 0.40603	1 - 0.30704	2 - 1.10205	2 - 0.812062	2 - 0.614072
ABUJA	—	135351	135351	0.003200551	0.006401	0.012802	0.019203	0.022404	0.028805	0.038497	0.044808
ALL	16846633	25444275	42289908	1	2	4	6	7	9	12	14

KEY: *Italics & Bold* - Currently allocated [Steps (c) (i) & (iii) of COPROMUSPO]

Underline - Previously allocated [Steps (c) (ii) & (iii) of COPROMUSPO]

TABLE 4 (CONTD.)

	P6	P7	P8	P9	P10	All
IDENTIFICATION CODE OF POST-TYPE	1	1	1	1	1	10
PREVIOUS TOTAL POST-PERIODS OF POST						
CURRENT QUANTITY OF POST-TYPE	1	1	1	1	1	14
CURRENT TOTAL POST-PERIODS OF POST-TYPE	2	2	2	2	2	24
CURRENT (CUMULATIVE) TOTAL POST-PERIODS TO THE POST-TYPE UNDER CONSIDERATION	16	18	20	22	24	24

| ETHNIC/ CULTURAL CONSTITUENCY | PREVIOUS CUMULATIVE VOTE (1979 Election) | CURRENT VOTE (1983 Election) | CURRENT CUMULATIVE VOTE (1979 & 1983 Election) | PROPORTION OF CURRENT CUMULATIVE TOTAL VOTE | CONSTITUENCY'S SHARE OF THE CURRENT (CUMULATIVE) TOTAL POST-PERIOD TO THE POST-TYPE UNDER CONSIDERATION (EXPRESSED IN INTEGER AND DECIMAL / NEGATIVE PARTS) | | | | | |
					P6	P7	P8	P9	P10	All
ANAMBRA	1209038	1158283	2367321	0.055978391	2-1.0435	2-0.9924	2-0.88043	2-0.768475	2-0.65652	2
BAUCHI	998683	1782122	2780805	0.065755759	1.052092	1.183604	2-0.68489	2-0.55337	2-0.42186	2
BENDEL	669511	1099851	1769362	0.041838871	*1-0.33058*	1-0.2469	1-1.6322	1-0.079545	1.004133	-
BENUE	538879	652795	1191674	0.028178685	0.450859	0.507216	0.56356	0.56356	0.67629	-
BORNO	710968	718043	1429011	0.033790828	0.54065	*1-0.39177*	1-0.32418	1-0.32418	1-0.18902	1
CROSS RIVER	661103	1285710	1946813	0.046034931	1-0.26344	1-0.17137	1-1.00793	1.012768	1.104838	1
GONGOLA	639138	723956	1363094	0.032232134	0.51571	0.58018	0.64464	0.70911	*1-0.22643*	1
IMO	1153355	1588975	2742330	0.064845968	1.037535	2-0.832773	2-0.7031	2-0.573389	2-0.4437	2
KADUNA	1382712	2137398	3520110	0.083237589	1.331801	1.498277	1.66475	*2-0.16877*	2-0.0023	2
KANO	1220763	1193050	2413813	0.057077755	1-0.08676	1.0274	1.141555	1.255711	1.369866	1
KWARA	354605	608422	963027	0.022772029	0.364352	0.409897	0.455441	0.50098	0.54653	-
LAGOS	828414	1640381	2468795	0.058377876	1-0.06595	1.050802	1.176558	2-0.715687	2-0.59893	2
NIGER	383347	430731	814078	0.019249935	0.307999	0.346499	0.384999	0.423499	0.461998	-
OGUN	744668	1261061	2005729	0.047429077	1-0.24115	1-0.14629	1-0.5144	1.043418	*2-0.861726*	2
ONDO	1369849	1828343	3198192	0.075625419	2-0.78999	2-0.63875	2-0.4875	2-0.33624	2-0.18499	2
OYO	1396547	2351000	3747547	0.088615634	1.41785	*1.59508*	*2-0.22769*	2-0.05046	2.126775	2
PLATEAU	548405	652302	1200707	0.028392282	0.454277	0.51106	0.56785	0.62463	0.68141	-
RIVERS	687951	1357715	2045666	0.048372439	1-0.22604	1-0.1293	1-0.0355	1.064194	1.160939	1
SOKOTO	1348697	2837786	4186483	0.098994848	2-0.41608	2-0.21809	2-0.0201	2.177887	2.375876	2
ABUJA	—	135351	135351	0.003200551	0.051209	0.05761	0.064011	0.070412	0.076813	-
ALL	16846633	25443275	42289908	1	16	18	20	22	24	24

KEY: *Italics & Bold* - Currently allocated [Steps (c) (i) & (iii) of COPROMUSPO]
     Underline - Previously allocated [Steps (c) (ii) & (iii) of COPROMUSPO]

TABLE 5

The method of Co-ordinated Proportional Representation by Multiple Unequal Scarce Posts (COPREMUSPO) applied to the hypothetical sharing of the (Federal) Executive Council positions among the political organizations in Universal Democracy, using the results of the Nigeria's 1979 Presidential Election.

IDENTIFICATION CODE OF POST-TYPE		P1	P2	P3	P4	P5	P6	P7	P8	P9	P10	ALL
CURRENT QUANTITY OF POST-TYPE		1	1	1	1	1	1	1	1	1	1	10
CURRENT TOTAL QUANTITY OF ALL POSTS TO THE POST-TYPE UNDER CONSIDERATION		1	2	3	4	5	6	7	8	9	10	10
POLITICAL ORGANIZATION	CURRENT VOTE (1979 Election) / PROPORTION OF CURRENT TOTAL VOTE	POLITICAL PARTY'S SHARE OF CURRENT TOTAL QUANTITY OF ALL POSTS TO THE POST-TYPE UNDER CONSIDERATION (EXPRESSED IN INTEGER AND DECIMAL / NEGATIVE PARTS)										
GNPP	1,686,489 / 0.100108	0.10011	0.20022	0.30032	0.40043	0.50054	0.60065	1 - 0.29924	1 - 0.19914	1 - 0.09903	1.00108	1
NPN	5,688,857 / 0.337685	1 - 0.66231	1 - 0.32463	1.013055	1.35074	2 - 0.31158	2.02611	2.363795	3 - 0.29852	3.039165	3.37685	3
NPP	2,822,523 / 0.167542	0.16754	0.335084	1 - 0.49797	0.76017	1 - 0.16229	1.00525	1.172794	1.340336	1.507878	2 - 0.32458	2
PRP	1,732,113 / 0.102817	0.10282	0.20563	0.30845	1 - 0.58873	1 - 0.48592	1 - 0.3831	1 - 0.28028	1 - 0.17746	1 - 0.07465	1.02817	1
UPN	4,916,651 / 0.291848	0.29185	1 - 0.41630	1 - 0.12446	1.16739	1.45924	2 - 0.24891	2.04294	2.33478	3 - 0.373368	3 - 0.08152	3
TOTAL	16,846,633 / 1.000000	1	2	3	4	5	6	7	8	9	10	10

KEY: *Italics & Bold - Currently allocated*

TABLE 6

The method of Co-ordinated Proportional Representation by Multiple Unequal Scarce Posts (COPREMUSPO) applied to the hypothetical sharing of the (Federal) Executive Council positions among the political organizations in Universal Democracy, using the results of the Nigeria's 1983 Presidential Election.

IDENTIFICATION CODE OF POST-TYPE	CURRENT VOTE	PROPORTION	P1	P2	P3	P3A	P4	P5	P5A	P6	P7	P8	P9	P10	ALL
IDENTIFICATION CODE OF POST-TYPE			P1	P2	P3	P3A	P4	P5	P5A	P6	P7	P8	P9	P10	ALL
CURRENT QUANTITY OF POST-TYPE			1	1	1	1	1	2	2	1	1	1	1	1	14
CURRENT TOTAL QUANTITY OF ALL POSTS TO THE POST-TYPE UNDER CONSIDERATION			1	2	3	4	5	7	9	10	11	12	13	14	14
POLITICAL ORGANIZATION (1983 Election)	CURRENT VOTE	PROPORTION OF CURRENT TOTAL VOTE	POLITICAL PARTY'S SHARE OF CURRENT TOTAL QUANTITY OF ALL POSTS TO THE POST TYPE UNDER CONSIDERATION (EXPRESS INTEGER AND DECIMAL/NEGATIVE PARTS)												
NPN	12081471	0.474839	1 - 0.5252	1 - 0.0503	2 - 0.57548	2 - 0.10064	2.3742	3.32387	4.27355	5 - 0.25161	5.22323	5.69807	6.17291	7 - 0.35225	7.
NPP	3557114	0.139806	0.139981	0.27961	0.41942	1 - 0.44078	1 - 0.30097	1 - 0.02136	1.25825	1.39806	2 - 0.46213	2 - 0.32233	2 - 0.18252	2 - 0.04272	2
(GNPP) (NAP) (PRP)	(643805) (284509) (969167)	(0.025034) (0.011182) (0.038091)													
PRP-GNPP-NAP	1897481	0.074577	0.07458	0.14915	0.22373	0.29831	0.37289	1 - 0.4780	1 - 0.32881	1 - 0.25423	1 - 0.17965	1 - 0.10508	1 - 0.0305	1.04408	1
UPN	7907209	0.310778	0.31078	1 - 0.37844	1 - 0.06767	1.24311	2 - 0.44611	2.17545	3 - 0.20300	3.10778	3.41856	4 - 0.27066	4.04011	4.35089	4
Total	25443275	1.000000	1	2	3	4	5	7	9	10	11	12	13	14	14

KEY: Italics & Bold - Currently allocated

NOTES:
(i) The number of positions on the Federal Executive Council in 1983 was presumed to increase by four over the previous period of rule (1979) by the creation of two new post-types p3A (one position) and P5A (two positions) and by increasing the post-type P5 to two positions.

(ii) PRP, GNPP and NAP were different political organizations at the 1983 elections but analysis shows that in Universal Democracy, neither GNPP nor NAP nor both of them combined could have a position on the Executive Council.
The presumption here is that both organizations would team up with PRP to enhance its position, even though it would have a (lower) position on the council without them. Hence the name PRP-GNPP-NAP

TABLE 7

Summary of the ethnic/cultural constituencies' hypothetical shares of the (Federal) Executive Council positions in Universal Democracy, using the results of the Nigeria's 1979 and 1983 Presidential Elections.

ETHNIC/CULTURAL CONSTITUENCY	VOTES CAST						EXECUTIVE COUNCIL POSTS FOR CONSTITUENCIES		
	PREVIOUS CUMULATIVE (1979 Election)		CURRENT (1983 Election)		CURRENT CUMULATIVE (1979 & 1983 Elections)		PREVIOUS POST (1979)	CURRENT POST (1983)	CUMULATIVE TOTAL NUMBER (1979 & 1983)
	Number	Proportion	Number	Proportion	Number	Proportion			
ANAMBRA	1209038	0.071767338	11538283	0.0455241	2367321	0.055978391	P6	P5	2
BAUCHI	998683	0.059280866	1782122	0.0700429	2780805	0.065755759	P8	P3	2
BENDEL	669511	0.039741532	1099851	0.0432275	1769362	0.041838871	-	P6	1
BENUE	538879	0.031987341	652795	0.0256568	1191674	0.028178685	-	-	-
BORNO	710968	0.04220238	718043	0.0282213	1429011	0.033790828	-	P7	1
CROSS RIVER	661103	0.039242441	1285710	0.0505324	1946813	0.046034931	-	P5A	1
GONGOLA	639138	0.03793862	723956	0.0284537	1363094	0.032232134	-	P10	1
IMO	1153355	0.068462048	1588975	0.0624516	2742330	0.064845968	P7	P3A	2
KADUNA	1382712	0.08207646	2137498	0.0840064	3520110	0.083237589	P2	P9	2
KANO	1220763	0.072463322	1193050	0.0468905	2413813	0.057707755	P5	-	1
KWARA	354605	0.021049013	608422	0.0239128	963027	0.022772029	-	-	-
LAGOS	828414	0.049173862	1640381	0.064472	2468795	0.058377876	P9	P4	2
NIGER	333347	0.022755111	430731	0.016929	814078	0.019249935	-	-	-
OGUN	744668	0.044202779	1261061	0.0495636	2005729	0.047428077	P10	P5A	2
ONDO	1369849	0.081312925	1828343	0.0718595	3198192	0.075625419	P3	P2	2
OYO	1396547	0.082897692	2351000	0.0924016	3749547	0.088615634	P1	P8	2
PLATEAU	548405	0.032552796	652302	0.0256375	1200707	0.028392282	-	-	-
RIVERS	687951	0.04086112	1357715	0.0533624	2045666	0.048372439	-	P5	1
SOKOTO	1348697	0.080057362	2837786	0.1115338	4186483	0.098994848	P4	P1	2
ABUJA	-	0	135351	0.0053197	135351	0.003200551	-	-	-
ALL	16846633	1	25443275	1	42289908	1	; 10	14	24

NOTE:

It can be seen that in 1983 five more constituencies would have had positions on the Executive Council than in 1979, so that in one or two more periods of rule all the constituencies would have had at least a position in the Executive Council, thereby eliminating the problem of ethnic/cultural marginality in political matters.

21

THE PRINCIPLE OF HOMOGENEITY OF CANDIDATES

This is the principle that there must be partisan and/or cultural homogeneity of the candidates for a political post.

The principle stems from the majority vote concept coupled with social justice or social democracy. The process of electing political officeholders by the majority vote of the selectors is not just competitive; it is eliminative, in the sense that only the choice of the majority wins a post while the other contestants win nothing. Therefore the process has to be seen to be fundamentally fair, to obey the laws of social democracy for it to be democratically acceptable.

It is generally accepted that people are differently qualified, experienced and endowed for something and that qualification, experience and endowment are personal attributes. Therefore when two or more persons contest for something that only one of them may have, human nature accepts that the best of the contestants on his personal merits should win. When this happens, both the losers and the onlookers are satisfied, good sense prevails and peace reigns. The loser then can congratulate the winner.

However, where it is obvious that the best of the candidates does not win, the loser feels cheated and revengeful, and even the spectators feel that something is wrong that needs to be redressed: pandemonium may ensue, unrest and instability may result. This has been the observation in all spheres of life, e.g. disturbances in football fields. In order to avoid such an unsatisfactory situation in the political arena, it is necessary to ensure in the interest of good sense and fair play, that the best of the aspirants on personal merits for a public office eventually occupies it, even when the election is made by the majority vote of the people/electors.

This implies the elimination of anything that will prevent the best candidate on his personal merits for a political office from winning in a competitive election process (by majority vote). Now, differences in competence for a particular political post may exist between two professions or between the sexes or between youths and adults, but not between one religion and another nor between one ethnic, regional or geographical group and another, nor between persons of different policies per se, as every ethnic group or every religion or every political group is capable of having qualified and experienced people for every political post, judicial, legislative and executive. This is to say that within a polity, a person may be more competent than another for a political post because of differences in their professions or in their ages (or experience) or in their sexes or other personal endowments but not because of differences in their religions or in their ethnic origins or in their partisan beliefs per se. For instance, a medical personnel may be best as the Minister of Health, a lawyer as Minister of Justice, a female as Minister of Women Affairs, and a youth as Minister of Youth Matters; but it is outrageous to say in the same country/polity that a Muslim is best as Minister of Defence or a Christian as Minister of Agriculture.

Therefore, it is right to say that differences in age, gender, education or profession are related to the personal merits or competence of individuals for a political office and so should be left to competition among individuals rather than being made the basis of group representation of voters.

However, differences in ethnicity, religious beliefs and partisan beliefs do not have direct bearings on an individual's ability or competence for a political office and so should be excluded from competition among individuals for a political post. Otherwise, they lead in reality to competition among, and consequently the elimination of, alternative partisan, ethnic or religious groups of the society rather than competition among and elimination of individuals as intended. This is so because, as noted by Rodee *et al* in *Introduction to Politics*, shared cultural (i.e. ethnic and/or religious) characteristics are the foundations of a sense of unity, a common purpose and political consensus and so have a strong appeal on the voters at elections.

In fact, most West European nations are defined along cultural lines/boundaries: the French, the Germans, the English, etc., are distinct ethnic (or racial) groups. The French are mainly Catholics; the English, Protestants; the Arabs, Muslims; etc., and so they are also distinct religious groups. Moreover, if the contestants for a political post model such voters' interests which do not relate to merit but which have a strong appeal on voters, then in voting, the voters are free to and will surely consider these extraneous non-merit-related factors in addition to the candidates' personal merits for the political post to be held.

The voters may even attach more weight to the extraneous voters' interests than to the candidates' personal merits for the post and therefore vote solely according to these extraneous factors to the exclusion of the relevant personal merits of the candidates for the office to be occupied. In fact, historical experience confirms that in such circumstances, citizens vote more on the basis of their personal interests than on the basis of the candidates' merits for the job to be done. The case of late Chief Obafemi Awolowo is still fresh in the memory of Nigerians. This is the man of whom Chief Odumegwu Ojukwu, the former leader of the defunct Biafran State (1967 – 1970), wrote in his book *Because I am Involved*:

> At his death, I had the singular honour of proposing for him this epitaph that has endured – he was the best President that Nigeria never had... Nigeria would have benefited from his presidency because of his innate presidential qualities. Nigeria must continually regret that he never, for many reasons, had the opportunity to serve at the presidential level. Awo was a leader of great stature. (pages 152-3)

Thrice Awo tried to become the prime minister or president of Nigeria and thrice he failed. Why? Because Awo was in an heterogeneous society where the candidates modelled alternative partisan and cultural (i.e. ethnic and religious) interests, which were more effective as the basis of selection by voting than were the candidates' personal merits for the political office.

The inevitable conclusion from the above theoretical and historical analyses is that matters such as cultural (i.e. religious, ethnic) and partisan differences, which have little or no relevance to the competence of individuals for political office but border on the voters' interests and hold a very strong appeal on the voters, should be eliminated from, or emasculated in, the process of selection by majority vote, in order to base the process solely on merit and so make it fair and hence socially democratic.

This means that there must be partisan and/or cultural homogeneity of the candidates for a political post. Otherwise, the process will not be a merit selection but in reality a partisan or cultural majority representation process, which, as the principle of Universal Representation of Voters shows, is undemocratic because it is inconsistent with the concepts of the political liberty and political equality of all the voters, in that it represents only the partisan or cultural majority of the voters and not all of them.

This principle is perfectly consistent with all the three democratic concepts of political liberty, political equality and political majority. In fact it synchronises the majority concept with the political liberty and political equality concepts. By providing that all the individual contestants for a political post must be from the same political party and/or the same cultural group of the people, the principle recognises the separation of the process of the universal representation of the various partisan and cultural groups of the people from the process of the election of an individual for a public office on his/her personal merits by majority vote.

In that way, it provides room for the fulfilment of the requirements of the political liberty and political equality concepts before the satisfactory application of the majority concept, thereby successfully marrying and uniting representation and competition. Thus, there will be universal cultural and partisan allocations of political posts, in accordance with the principle of Universal Representation of Voters.

The allocations are made equitable by being done in accordance with the appropriate cultural and partisan distributions of the popular votes in the General Universal Representation Election, cumulative votes for scarce posts and current votes, i.e., as the principles of equality of political rights provide for.

Then each of the posts is filled by majority vote and on the personal merits of the candidates by ensuring that all the individual contestants for a partisan political post must be from the same political party and cultural group of the people to which the post has been equitably allocated for the period of rule at the level of government concerned. Similarly, all the individual candidates for a non-partisan elective post must be from the same cultural group to which the post has been equitably allocated for the period of rule concerned.

This principle also implies that the personal qualification of individuals for a political post may include such merit-related factors as freedom to vote in a general representation election, educational level, sex, age, profession and experience, whenever necessary, and that these factors need not be separately represented as some people sometimes clamour for.

The principle of Homogeneity of Candidates has been used in one form or another in the existing majority rule systems of government. For example, for Nigeria's Fourth Republic (1999-2003) where there were only three political parties, two of the three parties, the Alliance for Democracy (AD) and the All Peoples Party (APP) combined together to present a presidential candidate to fight it out with the candidate of the third party, the Peoples Democratic Party (PDP). Both candidates were Yoruba and Christians from the South-West geopolitical zone of the country. Thus, there was cultural homogeneity of the presidential candidates, though there was no partisan homogeneity. The cultural homogeneity of the candidates helped to douse political tension in the country later because even though the losing AD - APP alliance candidate challenged the winning PDP candidate in court for alleged gross election rigging, the matter was eventually allowed to rest mainly because the winner was a Yoruba man and there was no point for the Yorubas to continue to fight themselves. So a victory was won for the principle of Homogeneity of Candidates for political office. Another example is seen in the zoning formulae adopted by the ruling party, PDP, in filling major political offices among the six geopolitical zones into which the then 36 states of Nigeria have been grouped. Within the first two years of the Republic, the President of the Senate, the upper legislative chamber, was changed twice without any difficulty because the PDP had zoned the political post to the Ibos of Nigeria's South-East geopolitical zone. In this case, there was both partisan and cultural/geo graphical homogeneity of the candidates for the senate president because the post was to be filled from the ruling party. Thus although the zoning formula was arbitrary and political party based and so might prove to be eventually unsatisfactory over time, nevertheless it worked to produce a peaceful change of political officeholders because there was partisan and cultural homogeneity of the candidates for the political office concerned, as the principle of Homogeneity of Candidates provides.

It is noteworthy that where subjectivity cannot be eliminated totally from merit selection of individual political officeholders, it should be better to use the method of selection by lot and for the political officeholders to serve for short periods of time, say one year at a time, depending on the number of qualified aspirants for a post, in order to afford more willing and qualified people the opportunity to participate directly in government. Whether selection is by merit election or by lot selection, however, there must be partisan and/or cultural homogeneity of the qualified candidates for a post.

22

THE PRINCIPLE OF
SHIFTING MAJORITY WILL

This is the principle that the general will or public policy is the will of a shifting, not a permanent, majority of the people.

It stems from political reality in addition to the concept of the political consensus or collective decision-making by majority vote. The majority vote concept implies that the general will or the will of the people is the will of the majority of the people. Now in a normal plural society, the citizens have different interests on different issues, and the particular people or groups of people constituting the majority of the society may therefore vary or shift with issues.

This means that in reality, there are shifting majorities and shifting minorities of the people as issues change. It then follows that in direct political democracy, the public will or the will of the people is the will of a shifting, not a permanent, majority of the people. By extension to representative political democracy, this means that the general will is the will of the representatives of a shifting, not a permanent, majority of the voters.

One implication of this principle is that for a political system to be realistic, it should, as issues change, be capable of shifting majorities and minorities in the formulation and making of public policies without a change of government. It implies that a 'government and opposition' system is unnecessary, and that the executive, which formulates the policy of the state, need not, in fact, should not be tied to the will of a fixed or particular majority of the legislators/electorate, i.e. it should not be partisan. It implies that the system of government be such that the government does not fall because of shifting majorities.

The principle ensures a realistic political system and continuity of public policies and programmes. It recognises the fact that political consensus, the general will or the public policy is to be reached not in the polling booth but in parliament and cabinet, as no single party can have the right policies on all the issues in the society, especially in a plural society. Both parliamentary and presidential systems (except in Switzerland and perhaps South Africa lately) are at variance with this principle. In the parliamentary system, the general will on all issues is the will of the majority party or coalition; the debate in parliament is perfunctory. The minority party or parties, however bright its/their policies on some issues may be, has/have little or no chance to influence and contribute meaningfully to the general will without the government falling. In the presidential system of government, public policy is often the will of the president or of his/her advisers. Lobbying and corrupt practices thrive to get the legislators to conform to the president's wish. The wishes of the people are often trampled upon.

The principle implies a system of government in which the legislature and the executive each comprises members from at least three political parties, each representing less than 50% of the electorate, and so in which public policy on any issue may result from any combination of the political parties without a change of government.

In a free political party system, there are many political parties and the parties representing the majority of the voters may result from different combinations of parties. For example, in a three party system with the following partisan distribution of votes: A = 35%, B = 27%, C = 38%, the parties representing the majority of the voters may be at least A and B = 62% or A and C = 73% or B and C = 65%.

Any of these three combinations may occur during an issue, since the parties represent alternative groups of policies on national issues. Moreover, as issues change, the operative combination could also shift, since different groups of citizens or political parties could have different policies on different issues. That is, as issues change, there will be shifting majorities (i.e. A and B, A and C, B and C) and shifting minorities of parties (i.e. B, C or A). Therefore in a free political party setting, i.e. multiparty setting, the will of the people is not the will of a particular majority coalition of parties but rather, the will of the shifting combinations or alignments of parties that represent the majority of all the voters as issues change. This gives all the parties the joy of participation, contribution and sense of belonging; and the resulting public policy will be nationalistic. Policy inconsistency, which is a feature of majority rule systems as government swings from one political party to another and which stands in the way of meaningful progress and advancement in the development of the young states, would disappear and rapid consolidated development would occur.

The national or general will cannot realistically be the will of a permanent majority. In any situation where it is the will of a permanent majority, it is sectional and so there will be dissatisfaction and instability eventually; but where it is the will of a shifting majority then there is a chance of stability, as the will of the state will be nationalistic. A forced two-party political system is not the solution to political instability in a multiparty country/polity, as it does not guarantee a shifting majority in public policy making. Virtual two-party system in the U.S. has endured mainly because power has swung between the two-parties, which is made possible largely because of the predominantly white, English speaking and protestant electorate, which is split between the two parties interspersed by the minorities.

The cultural structure of the U.S. has so far helped swinging thus averting rule of exclusion periodically. However, where the situation is different and the structure of a polity is unrealistically modelled by a two-party system without swinging, there will be instability and unrest. This is what has been happening in the recent past in Nigeria, Ghana, Somalia, Liberia, Rwanda etc.

The Swiss political system is perfectly in line with this principle and it has survived and very well too. In Switzerland, members of the executive will not be expected to resign because a bill introduced by them, however important it may be, has failed passage in the legislature. They will simply drop the matter, or remodel the bill to meet the criticism that has caused its defeat.

Nigeria and other young states need this principle very much because it is in tune with their pluralism and nature. There is therefore no need for a forced two-party system in a truly multiparty system, as that is undemocratic and will eventually lead to chaos.

It is even very uncertain if a two-party system will endure in the U.S. if the cultural representative of about 25% non-white voters there continues to be kept out of occupying the White House for long. Times are changing. For instance, who could for once have envisaged earlier the type of rumpus that attended the year 2000 presidential election between former Vice-President Al Gore and the eventual winner, President George W. Bush?

23

THE PRINCIPLE OF COLLECTIVE RESPONSIBILITY OR SUBORDINATION OF WILL

The third principle implied by the concept of decision-making by the will of a majority of the decision-makers is that the individual political officeholder should have the democratic culture of subordinating his or her own will to his/her party's collective will and subordinating both personal will and party's will to national or.state will whenever necessary.

This principle, which has been known in the political arena for a long time, stems from the fact that collective decision-making by the majority vote of all implies that the resulting decision is binding on all concerned. Therefore a party's will, as the decision of the shifting majority of the party members, is binding on all the party members. This means that, as far as party or political matters are concerned, party members are to subordinate their individual wills to their party's will and that the individual citizens, who are obliged to have delegated their mandates or shares or participation in government to the parties, are to do likewise.

Similarly, a general or national will, as the decision of the representatives of a shifting majority of the citizens in representative political democracy, is binding on all the citizens, who are obliged to have delegated their shares or participation in government to their chosen political representatives or parties. This means that all citizens, including party members, are to subordinate their individual wills and party wills to central, public or state will.

Two implications of this principle are as follows. Firstly, there must be party voting in the legislature and in the executive, i.e. all members of a political party in a legislative house or in the executive must vote together as a block. Secondly, a political party has the right to appoint or remove its members in government (i.e. in the legislature and in the executive). These two implications are consistent not only with each other but also with the principle of Group Representatives for Voters.

Since by the principle of Group Representatives for Voters, the partisan political representatives of the citizens in government are political parties, the will of a political party's members in government is the party's will; therefore there must be party voting and this is ensured by the right of a political party to appoint and remove its members in government.

A third implication of the principle is that only democrats and not fundamentalists should be elected into a (democratic) government. This is the essence of true representative political democracy and no one should be exempted from it. The president or prime minister should lead the way; he must be a living example of what is expected from his followers. He must be able to lead a strong team comprising members from political parties other than his own. This implication reinforces the fact revealed under the previous principle that partisan homogeneity of the executive is unnecessary, so long as the members are democrats.

This principle has the potentiality of resolving some knotty issues in representation. There is currently in the political arena a lack of clear-cut relationships between the electorate, political parties and political officeholders. For example, Jacobsen and Lipman (p.126) reported that:

> there are wide differences of opinion as to the proper duty of a political representative. One theory holds that he is primarily an agent of his constituents committed to follow their instructions and their wishes and to look out for their local interests. A contrary theory holds that the representative is an officer of government and should act for the people of the state as a whole, rising above parochial considerations. A third concept holds that he should consult and act with leaders of his party, subordinating his own personal convictions and the transient interests

of his constituents to the general programme adopted by the party.

Jacobsen and Lipman then added a fourth theory, their own: 'In practice, a representative should try to conform to all these theories.' Which of these four theories is democratic? Who, according to true representative political democracy, are the people's political representatives: political parties or individuals appointed on the platforms of political parties or independent candidates? These questions arose because of the personalisation of politics and can be resolved by the principles of Group Representatives for Voters and Subordination of lower will to higher will as follows.

As the partisan political representative of a citizen is a political party and not an individual (see the principle of Group Representatives for Voters), a political party member in government is not a citizen's partisan representative but rather a political party's agent in the field. The political officeholder's political representative in government is not the political officeholder in government himself or herself but rather the political party, whose agent he or she is. The political party member in government is not the partisan political representative of himself or herself in government because the partisan political representative in government of any citizen is a political party, a corporate body and the political party member in government is an individual citizen.

As a citizen, the political party member in government, like any other citizen, has by his vote subordinated his will to that of the political party of which he is an agent in government to speak for him or her. The political party member in government has, like any other citizen, by his vote contracted his party to represent, act or speak for him or her in political matters. He or she can therefore not pursue his or her own personal will in government.

Although he has been appointed into a position allocated to a cultural/ethnic or geographical constituency, nevertheless he is more a symbol of national unity, a symbol of what gives the state its most visible and complete expression of the nation, than primarily an agent of his constituents. By the principle of Political Party Dominance, he is secondarily an agent of his constituents but primarily an agent of his political party, to which he and (some of) his constituents have given the right to act for them in government and whose wishes he ought to follow in government.

He is therefore not primarily to follow his constituents' instructions and wishes or primarily to look out for their local interests over national interests in government, even though he is expected to do so if, when and where expedient, reasonable and convenient so that his constituency is not cheated.

The political party member in government therefore has a duty to himself, his constituency, his party and his country. Firstly, as a citizen he has temporarily delegated his political right or share in government to his chosen political party for a (fixed) term and can now only advise it through the press, memos etc. As a member of his political party, he has a right to air his views or opinions and those of his constituents on any national issue and take part (including voting) in the party's deliberations to arrive at the party's policy or stand on any issue in which a new or modified policy is required. As a member of a cultural/ethnic constituency on the platform of which also he is in government, he should even vote along with members of his cultural/ethnic constituency if necessary and subordinate his own personal will to the will of a majority of members of his cultural/ethnic constituency in his political party in arriving at the party's general will or policy on an issue.

Secondly, as a political party's member in Parliament, he has a duty to uphold the party's views or policy on any national issue in the process of making public policy. In this regard, he should consult and act with leaders of his party, subordinating his personal convictions and the transient interests of his constituents to the general programme adopted by the party.

However, (using the words of Appadorai pp. 528-9 and Burke) so that deliberations in Parliament (or Executive) may not be ineffective, so that party policies may not be "authoritative instructions, mandates issued," which party members in Parliament are "bound blindly and implicitly to obey, to vote and to argue for," to maintain as agents and advocates against other agents and advocates, and so that 'the general good resulting from the general reason of the whole' may guide, parliamentary (and executive) post holders of a party should whenever necessary or expedient be the party's opinion makers and whenever necessary the decision of a majority of them should be acceptable as a political party's decision or will.

This will avert the 'absurd state of affairs in which the determination precedes discussions, in which one set of men deliberates and another decides and where those who form the conclusion are far away from those who hear the arguments'. But this should not replace the need for regular or occasional deliberations at a party level to arrive at the party's general will on national issues, which will guide the party's political office occupiers in their deliberations and voting on national issues.

Thirdly, as a member of the executive to formulate and execute the general/public or national policy, the political party member has a duty to uphold the public will, irrespective of whether or not it agrees with his own will or his party's will, because by the principle of subordination of lower will to higher will, public will, which is superior to his own will or to his party's will, overrides these other two 'inferior' or lower wills. In this respect, he is an officer of government and should act for the people of the state as a whole, rising above parochial considerations.

However, in the formulation of the public will, the political party member, as a member of the executive, has a duty to uphold his party's will, because the public will is the will of the parties representing the majority of the voters and so he should endeavour to see that his party's will becomes, or is taken into consideration while shaping, the public will or any part of it. In this respect, he should consult and act with other (executive) members of his party, subordinating his own personal convictions to the general programme adopted by the party and/or to the will of the majority of the (executive) members of his party concerned.

It is interesting to record that the Swiss constitution provides that 'members of the two Councils (the Council of States, the upper Chamber, and the National Council, the lower Chamber) shall vote without instructions.' This may be taken to be against the principle of Political Party Dominance, if party voting is regarded as voting with instructions. However, in Switzerland there are many institutions, like in direct political democracy, which make the Swiss democratic system to be unique and not solely dependent· on the political party based representative democratic system. One of such institutions is the referendum, which makes it compulsory for all constitutional laws to be submitted to the people, the general electorate, for approval or rejection. Even in respect of ordinary laws, the constitution in Article 89 says: "federal laws are submitted for acceptance or rejection by the people if a demand be made by 30,000... citizens or by eight cantons. Federal decrees which are of general effect and are not urgent are likewise submitted on demands." Moreover, although the National Council, which consists of 196 to 200 members, is elected by proportional representation, the Council of States, comprising 44 members, two from each full canton and one from each half-canton, is elected by the people in all but four cantons and by the cantonal Legislatures in the exceptional four cantons.

It should be noted that in Universal Democracy, the people have the right to introduce private bills in the legislature, and if the legislators refuse to pass them, then such bills must compulsorily be submitted to the general electorate (in a referendum) for approval or rejection. In this way, the people can make their government do their will on any matter, as they are sovereign, and so will not often have to resort to rebellion, revolution or civil war to resolve issues with their governments. Such a bill will not go directly to the electorate in the first instance in order not to undermine the authority of the legislature.

24

SUMMARIES OF THE PRINCIPLES OF UNIVERSAL DEMOCRACY

This section briefly summarises the twenty principles of Universal Democracy that have been fully discussed in chapters four to twenty-three. Each principle has its basis in one aspect or the other of the definition of True Representative Political Democracy (T.R.P.D.) given in chapter three and is complete with its institutional measures. The principles are therefore amplifications of the definition or meaning of true representative political democracy or of the concepts on which it is based. They enable the political institutions and structures that are consistent with Universal Democracy to be established or identified. The summaries are hereby itemised below for ease of reference.

1. *Separation of Powers:* The three governmental powers, namely legislative, executive and judicial powers, should be exercised by separate branches or arms of government with no overlapping political membership if tyrannical governments are to be avoided and if the liberty of the citizenry is to be guaranteed. A branch or arm of government is here defined as any unit or department of government solely exercising the whole or a part of one of the three governmental powers – namely legislative, executive and judicial powers – and having no member holding political office in any other department of government.

Any one of the three powers may be exercised by more than one branch of government but no two of the three powers should be exercised by the same branch or arm of government and no two branches of government must have overlapping political membership.

Therefore, those who execute laws should participate neither in their making nor in their adjudication; those who adjudicate laws should participate neither in their making nor in their execution; and those who make laws should participate neither in their execution nor in their adjudication. Moreover, each branch or arm of government should derive its powers direct from the mandates of the electorate and therefore not be under the control of any other branch or arm by appointment, funds control or otherwise.

2. *Universal Representation of Voters:* Every citizen (voter) has a right to a share in government through his/her personally chosen partisan and cultural representatives, if every citizen (voter) truly has the right to a representative share in government. Therefore, one's partisan and cultural political representatives are one's personal choice, made by voting at a general universal representation election.

This principle confirms that the majority concept is not involved in the selection of the political representatives of the people. Firstly, because a person is an individual and not a multitude and secondly, because each voter has to be represented by his/her own choice and not necessarily by the choice of the majority voters without him/her, if he/she truly has a share in government through his/her representatives. Therefore the single-member electoral systems, – i.e. the simple plurality (or first-to-pass-the-post) system, the majority system and their variants such as the double-ballot system – all of which are based upon the majority representation notion, are unsuitable for representing the voters because they represent not all voters but only those who vote for the single winners. Rather, there should be universal partisan and cultural representation of all voters which should be effected by allocating the political posts concerned to all the cultural constituencies into which the people have grouped themselves and to all political parties that they have voted for, in accordance with the relevant principles of political equality (see below). In true representative democracy, political representation is not the right of only the majority but rather the right of all voters.

3. *Universal Suffrage:* Every free citizen has a right to vote in a general universal representation election to choose or elect personally his or her own partisan and cultural political representatives in government if he/she truly has a right to representative participation in government. Therefore, there should be universal (free) adult suffrage at the election, assuming that children or minors are still under their parents. There should be no qualification in respect of sex, birth, wealth, status, profession, etc.

4. *Appropriation of Political Right:* A citizen has to vote in a general representation election in order to be represented in government, i.e. have representative participation in government, if his/her representative in government is truly his/her personal choice made by voting. Therefore, the sharing, allocation, zoning, or apportionment of political posts such as parliamentary seats and executive posts should be done on the basis of votes and after the General Universal Representation Election (GURE) for the current period of rule and not on the basis of population, or arbitrarily as is currently the case.

5. *Free and Fair Elections:* The candidates for elections should freely come up, every voter should be free to choose among them as he or she likes/wishes, and the election results should neither be suppressed nor interfered with in any way. Accreditation of voters, electronic voters registers, freedom to vote anywhere one likes, voting in the presence of all, secret balloting, counting of votes in the presence of all and compulsory announcement of results in the presence of all immediately after counting of votes is finished, etc., are measures that ensure this principle. So also are the conduction of the representation and merit elections centrally by the electoral commission and the public funding of the elections, among other measures.

6. *Group or Corporate Representatives for Voters:* The political representatives of the citizenry in representative political democracy are not individuals but rather corporate bodies or groups, if the concepts of the political liberty and the equality of the political right of the citizenry and of public policy being the will of the majority of the voting public are acceptable. Therefore, the voting public should

select groups or corporate bodies instead of individuals as their partisan political representatives in government. Thus in the General Universal Representation Election, the people will vote as distinct cultural/geographical constituencies for their cultural representation and select political organisations/parties for their partisan representation. Therefore, "independent" individual candidates are ruled out in the representation election.

7. *Free Grouping of Citizens:* The grouping of the people into political units such as political associations and cultural/geopolitical constituencies for the purpose of their political representation should be free if the people truly have political freedom/liberty. Therefore, all political organisations, as alternative homogeneous bodies of policies on current national issues, that score enough votes for at least a political post in the executive branch of government in a period of rule must have legislative and executive participation in government as political parties for the period of rule; and all distinct cultural/ethnic groupings or suitable combinations of them should have legislative, executive or judicial participation in government as often as their respective cumulative voting strengths will allow. Moreover, compulsory lumping together of different cultural/ethnic groups into a state (or canton) or local government area is undemocratic.

8. *Non-Transferability of Delegated Mandates:* A political representative may not make political appointments outside himself or itself if the focus in governance is not to shift from the ruled to the ruler and if good and responsible government is to be maintained. Therefore, only an elected or selected corporate political representative or a corporate part of it appointed by it may make political appointments and the political appointee(s) must be part of the appointing body. Thus, the political parties elected at the current general representation election as the partisan political representatives of the people (or their appointed subsets) or the cultural constituencies or their non-partisan professional bodies (or their regional branches) may make political appointments from among their members.

9. *Periodic Representation of Voters:* Every citizen has the right to renew periodically his or her choice of political representation in government, if the ruler must be regularly subjected to the control of the ruled to check abuse of delegated power. Therefore, every government must have a fixed life, i.e. political representation must be for a limited period at a time – a definite period of rule.

10. *Separation of Elections:* The election for the universal representation of the voters should be separated from, and should come before the election(s) for the selection of the individual political office occupiers on merit by majority vote, if the concepts of the political liberty and equality of political rights of the citizens are to be compatible with the concept of decision-making by majority vote. Therefore, there must be two sets of election in a polity. There must be a general election, termed as the General Universal Representation Election (GURE), in which the candidates will be expressly political parties and the people will vote as distinct cultural/geographical constituencies, on the basis of which they will also be represented.

The partisan and cultural votes' distributions of this election, whose purpose is the universal representation of the citizens, will be the basis of the partisan and/or cultural allocations of partisan and non-partisan political posts. The election will precede (and be separated from) any other general, partisan or cultural elections, termed the Merit Elections, or any lot selection, whose purpose is to select the individual political post occupiers.

11. *Limited Separation of Representation:* Factors of representation are to be separated as far as representation of voters in terms of each of them is desirable and easy, if the separation of factors is to be realistic and beneficial. Therefore, only a two-dimensional representation system involving cultural/ethnic (or geographical) constituencies and political parties should be used but a three-dimensional system involving religion in addition should be avoided for its complexity. Also, there must be separate allocations of the political posts (through which representation of voters is effected) to cultural constituencies and to political parties independently of each other, each of the two types of allocation being independently based upon the polity's total

vote at the General Universal Representation Election (GURE), at the level of government desired.

12. *Political Party Dominance:* The political party rather than the cultural constituency should predominate in the matter of the right to elect or remove individual partisan political office occupiers and decide upon public policy, if a political party is truly appointed a political representative by, and truly aggregates opinions/interests across, the cultural constituencies. Therefore, a political party must have the right to appoint or remove (i.e. change) its members in government. Moreover, there may not be carpet crossing of partisan political officeholders because they are holding not personally acquired posts but corporately acquired posts.

13. *All-Branch Representation of Voters:* Every voter should be represented – that is, have his/her chosen political representative(s) in every one of the different branches or arms into which governmental powers are divided, if every voter is entitled to the same political right. Therefore, at each level of governance, each of the branches or arms into which governmental powers are divided should be run by all the political parties in every period of rule and by members of all the cultural constituencies at the appropriate level either in every period of rule or in a cycle or a reasonable number of periods of rule. This implies a multicultural and all-party Executive, i.e. a non-partisan, non-sectional Executive, among others.

14. *Proportional Representation of Voters:* The number of political posts that may be held by any group is directly proportional to the number of votes cast or won (in the General Universal Representation Election) during a period of rule, if all votes are politically equal. Therefore, a number of political posts of the same type or of equal rank in sufficient quantity should be shared among a number of alternative political parties or cultural (e.g. ethnic or geographical) constituencies in a period of rule in direct proportion to the political parties' or cultural constituencies' shares of the popular vote for the period of rule.

The idea of equality of constituencies or subgroups, by which various cultural constituencies, zones, sections, states or regions of a country, despite their respective number of voters, have equal number of seats in a lower or upper legislative chamber, is therefore inconsistent with the democratic concept of equality of political rights of all the voters of the different constituencies or subgroups; it is therefore undemocratic and must be discarded.

15. *Rotation of a Scarce Political Post-Type:* All voters are entitled by equality of political right to be represented by a scarce political post in rotation or in turn. A type of political post is taken to be scarce when the available number of the type of political post cannot in a period of rule go round all the alternative groups to be politically represented through it when its number is numerically shared among them in proportion to their voting strengths. Therefore, the cumulative quantity (tagged "post-period" in this book) of the scarce political post since inception up to the present period of rule should be shared among the relevant alternative cultural constituencies in the present period of rule to determine which constituency (or constituencies) should have the post-type in the period of rule. The order of rotation of the scarce post-type among the alternative constituencies is thereby automatically determined. There is no rotation of a scarce post-type among political parties.

16. *Proportional Rotation of Scarce Political Post-Types:* The share of the cumulative quantity (i.e. post-period) of a scarce political post-type or post-types that may be equitably held by a section of a polity in the present period of rule is directly proportional to the number of cumulative total votes cast over the periods of rule concerned to date, if all votes are politically equal (over the years). Therefore the cultural sharing of a scarce post's or of scarce posts' cumulative quantity over the periods of rule to date should be done (in the present period of rule) in direct proportion to the cultural constituencies' shares of the cumulative popular vote over the periods of rule concerned to date.

17. *Co-ordinated Proportional Allocation of Multiple Unequal Scarce Posts:* Multiple unequal scarce post-types should be allocated to alternative groups by the progressive (i.e. stage-wise) combined proportional representation by, or rotation of, each post-type with all its superiors to achieve equal qualitative and/or quantitative

representation of voters by such combined posts within or over periods of rule. Therefore the allocation of multiple unequal scarce political posts must follow the following steps:

(a) Ranking of the unequal scarce political post-types in the descending order of importance.

(b) Allocating the post-types in turn, one post-type at a time, and starting from the most important one.

(c) Allocating a post-type to the cultural constituencies by the method of Co-ordinated Proportional Rotation of Multiple Unequal Scarce Posts (COPROMUSPO) as follows.

    (i) Integer sharing the combined post-periods of the post-type and of all its superiors among the cultural groups concerned in direct proportion to the groups' shares of the cumulative popular vote over the periods of rule concerned, subject only to rounding-off errors.

    (ii) Considering for each group, its actual combined share to date and stage (i.e. past and present periods of rule) of the combined post-periods of the post-type and of its superiors.

    (iii) Finding the difference between (i) and (ii) above for each group and ensuring that it is non-negative, i.e. either zero or a positive number – reviewing (i) if necessary (i.e. if the difference is negative).

(d) Allocating a post-type to the political parties by the method of Coordinated Proportional Representation by Multiple Unequal Scarce Posts (COPREMUSPO) as follows.

    (i) Integer sharing the combined current total quantity of the post-type and of all its superiors among the political parties in direct proportion to the parties' shares of the current popular vote for the current period of rule, subject only to rounding-off errors.

    (ii) Considering for each political party, its combined share to stage (i.e. previous and present stages) of the combined current total quantity of the post-type and of its superiors.

(iii) Finding the difference between (i) and (ii) above for each political party and ensuring that it is non-negative – i.e. either zero or a positive number – reviewing (i) if necessary (i.e. if the difference is negative).

18. *Homogeneity of Candidates:* There must be partisan and/or cultural homogeneity of the candidates for a political post, if the best of the candidates on personal merit for the post is to be selected by a majority vote, or by lot. Therefore, all the individual contestants for a partisan political post must be from the same political party and cultural subgroup of the people at the level of government concerned. It is assumed that the political post has first been equitably allocated to the political party and the cultural group. Similarly, all the individual candidates for a non-partisan elective post must be from the same cultural group to which the post has been equitably allocated for the period of rule concerned. All the candidates must be free adults qualified to vote in a general representation election.

19. *Shifting Majority Will:* The general will (or public policy) is the will of a shifting, not a permanent, majority of the people, if the particular people constituting the majority of the society really vary/shift with issues. Therefore, if public policy is to be nationalistic and thereby ensure national stability, cohesion, integration and sense of belonging, the executive that formulates and executes the policy of a polity should not be tied to the will of a fixed or particular majority of the legislature/electorate. It should therefore also not be partisan in composition, i.e. there should be an All-Party Executive.

20. *Collective Responsibility or Subordination of Will:* The individual political officeholder should whenever necessary subordinate his/her own will to his/her party or group's collective will and should subordinate both personal will and party will to national or government will, if the decision of the majority of a group is truly binding on all members of the group. Therefore, only democrats should be elected to hold political office and a government or an executive need not be partisan in composition. There must also be party voting in Parliament and Executive.

PART THREE

Institutions and Structures of Universal Democracy

25

POLITICAL PARTIES IN UNIVERSAL DEMOCRACY

This chapter attempts to define a political party and discusses various issues about political parties such as their members in government, their establishment, composition, and number, among other things.

Definition of a Political Party

Various writers have defined a political party in several ways. Some of the definitions that have been given include the following:

1. 'A group ·with supporters which in the opinion of the group have similar principles' (A.M. Potter).
2. 'An organised power that seeks to control both the personnel and policy of a government' (E. Sait).
3. 'An internal power group whose status has been formalised – it functions as part of the regime' (Laswell and Kaplan).
4. 'A regular and permanent organisation of a certain number of people concerned with either conquering power or keeping it' (Raymond Aaron).
5. 'Any group, however loosely organised, seeking to elect governmental officeholders under a given label' (Epstein).
6. 'A body of men united, for promoting by their joint endeavour the national interest, upon some particular principle in which they are all agreed' (Edmund Burke (1729-1797)).

7. 'A group of people who share a common conception of how and why state power should be organised and used'.

8. Political parties are 'all the otherwise varied groups that provide labels under which candidates seek election to governmental office' (Greenstein and Polsby).

9. 'An organised group of citizens who act together as a political unit, have distinctive aims and opinions on the leading political questions of controversy in the state, and who, by acting together as a political unit, seek to obtain control of government' (A. Appadorai).

From these definitions, six points appear relevant to political parties. First, a political party is an organisation and differs from an unorganised or amorphous group of persons. Secondly, a political party is different from any other organised interest groups in the society, such as trade unions or pressure groups, in that it seeks direct rather than indirect political power. Thirdly, a political party has distinctive aims and opinions or, as Appadorai (p.538) puts it, 'a common body of principles and policies' and its members work together as a political unit to see that those principles and policies are adopted by the government of the day. Fourthly, 'every political party takes a name as a descriptive label (Liberal, Democrat, Labour, Republican, Conservative, Nationalist, Christian, Socialist, or Buddhist), which is intended to convey to the world and to the party members as far as possible the principles which dominate the party' (Appadorai, p. 154). Fifthly, a political party, if it is worth the name, must at a general election win enough citizens' votes to be able to represent them in government, i.e. to hold political posts. Lastly, the members of a political party should have the necessary qualifications for any political post, as a political party's members should be able to hold any political post.

From the foregoing and from our 'sympathetic understanding' (Davies) of the functions performed by political parties in the society, the following definition of a political party emerges.

A political party is any organised group of citizens with the necessary qualifications for every partisan political post, under a given label, with a common policy on every national issue and having enough citizens' votes for political office.

It is clear from this definition that a political organisation contests the general election and does not become a political party for a period of rule until it has scored sufficient votes at the General Universal Representation Election (GURE) for the period of rule.

A Political Party's Member in Government

Since all the members of an elected political party have chosen the political party as their political representative, they have delegated their rights to a share in government to the party and the question of their choosing another political representative does not arise. This is in consistency with the concept of the political equality of all voters that no party member has any undue advantage over other citizens in the selection of the government.

Moreover, the political posts that have been won by the political party belong to the political party as a distinct entity. Therefore the members of the political party to occupy its political posts in government must be selected not on the basis of their individual representation but rather by lot or on the basis of their personal merits for the posts to be held. Therefore the aspirants for a political post must compete purely on the basis of their personal merits for the post and the best of them on personal merit for the post selected by a majority vote of all the members concerned.

Now by the principle of Homogeneity of Candidates, a selection on merit may be made by majority vote only when the candidates are from the same political party and are a culturally homogeneous set. Therefore, a political party's candidates for a partisan political post only need to be culturally homogeneous if the selection by majority vote is to be made on the basis of the personal merits of the candidates only.

This implies a cultural allocation of political positions before the merit (or lot) selection. Moreover, by the principle of Non-Transferability of Delegated Mandates, a political party's agent in government must be a member of the political party. Hence, a political party's agent in government is one of its members selected by lot or majority vote from a culturally homogeneous set of its aspirant members for a political post.

By the principle of Non-Transferability of Delegated Mandates, only the political parties elected during the current period of rule should make a political appointment from among their members. Therefore, the selection on merit should be made by the majority vote of the members of the political party concerned, as some other parts of this book expatiate.

Depending upon a polity's preference, political development and political culture, it may be desirable to take the members of a political party for the purposes of merit selection as its members in the legislature and the executive who can be easily identified instead of all the registered members of the political party who cannot sometimes be easily identified. Members of the legislature and of the executive at the lower levels of government may also be included in the electorate for a particular level.

Who Establishes Political Parties: The State or the Citizens?

By the principle of Political Party Dominance, the citizens are represented in government policy-wise by political parties, which are organised groups of qualified citizens modelling alternative bodies of policies on national issues of controversy.

The existence of multiple national issues of controversy and of multiple alternative policies on each of such issues means the existence of multiple alternative bodies of policies on national issues of controversy, which must be given expression to in a free society.

Since some citizens belong to every one of the alternative bodies of policies on national issues of controversy and since citizens are represented on the basis of the bodies of policies, then the universal representation of the citizens by their preferred bodies of policies on national issues (see the principle of Free Grouping of Citizens) implies one of two alternatives. Either there is establishment by the State of *all* the alternative bodies or combinations of policies on national issues of controversy so that every citizen may have the choice to be represented by his preferred body of policies, or there is the freedom by the citizens to establish *any* of the bodies of policies that they wish.

Now, it is a most difficult and undesirable task for the State to establish all the viable alternative bodies of policies on national issues of controversy because there are too many alternative bodies to establish. For example, if there are only two sides to an issue (and there are often much more than two) and if there are ten issues of controversy, then there are (may be) as many as one thousand and twenty-four (2 to power 10 = 1024) combinations of bodies of policies on the ten issues and hence as many as one thousand and twenty-four possible political organizations for the State to float. And the State cannot justifiably float some of the bodies and leave out the rest without infringing on the doctrine of the political liberty of the citizenry or the principle of Free Grouping of Citizens, which requires all the bodies to be floated.

On the other hand, if the citizens have the responsibility to establish the bodies of policies themselves, many of the bodies especially those with small followership in the society, may not be given expression to and the citizens will nevertheless feel obliged to align with one of the available alternative bodies as no one will feel that any one body of policies has been imposed upon him, since he can readily float another alternative if he is able and willing.

Therefore, not the State but the citizens should be free to establish any of the alternative bodies of policies on the issues of controversy in the society that they wish. Therefore the citizens and not the State should establish political parties.

Need Political Parties be Policy-homogeneous ?

If political parties are policy-heterogeneous, then each of them will have alternative policy subgroups. Therefore, the party-in-government will be policy-heterogeneous, i.e. without one voice on controversial issues in government. Party voting in parliament or executive (in accordance with the principle of Political Party Dominance) will therefore be difficult or impossible.

There will be tendencies for political subgroups within a party to cooperate with similar policy subgroups in another party. This is exemplified by the Action Group (A.G.) party crisis and the resulting formation of a splinter party, firstly as the United People's Party (U.P.P.) and later as the Nigerian National Democratic Party (N.N.D.P.), in Nigeria in the early 1960s (Crowder, pp. 262-4). The result is that the political party system will not be cohesive: it will be weak, possibly thereby resulting into anti-party activities by the party members.

A policy-heterogeneous political party would distort the political party representation system. The true basis for a voter to choose a political party in the General Universal Representation Election (GURE) is its opinions on the (major) issues of controversy in the polity agreeing with the voter's. Thus if at election time a political party is policy-heterogeneous, i.e. has more than one policy or opinion on an issue, a voter may be confused and so either not vote for it or make his choice using other criteria such as ethnicity and religion. Moreover, if the party-in-government is policy-heterogeneous, it would not be pursuing with its whole voting strength the policy for which its voters chose it. An alternative policy with minority voters' support may thereby inadvertently become public policy. Thus, the political party system would fail to provide a true model of a polity's opinion (or policy) complexion.

Therefore, in view of all the above, political parties need be policy-homogeneous groups.

Composition of a Political Party

By definition, a political party is a policy-homogeneous group in that it has a single policy on each issue of controversy in the society. A political party is supposed to fill any political post allocated to it with its member from the cultural group to which the post is also allocated. Moreover, any post may be allocated to any cultural group, and if partisan to any political party.

Also every post may carry some requirements relating to age, gender, education, profession etc. Therefore, a political party must not only comprise some of the members of all the cultural groups but also contain them in sufficient number and quality to enable it hold any political post. In other words, there must be in a political party members from each cultural group who have the requisite qualifications for each post that may be allocated to the group. This is the requirement for a political association to be able to canvass for votes. This requirement, which is democratic (since it stems from democratic requirements), will result in, viable political parties and eliminate mushroom or religious, fundamentalist political or ethnic parties. The body responsible for elections in a country must see that these requirements are fulfilled before it registers a political organisation to participate in the General Universal Representation Election in any period of rule.

How Many Political Parties?

By definition, a political party must:

a)   be an organised group of citizens seeking partisan political post.

b)   have a given label.

c)   have a common body of policies on national issues of controversy distinct from that of any other similar organised group of citizens.

d)   have members (from every cultural constituency) with necessary qualifications for all types of partisan political post.

e)   have enough citizens' votes for political office.

The requirement (e) implies that a political organisation that aspires to become a political party must, in addition to satisfying the previous four requirements, contest the General Universal Representation Election and win votes sufficient for at least one political post in each branch or arm of government. An aspiring political party needs to have sufficient votes for a political office in all branches or arms of government and not just in any one branch in order that the principle of All-Branch Representation of Voters would not be pre-empted.

The principle of All-Branch Representation of Voters requires all voters to have partisan representation, and hence partisan representative participation, in all branches of government in every period of rule. It will be pre-empted if a political party, which has the duty of representing voters, is able to represent its voters only in some and not all of the branches of government. Therefore for consistency with this principle of representative political democracy, a prospective political party must win enough votes to hold at least a political post in each branch or arm of government to become a political party. Assuming that the political posts in all branches or arms of government are allocated on the basis of the results of one general election, the General Universal Representation Election (GURE), which this book recommends, the above requirement is satisfied if a political organisation wins sufficient votes in the election to hold at least a political post in the arm or branch of government with the smallest number of political posts. This is because it is this branch or arm of government that requires the largest number of votes per political post according to the principle of Proportional Representation of Voters.

Hence, since the number of political posts in government is limited and since the political posts are allocated to the alternative partisan groups in proportion to the votes they win, as the principles of equality of political rights require, the universal partisan representation of voters in each branch or arm of government in every period of rule imposes an upper limit on the number of partisan groups (i.e. political parties) in government in any period of rule, as has been discussed in some more detail in other parts of this book.

Summary

A political party is a "ruling house" that provides partisan political officeholders, e.g. legislators. All citizens interested in partisan political posts shall join or form political parties (in accordance with their partisan beliefs). Through the General Universal Representation Election (GURE), all citizens shall vote for the political party whose policies they share, to define its political strength and consequently the partisan political posts to which it is entitled (in the polity for a period of rule). Then through lot selection or party merit elections, qualified party aspirants fill a political party's allocated political posts to represent its voters (in government).

26

THE LEGISLATURE IN
UNIVERSAL DEMOCRACY

The legislature is the arm/branch of government that makes laws. All citizens/voters are entitled to participate in the making of laws. Therefore, all voters should be represented in the legislature i.e. the legislature should be fully representative.

As reported by Appadorai (p.550), most modern constitutions provide for a legislature of two chambers, the lower and the upper.

Arguments have been advanced for and against the need for a second chamber in modern constitutions. Here are some of them as given by Appadorai (p. 550 - 552).

(1) It is a safeguard against the despotism of a single chamber. Critics of this argument say a second chamber causes delay and it is expensive, pointing out that other safeguards exist and are possible, e.g. the suspensive veto of the executive, a second or even third vote in the same chamber after an interval.

(2) It serves as a check upon hasty and ill-considered legislation.

(3) It helps to provide adequate representation of the aristocratic element of the community. As social democracy is against special privileges of birth, wealth, status, profession, etc., this argument is undemocratic in Universal Democracy.

(4) It is the best way of providing adequate representation to certain interests in a country, such as labour, women, etc.,

which need representation but which, for want of proper organisation or other reasons, may not get such representation in the Lower House. Labour, women, landlords and chambers of commerce were thus given special representation under the government of India Act, 1935. This argument is undemocratic in Universal Democracy because it is inconsistent with social democracy, which is against special privileges of sex, profession etc. Rather, it should be ensured that no hindrance is placed in the way of the representation of any interests. All interest groups should have qualified aspirants for various political posts and offices, who should form or join political parties.

(5) It makes it possible for people of political and administrative experience and ability (who for reasons of age, finance, or health are not likely to try to enter the Lower House through the arduous process of electioneering) to be brought into public life and made available for the service of the state. This argument is undemocratic because in true representative political democracy, legislators must be political party members selected competitively on their personal merits. However, the principle of Homogeneity of Candidates and other possible measures would make electioneering hardly arduous and therefore attractive to more people than in the past.

(6) In federal states, it affords an opportunity for giving representation to the component units of the federation as units, the Lower House being constituted on a population basis. This argument of the second chamber embodying the federal character of a country is often countered by the fact that experience shows that members often vote on party, rather than state lines. Moreover, the argument is undemocratic in Universal Democracy because it is inconsistent with the principle of Appropriation of Political Right and the principle of Proportional Representation of Voters, among others.

(7) It is in conformity with the experience of history, which has been in favour of two chambers. No major state, it is argued, whatever its form of government, has been willing to dispense with a second chamber.

It is clear from the above that only arguments (1), (2) and (7) are valid for consideration in Universal Democracy.

The main consideration in constructing an Upper House is that the Upper House should be differently composed from the first. This is to make legislative measures receive consideration a second time by a body different in character from a primary representative Assembly, preferably with superior or supplementary intellectual qualifications and age to avoid duplication. Differentiation between the two Houses is usually brought about in the following ways:

(1) In the method of choice of members. This can be seen from a study of current practice in various existing legislatures. However, this is unnecessary and there is no room for it in Universal Democracy.

Rather, differentiation between the Lower House and the Upper House should be brought about in the level of constituencies used (see the principle of Free Grouping of Citizens) and in the number of the total membership of each House. Primary or secondary cultural/ethnic constituencies may be used for the Lower House while secondary or tertiary cultural/ethnic constituencies are used for the Upper House, the constituencies used for the Upper House being one level higher than those for the Lower House.

Also the total membership of the Upper House should be much smaller than that of the Lower House. Thus in these two ways, each member of the Upper House will represent a much larger area of the polity or a superior cultural grouping and a much larger number of citizens than each member of the Lower House. It will indeed be an upper or senior legislative chamber.

(2) In the tenure of membership. In the U.S.A., members of the Lower House are elected for two years; but members of the Upper House for six years; in France (under the Third Republic), the corresponding periods were four and nine years. Moreover, the idea of partial renewal is applied to members of the Upper House, one-third for instance, retiring every two years in the U.S.A. and in India. However, differentiation in the tenure of membership and partial renewal of membership of the Upper House do not make the Upper House to be a body different in character from the Lower House.

Moreover, the two measures will introduce complications into the political system as more than one set of periods of rule will become applicable and the same General Universal Representation Election cannot apply to the various branches/sub-branches of government. Therefore differentiation in the tenure of membership and partial renewal of membership are unnecessary and disadvantageous. They should not be used in Universal Democracy.

(3) In qualifications for membership. In the U.S.A. for membership of the House of Representatives, the age qualification is twenty-five; but for membership of the senate, it is thirty. Differentiation may also be made by prescribing educational qualifications, as was done for membership of Indian Council of State. Age and educational qualifications are permitted in Universal Democracy but there should be no qualifications regarding property ownership, sex, profession, status, etc., as these are against social democracy.

As social democracy is against special privileges of birth, wealth, status, profession etc., True Representative Political Democracy (T.R.P.D.) is against the Upper House being a hereditary body as in Britain, or a nominated body as in Canada and Italy, or a partly nominated and partly elected body as in India. Whether one or two chambers are used, they should be constituted according to democratic principles, many of which this book describes. The legislative chambers are required to make laws or public policies by a simple majority vote of all of their members and democratic public policy is the will of the majority of the voters.

Democratic public policy making therefore requires/demands that the legislators in a House of Parliament represent the same number of voters so that any majority of them may represent a majority of the voters. In this way, the will of any majority of all the legislators will be tantamount to the will of a majority of the voters. This means that all legislators should be political party members, i.e. no independent candidates are allowed as legislators, that the parties should be elected by the PR electoral system and that the legislators whether for the lower or upper house should be selected by lot or party merit elections, all as described in this book.

27

THE EXECUTIVE IN
UNIVERSAL DEMOCRACY

According to Garner, 'the term executive is used broadly to mean the aggregate or totality of all the functionaries and agencies which are concerned with the execution of the will of the State as that will has been formulated and expressed in terms of law.' In this sense, as pointed out by Appadorai, the term includes both those (like the president in the U.S.A. and the cabinet in Britain) who 'exercise supreme control' and those subordinate officers (like policemen and clerks) who 'simply carry out orders'.

In this book, as is common in political science, the term executive will, in the words of Appadorai (p.556), be restricted to those whose primary duty is that of 'seeing that laws are enforced' rather than that of 'doing the things which the laws call for', the term civil service being used to refer to all other executive officials taken together.

The Functions of the Executive

These functions can be summarised as follows.

(1) Administrative: This is the 'direction and supervision of the execution of laws'. For the efficient performance of this function, the executive 'is vested with the power of appointing and removing the higher officials, directing their work and exercising disciplinary control over them'. (Appadorai, p. 557).

(2) Military Power: This includes the power of the supreme command of the army, navy and air force and, in some States (e.g. Britain), the power to declare war. In the U.S.A., Congress alone can declare war (ibid).

(3) Diplomatic Power: This is the power to represent the State in its relations with other States, conduct negotiations with them, and conclude treaties. Some States (e.g. the U.S.A. and France) require the consent of the legislature for the validity of treaties.

(4) Legislature: This is mainly the power to formulate the policies that are presented to the legislature.

(5) Judicial: This includes the power of pardon for those that have been found guilty by the judiciary.

Should the Executive be Chosen from Parliament?

Many countries choose their executive fully (e.g. Switzerland by convention though not by constitutional provision and Britain by constitutional provision) or partly (e.g. Japan) from Parliament. The merit of choosing members of the executive (fully or partly) from Parliament is that it makes duly elected personnel available for the executive without a fresh election.

This assumes that the members of Parliament are duly constituted, otherwise the method will be outright unacceptable, and that those selected from the legislature are not replaced, because if they are, then the advantage is lost as the selected members of the executive could have been chosen in the first place by the method used for the replacement.

Considered against true representative political democracy, the method has the shortcoming of violating either the principle of Separation of Political Powers, which touches on the liberty of the citizens, or the principle of All-Branch Representation of Voters, which touches on the equality of representation of voters. It is inconsistent with the principle of Separation of Political Powers if the members of the executive so elected from the legislature remain members of Parliament, as is the case in Britain, but inconsistent with the principle of All-Branch Representation of Voters if they resign their membership of Parliament thereafter, as is done in Switzerland.

Where the members of the executive retain their membership of Parliament, then the procedure implies that the Parliament and the executive are joined, i.e. they are both in one and the same branch of government, that the executive is a part, a department, (in fact the leading or controlling department) of the legislature and is in that respect undemocratic, as it contravenes the principle of Separation of Political Powers, which requires executive and legislative powers to be in different branches of government. (No wonder the government falls when the executive no longer controls the Parliament).

Where the members of the executive selected from the Parliament resign their membership of Parliament thereafter (and there is no replacement), as in Switzerland, the citizens that such members of the executive formerly represented in the legislature will now be without representation in this branch of government, and those now represented in the legislature would be without representation in the executive.

This means that the cessation of the selected persons' membership of the legislature ensures compliance with the principle of Parliament and executive being separate branches of government, and the same person or group of persons who makes the law would not apply or enforce it; but it now makes the method to err on the part of equality of representation of voters because all the people previously represented in the legislature are now represented in either the legislature or the executive but not both. Therefore they are now unequally represented (or more unequally represented if they were formerly unequally represented), since the legislature and the executive are different and unequal branches of government, across which rotational representation of voters does not take place.

The situation is thus unsatisfactory because it may result in some cultural/ethnic or solidarity groups in a country being permanently represented in both the legislature and the executive whereas some are permanently represented in one or the other but not in both of the branches or arms of government and this may cause discontent and agitation.

It can be concluded from all the above that the method of selecting members of the executive from Parliament is unsatisfactory, being inconsistent with some of the basic principles of true representative political democracy. The method is therefore unacceptable for a democratic executive, which should be chosen independently of the legislature. Fortunately the advantage which the method has, that of securing duly elected personnel for the executive with the same election used for the legislature, is available without the method's attendant undemocratic shortcomings.

Through the election of political parties instead of individuals at the General Universal Representation Election (GURE) and through the Party Merit Elections thereafter to select the individual political officeholders, the advantage is guaranteed, as the political parties need be elected only once during a period of rule and all the party merit elections can be done at the same time thereafter.

It should be pointed out that nothing in the foregoing prevents a particular legislator from occupying an executive post earmarked for his/her cultural constituency and political party, provided he is replaced and his replacement in the legislature is elected from his political party and cultural/ethnic constituency.

Partisan or Representative Executive?

True Representative Political Democracy implies a non-partisan or an all-party executive. The rationale for this truism is as follows. By the principle of All-Branch Representation of Voters, all the political parties should participate in each branch of government in every period of rule. But, according to the principle of Separation of Political Powers, the executive is a separate branch of government. Therefore all the political parties should participate in the executive. It follows from this conclusion that universal democracy implies a non-partisan i.e. a representative or an all-party executive.

The principle of Shifting Majority Will also implies a representative executive. Noting that:

(a) the will of the state is the will of the legislature;

(b) the will of the legislature on an issue is the will of the combination of political parties that represent the majority of the voters on that issue;

(c) the combination of political parties that represent the majority of voters may vary from issue to issue as different political parties may have different policies on different issues and as no fixed set of parties may have the best policies on all the issues of controversy;

then it follows that the will of the state is the will of a shifting or different combinations of the political parties. Therefore there is no need for the executive to comprise only the representatives of a fixed majority of the voters, since they are executing the will of different combinations of political parties.

Coalition governments are examples of executives with more than one political party, but not a non-partisan executive. That is one of the reasons why they are generally unstable because they are inconsistent with true representative political democracy. The Swiss Collegial Executive is a living example of a non-partisan executive. It is not based upon a party majority in the legislative bodies; its members are elected not only from different party groups but also from party groups fundamentally opposed to each other.

The British Executive is a partisan executive, as (in the words of Jacobsen and Lipman) the 'titular monarch formally authorises the leader of the majority party in the House of Commons to be prime minister,' who chooses his or her 'cabinet from among the members of Parliament – the greatest number of seats being given to members of the House of Commons, almost always selected from the majority party'.

Jacobsen and Lipman has described the 'chief defect' of a partisan executive as an overemphasis on party, rather than the nation or the country, which keeps many important matters (other than party interests) from receiving an adequate hearing.

However, the partisan executive in the U.K. is checked by the titular monarch who, said Peel, 'after a reign of ten years, ought to know much more of the working of the machine of government than any other man in the country' and who, as Appadorai said 'is in a position to rise above parties and partisanship, for his or her personal fortunes are hardly affected by party politics'. In other words, the titular monarch acts as a sanction, an independent umpire to achieve authority with responsibility with the British 'party cabinet' (Jacobsen and Lipman).

In the determination of policy and in administration, as Appadorai wrote, the British monarch has, in Bagehot's often quoted words, three rights: the right to be consulted, the right to encourage, the right to warn. As Appadorai emphasised, the right of the monarch to be consulted is an important one and it is on record that more than one monarch insisted on this right.

Monarchy is itself undemocratic, but as a vestige of tradition of the past, it helps to explain why party executive has survived in some countries, particularly the U.K. and perhaps Belgium, even though under severe pressure. The Belgium monarchy is a political institution that cuts across the cleavages of Belgium society, helping to moderate conflict instead of aggravating it (Rodee *et al* p.308).

> Identified exclusively with neither one Belgian community nor the other, constantly exhorting Belgium's people and governing elite to compromise their differences in the interest of all, King Baudouin I (of Belgium) has worked for continuity and stability in a political system that, without a reigning monarch, might long ago have come apart at the seams.

An attempt in modern states to mimic monarchy and appoint ceremonial presidents to perform the role of monarchs in Parliamentary systems and so bring stability failed to produce the desired results (e.g. Nigeria's first republic). It must be accepted that no ceremonial president, elected or appointed, can truly be a political institution that cuts across the cleavages of modern societies like there is in the U.K. or in Belgium. Only a representative executive can be.

The criterion of good/responsible government is being responsive to public opinion without being inconsistent in policy. Political or policy inconsistency is a feature of partisan executive as government swings from one political party to another. The following account by Chuba Okadigbo (1987, page 133) illustrates policy inconsistency in the Nigerian polity as government changed from one hand to another.

> In 1976, the Federal Military Government adopted his (i.e. late Chief Obafemi Awolowo's) Free Primary Education Programme. This was cancelled in 1979 by the Shagari government which, however, tried to implement same in 1983. In 1985, the programme of Free Education was again cancelled by the Buhari/Idiagbon junta.

The Obasanjo government of Nigeria's Fourth Republic (1999-2003) has again adopted the programme (somehow).

With a representative executive, policy inconsistency will be absent because, whoever the president may be, whether from a majority cultural/ethnic constituency or a minority one and from whichever political party, all the political parties in Parliament are always in the executive and so there is the best chance for the laws enacted by Parliament to be executed in the best interest of all. With a representative executive, policies will wear a national or countrywide outlook rather than a partisan outlook.

It is based on the premise that all voters should be represented in the executive, as the new South Africa has done. There will be no policy elimination at the polls as in the case of the single party Executive, but all the parties that are in the legislature will also be in the executive. The method of executing policies to be pursued by the executive would always be arrived at by the majority vote of the policy heterogeneous cabinet members after considering the alternative methods in their pure or modified forms.

The selection of a representative or non–partisan executive can start with the results of a General Universal Representation Election. What is required is the partisan and cultural distributions of voters in a central or national election for the current period of rule. A separate central or national election purposely for the executive is unnecessary: the result of the General Universal Representation Election (GURE) will do.

The parliamentary system of government is based upon a partisan executive. The presidential system of government is also based upon the partisan executive. The representative executive is recommended for the new states and the old states that have problems. But why partisan executive, which necessarily excludes people from the minority parties? Because whether we accept it or not, the majority camp is represented in the executive whereas the minority camp is not.

This implies that only those who voted for the majority party or majority coalition of parties have the right of political representation in the Executive. This is against the concepts of political liberty and equality of political right, as represented by the principles of Universal Representation of Voters and All-Branch Representation of Voters. It is therefore undemocratic.

This arrangement may still be unsatisfactory even where all cultural groups are represented, because of two reasons. First, if all the officeholders come from the majority party, then a cultural constituency whose majority voted for the minority party will not be fully satisfied as having been represented by one of their members from the majority party. And this situation cannot be satisfactorily remedied by the majority party selecting some officeholders from the minority party (as President Obasanjo of Nigeria did in 1999) because by the principle of Non-Transferability of Delegated Mandates, it is undemocratic for the majority party to select someone from outside itself to occupy its political post. Even the minority party may turn down the request and refuse to participate as an appendage to the majority party.

One of two situations may result in the polity. Either there will be a mass deflection of the polity to a political party, resulting effectively in a one-party system (the Nigerian 2003 elections point towards this) or else resentment and frustration will deepen in the minority camp, resulting in disunity and instability in the country. No wonder many notable citizens are often declared rebels in their own country. None of the two situations is desirable in a country.

Moreover, no single party has the best policies for society on all issues; so partisan executive is against the principle of Shifting Majority

Will on all issues as debates are perfunctory in parliamentary systems and lobbying and corruption thrive in presidential systems – all in an attempt to prevent the true will of the majority from seeing the light of the day. Therefore the representative executive is the only way to ensure that the people are represented by their choice and that the best policies that enjoy the support of a (shifting) majority of the people on all issues emerge as public policies. It is the only way to stem the problem of political corruption and political refugees.

In this regard, the presidential system of government, as presently practised, whereby a citizen, called a president, is appointed by the plural or absolute majority votes of the voting citizens as their representative and he/she subsequently appoints (with or without the ratification of the national assembly) the remaining members of the executive bodies, is inappropriate for heterogeneous societies because neither is he/she necessarily the best of the presidential candidates on merit, nor is he/she representative of the whole or best interests in the country, being representative of the interests of 'at best' only a fixed (not shifting) majority of the voters, who are just a part of the country. The 'at best' here signifies that the president represents a majority of the voters only in a two-party system. In a multi-party system (e.g. three or more parties) he would often represent a minority of the voters (e.g. Nigeria's Second Republic). It is noteworthy that none of the forty-four American presidents has ever come from the non-white population, which accounts for about 25% of American population. This is inconsistent with the concept of the political equality of all voters, which implies that about a quarter (i.e. over ten) of the American presidents ought to have been non-whites since about a quarter of the voters is non-white.

It is only a representative executive that can eliminate over-concentration of power in a few hands.

It needs to be added that a partisan executive is no armour against governmental instability. For example, in Nigeria's Fourth Republic, President Olusegun Obasanjo faced serious impeachment threats from his own political party-dominated legislature which were averted only by the goodwill of the people at large.

The just concluded Nigerian 2003 presidential, gubernatorial, and national and state assembly elections generated so much tension in the country that some well-meaning concerned citizens asked the winners, President Olusegun Obasanjo and his Peoples Democratic Party (PDP) to extend "hands of fellowship" and " olive branches" to their opposing political parties and their members. Some people even called for a one-year "interim or transitional government of national unity to be composed of persons nominated by the political parties and other interest groups", to be chaired by the incumbent President Obasanjo, and mainly for the purpose of "convening and organizing a National Conference for the restructuring of the Nigerian polity under a new Constitution..." and for "setting up a new and credible electoral system...", among other things. (*The Guardian* of Nigeria, Friday 23 May 2003, pages 1 and 2.)

The author notes that it is mainly the undemocratic absence of universal representation of the voters in both the legislature and the executive, resulting in the use of the partisan and single executive in the country, that has (more than anything else) brought about the tension and the problems. No such appeals or suggestions would arise in a polity where the democratic principle of universal representation of voters in every arm of government is already operative, as this book suggests, since all cultural/ethnic constituencies and all political parties would always be equitably accommodated in the executive as in the legislature. What is a "government of national unity" apart from an equitable multi-culture all-party executive? And why should it be "interim or transitional" in a polity, since it is the democratic thing to do?

A former Nigerian military Head of State from the Northern part of the country, retired General Abdulsalami Abubakar, who handed over the reign of power to President Olusegun Obasanjo on 29 May 1999, was reported to have "asked victors in the elections to have very large heart by accommodating every shade of opinion, stressing that the idea of winner takes all was not right for the country". The report added (among other things) that he "disclosed that the leaders were already making arrangement to organize a conference of all stakeholders in the country with a view to finding a solution to the present overheating of the polity". (*Nigerian Tribune*, Wednesday 4 June 2003, page 40).

In his inaugural speech at Eagle Square, Abuja on 29 May 2003 for the second elected term in office, President Obasanjo himself pledged to try "to heal the wounds from the elections..." and to use his "mandate to provide quality leadership for all of Nigeria and for Nigerians regardless of their political persuasions". President Obasanjo and his PDP in their second term in office would surely, as they did before (in 1999) without such prompting, form a broad-based government that would accommodate (some) other (willing) political parties. That would be highly commendable, as it is beyond the country's constitutional provisions but would enable (some of) the almost 40% of the voters that did not vote for him to have (some form of) representative participation in the executive arm of the national government, in line with the democratic requirement for 100% voter representation (i.e. representative participation) in every arm of a (representative) government, the executive arm inclusive, as this book shows. The author is of the opinion that, in addition, President Obasanjo and PDP should use their huge mandates to cure once for all the diseases causing the wounds and so ensure that the wounds are never opened up again, by seeing to a re-structuring of the Nigerian polity and to the effecting of the necessary amendments to the Nigerian Constitution along the democratic lines that this book describes. In that way, President Obasanjo and his PDP would not only be leaving a permanent priceless legacy of "sustainable democracy" (as Professor Jerry Gana, Nigeria's outgoing Minister of Information would say) for the Nigerian nation but also be writing their own names in letters of gold in the annals of Nigerian history.

Single or Plural Executive?

True representative political democracy implies a plural executive, in which final control rests with a body or council, rather than a single executive, in which final control rests with an individual. The rationale for this conclusion is as follows.

The principles of All-Branch Representation of Voters and Separation of Political Powers together imply an all-party and multicultural executive, one in which all the cultural constituencies and all the political parties participate, i.e. have their members. Moreover, the principle of Free Grouping of Citizens implies the existence of more than one political party as the people's partisan representatives and there may be more than one cultural constituency. Furthermore, for participation in the executive, a political party and/or a cultural constituency must have at least one member in the executive. It follows therefore that an all-party multicultural Executive in a plural society is a plural Executive, comprising more than one person, who are the respective members of the multiple political parties and multiple cultural constituencies having all the popular votes.

Also, according to the principle of Proportional Representation of Voters, each of the members of a branch or arm of government represents the same number of voters. Therefore, since all voters are politically equal, it follows that all the members of a plural executive are politically equal, that is, they are colleagues or co-ordinates.

The implication of all this is that representative political democracy expects a plural Executive in which final control rests not with one person but with all the members collectively as colleagues. By the doctrine of decision-making by majority vote, the final control is exercised through consensus or majority vote in which, according to the principle of Subordination of Will, members of the same party always vote together. Moreover, all members uphold the majority decision thereafter, again according to the principle of Subordination of Will or Collective Responsibility.

The single Executive is illustrated by the President of the United States of America, in whom *alone* the constitution of the United States vests the executive power (Potter *et al*). The President of the U.S.A. has his ministers, but they are strictly *his* ministers, named by him and dependent on him; they are his advisers and agents, not his colleagues. (Appadorai, E.A. Freeman in *Historical Essays*, Essay XII). So also is the Nigerian President.

The plural Executive is best illustrated by the Federal Council of Switzerland, in which the Swiss Constitution vests the supreme executive power of the land. The Swiss Executive has no prime minister but a president. The president is simply the chairman of the Federal Council and exercises the usual powers of a chairman (Appadorai). He does not select the other members of the Council and has no authority over them; they are his colleagues, not merely his agents or advisers (ibid). Executive acts are the acts of the Council as a body, not of the president personally. (E.A. Freeman, *Historical Essays*, Essay XII, Macmillan, 1986).

As Jacobsen and Lipman (p.146) have noted 'the highly successful operation of the Swiss collegial system is a challenge to theorists who insist on a single executive head...' The analysis in this book shows that such an insistence is in fact against true representative political democracy and must have stemmed from a selfish motive or may be one of those wrong conclusions from inductive analysis or informed by ignorance.

The British Executive also is reported to be a plural Executive. Jacobsen and Lipman reports (p. 138); 'Although the (British) king (or queen) is the formal symbol of leadership, the real executive powers are lodged, not in a single person, but in a cabinet which is composed of a prime minister and about twenty other ministers ... each of these individuals directs one department of government'. However, one may venture to say that the British Executive is (if at all) a weak plural Executive, since the British prime minister chooses his or her cabinet and so the executive may actually in practice function as a single Executive.

Those who advocate the single Executive because 'it secures the unity, singleness of purpose, energy and promptness of decision'

(Appadorai p.558) should remember that it is, as shown above, undemocratic and can cause the commonwealth to be dragged through the dirt by a small man as has happened to many countries in. the past, Nigeria inclusive. On the other hand, not only is a plural Executive democratic, it is also a maxim of experience that in a multitude of counsellors there is wisdom and therefore a collegial Executive is safer than a single Executive. (Representative Government chapter XIV and Appadorai, p. 559). E.A. Freeman (1986) wrote:

> The presidency of Washington and the presidency of Pierce are in Switzerland alike impossible... America, with her personal chief, runs a risk, which Switzerland avoids. As in all cases of risk, the more adventurous State sometimes reaps for itself advantages, and sometimes brings on itself evil, from both of which its less daring fellow is equally cut off.

The plural Executive certainly better suits a democratic State, unitary or federal. It is unwise, as it is undemocratic, to leave the destiny of millions of people in one man's hands, however great he may appear to be. Moreover, the fact that the president, as a single Executive, has to turn back to appoint arbitrarily some of the citizens whose representative he is as his own agents to share part of the burden that has been unwittingly imposed upon him shows the inadequacy and illogicality of the system. Granted that the system is used with checks and balances, it must be said that such measures are effective only in reducing the high tendency of the president to be a dictator, the proneness for which is very high because he may appoint and remove his ministers.

However, checks and balances neither remove the facts that the president is not necessarily the best of the aspirants on merit for the post to be held nor the fact that he is representative of only a part and not the whole of the country nor the paucity and irrationality in the idea of a country electing a single person to shoulder the responsibilities of several persons only for that one person to turn back on his electors and arbitrarily pick some of them to carry part of the burden that they have all thrust upon him.

It is noteworthy that in European countries, unlike in North and South America, executive authority is vested in cabinets rather than in presidents.

The single Executive is like a society or social club where all the members choose only their president and the president then appoints all the other members of his Executive. On the other hand, the plural Executive is like a society or social club where all the members elect the president as well as each of the other members of the Executive. I believe that the plural Executive is better for the same reasons that a modern society or social club prefers to elect each member of its executive rather than only its president.

With a plural Executive, the polity can spread its executive officeholders equitably among its various constituencies (cultural and partisan) and so better serves its own general interests rather than some narrower party or sectional interests which a single Executive necessarily serves, especially in a plural country/polity.

It is noteworthy that since the early 1990's, that great politician and elder statesman of Nigeria, Chief Anthony Enahoro, has been advocating a cabinet type of government for heterogeneous countries such as Nigeria. Even on 29 May, 2002, when he had the honour to be the chairman at the ceremony marking Nigeria's Democracy Day that was organised by President Olusegun Obasanjo's Federal Government, he reiterated in his speech that he did not believe that the presidential system of government was the best for Nigeria. This view is not at variance with the analysis here.

Nigeria and other countries should jettison the single Executive for the plural Executive. They should stop wasting scarce public funds on holding several unnecessary general elections, such as presidential, gubernatorial, national and state assembly, and local government elections. After the only necessary General Universal Representation Election (GURE), they should select their plural Executive and other political post occupiers by lot or (party) merit elections, all of which can take place on the same day, as explained further in other parts of this book.

Should the Chief Executive Make Political Appointment?

The Chief Executive may not appoint a non-representative into political office because doing so would violate the principle of Non-Transferability of Delegated Mandates, which forbids rulers in true representative political democracy from making rulers, as that would make Government to be removed from the people to the second degree of representation, which is not true representative democracy. Only the people, that is, the rulers and the ruled, the cultural constituencies and the political parties if they are directly elected, may make political appointments from among themselves.

Moreover, the Chief Executive may not make political appointments from the legislature or any other branch or arm of government because he would still be making political appointments outside himself, contrary to the principle of Non-Transferability of Delegated Mandates. He along with the other members of his plural executive may only make a selection from two nominees duly elected from the same political party and/or cultural constituency by members of the political party and/or cultural constituency, as discussed fully under the chapter on Elections and Electoral Systems.

Furthermore, the Chief Executive may not move members of the plural Executive from one political post to another in a universal democratic government. The reasons are as follows. First, holding of a particular post is, by the principle of Co-ordinated Proportional Allocation of Multiple Unequal Scarce Posts, a right of the political party and the cultural constituency to which the political post is for the time being allocated and only their member may occupy the post during the current period of rule. Also, the post must have been filled by the best-qualified candidate, through a competitive merit election. Furthermore, every member of the executive is a colleague, and not a subordinate or an agent, of the Chief Executive, who is only first among equals, as earlier discussed.

The prime minister in the parliamentary system or the president in the presidential system is allowed to make political appointments into the executive, which is inconsistent with true representative political democracy. The usual explanation for this undemocratic indulgence in these systems is that the prime minister or the president should be allowed to choose those he can work with to make for smooth running of government business. However, this slackness should not be tolerated in true representative ' political democracy because it amounts to a transfer of the prime minister's or president's status from that of a trustee, a representative, to that of the actual owner. It shifts the focus of the appointees' allegiance from the people to the prime minister or president. It leads to a betrayal of trust and to corruption. It encourages dictatorial tendencies in the president or prime minister. It lowers the responsibility of the Chief Executive to the 'share-holders' (i.e. the people) by making him a weak manager who can manage only those he himself assembles together.

A prime minister or president worth the name ought to be able to lead a strong team, a team assembled by the people, not just by himself or herself. The principal of a college, like the vice-chancellor of a university, usually does not appoint his/her members of staff and yet his/her success depends on how well he/she can lead them. The chief executive or managing director of a company or business concern or even a committee appointed by government often does not appoint his/her co-directors or co-members and yet he/she has to lead them to achieve the company's or committee's objectives if he/she is worth his/her salt.

It must be accepted that there is no political freedom or political equality for the citizens in the selection of their government if they select one or few members of government who will then exclusively select a much greater number of other political members of the same government. Those members of government who have to appoint their 'lesser' counterparts are clearly politically superior to any other person, in or out of government, in the selection of the government. Moreover, the allegiance of such a government will be more to those who appoint their counterparts than to the general electorate it is supposed to represent and serve.

Furthermore, why should a people elect an individual to shoulder the responsibilities of several persons, knowing fully well that the individual will afterwards turn back upon them and subjectively pick some of them to share the responsibilities with him? Where is rationality in such an arrangement? Where is the political liberty of all the citizens in the arrangement? Where is the political equality of all the citizens in it? And where is objectivity in it? Definitely nowhere.

Should the Executive Hold Office for a Fixed Term?

The full question is: should the executive hold office for a fixed term (as in the United States of America and Switzerland) or only as long as it commands the confidence of the legislature (as in Britain)?

True Representative Political Democracy expects the executive to hold office for a fixed term, as will be seen from the following analysis. First, by definition, a function of the executive is the execution of the will of the State as that will has been formulated and expressed in terms of law. (Garner). But by the principle of Separation of Powers, the legislature, not the executive, makes laws. The will of the State is thus the will of the legislature (subject to popular sovereign). Therefore, even though the executive may recommend measures for the consideration of the legislature, initiate bills and defend them in Parliament and even exercise a suspensive veto because the executive needs particular legislation for its works, nevertheless it is the duty of the executive to carry out the laws that the legislature has enacted and need not resign because a bill introduced by it, however important it may be, has failed passage in the legislature. The executive should simply drop the matter or remodel the bill to meet the criticism that has caused its defeat. If the bill is important and popular, it may go to the legislature as a private bill, which, if not passed, should compulsorily go to the electorate for approval or rejection.

Secondly, by the principle of Separation of Powers and the principle of All-Branch Representation of Voters, the executive, like the legislature, derives its powers direct from the mandate of the electorate; it is not appointed by or from the legislature. The mandate of the electorate, by the principle of Periodic

Representation of Voters, is given for a fixed term. Therefore, the executive, like the legislature and the Judicial Council, must have a fixed life.

Moreover, by the principle of Shifting Majority Will, the executive that may formulate the policy of the State should not be tied to the will of a fixed or particular majority of the legislators because the national will is, in True Representative Political Democracy, the will of a shifting not a permanent majority of the people. Therefore making the executive to hold office only as long as it commands the confidence of the legislature, as is necessary in the parliamentary system of government, is not only irrational but also inconsistent with Universal Democracy. It is necessary in the parliamentary system of government because the executive is arbitrarily tied to the majority party/coalition. If this condition is relaxed and the executive is drawn from all the parties in Parliament, then the situation will not arise that the executive does not command the confidence of the legislature and the parliamentary system would be more stable.

Ensuring a Responsible Executive

The executive executes 'the will of the State as that will has been formulated and expressed in terms of law' (Garner) by the legislature. The legislature, as the final decision maker in matters of legislation and finance and as 'the organ of public opinion on all matters of public importance' (Appadorai, p. 554) should have right to watch and compel the executive 'to justify all its acts before the legislature and before the public, i.e. openly; and if (any of) the men (and women) who compose the government (i.e. executive) abuse their trust or fulfil it in a manner which conflicts with the deliberate sense of the nation', the legislature must have power to expel such of them from office by court processes.

The executive members should therefore have the right of being present in the legislature when necessary, taking part in its discussions and introducing bills. But the executive members are not members of the legislature and cannot vote in the House.

The cabinet should operate on the principle of Collective Responsibility, taking its decisions by either consensus or majority vote. Every member of the executive should be bound by the principle of Subordination of Lower Will to Higher Will. As a safeguard of liberty, government officials should be answerable in a court of law for their conduct as government servants. Therefore the judiciary should be vested, in relation to the executive, with the power to review the acts of the executive. It is noteworthy, in this connection, that many States in Europe have established separate administrative courts for the trial of cases in which the government or its servants are parties (Appadorai, p. 569).

Summary

In summary, the executive in True Representative Political Democracy should have the following features. It is a cabinet type of Executive like the Parliamentary Executive but chosen independently of the legislature and holding office for a fixed term like the non-parliamentary or the presidential type. It is a multi-party and multi-culture executive with power vested in a cabinet or council and not just only in the president, who is the chairman of the cabinet or council. The Executive executes the will of the legislature whose duty it is to make laws for the polity.

28

THE JUDICIARY IN
UNIVERSAL DEMOCRACY

There is no better test of the excellence of a government than the efficiency of its judicial system, for nothing more nearly touches the welfare and security of the citizen than his knowledge that he can rely on the certain, prompt, and impartial administration of justice – Bryce in *Modern Democracies*, Vol. II, p.421 and A. Appadórai in *The Substance of Politics*, 11th Ed., p.567.

The primary duty of the judiciary is, as pointed out by Appadorai, 'to interpret law, to apply the existing law to individual cases, and, by so doing, to hold the scales even both between one private citizen and another, and between private citizens and members of the government.' This important role of the judiciary, Appadorai continued, makes it 'obviously essential to choose men of honesty, impartiality, independence and legal knowledge to fill the places of judges.'

As regards the duration of office of judges and their salaries and allowances, Appadorai (pp. 567-568) reported that it is now recognised that the preservation of judicial independence requires that judges should hold office for life – sometimes expressed as 'holding office during good behaviour', i.e. so long as they are not guilty of any crime known to the law – independent of the pleasure of the executive and the legislature, and that their salaries and allowances should not be diminished during their term of office. However, if they commit any crime known to the law, they should be tried in a court of law, like any other citizen. This leaves us with the methods of their appointments to consider.

According to Appadorai, there are three methods in vogue for appointing judges: nomination by the executive (e.g. in Britain, The French Republic, the U.S.A., Canada, Australia, South Africa, Germany, Italy and India), election by the legislature (e.g. in Switzerland and Russia) and election by the people (e.g. in some Swiss cantons and American states).

Relation of the Judiciary to the Executive

So that the judge might not behave with violence and oppression, so that the executive, as judge, may not sit in judgement over its own conduct, which is obviously injurious to freedom, and since members of the executive are not chosen for their capacity or training as judges, judicial and executive powers should not be joined in the same hands, 'whether of one, a few, or many.' i.e. no member of the executive should have judicial functions.

In other words, the executive should neither nominate nor appoint the judges; the executive should be vested with only the power of pardon in relation to the judiciary. Like the legislators and the members of the executive, the members of the Judicial Council, the non-partisan political body that should be vested with the power to appoint judges and see to the welfare and promotion of judges, should be appointed by the polity's relevant cultural constituencies and/or their appropriate learned/professional body components whose members are to fill the positions.

The Judicial Council posts will be allocated only culturally (i.e. ethnically or geographically) since the posts are non-partisan posts.

On the other hand, as a safeguard of liberty, government officials should be answerable in a court of law for their conduct as government servants. Therefore the judiciary should be vested, in relation to the executive, with the power to review the acts of the executive. It is noteworthy, in this connection, that many states in Europe have established separate administrative courts for the trial of cases in which the government or its servants are parties (Appadorai, p. 569).

The following two examples from the Nigerian political history reinforce the fact that the Executive should not have the power of appointment over the judiciary in a democratic polity. In Nigeria's Second Republic, the presidential election was in dispute and it was obvious that the dispute might reach the Supreme Court, the country's apex court, to decide the eventual winner. In the meantime, there was a need to appoint a new Chief Justice who would preside over the Supreme Court. The disputed president-elect had to have a hand in the appointment of the Chief Justice that would eventually sit in judgement in his (disputed president-elect's) case. This was so because the constitution allowed the president to appoint the Chief Justice. The president-elect was declared the winner. Many people felt that the arrangement was unfair to the other party. Moreover, during the military regime of late General Sani Abacha, the late Chief M.K.O. Abiola was kept in prison for a long time because the incumbent head of state did not appoint the additional judges that were then required to make the full complement of the judges to hear Abiola's case. Chief M.K.O. Abiola had allegedly won the Nigerian 1993 Presidential Election that was to usher in the Third Republic but which was annulled by the then military President Ibrahim Babangida, General Abacha's predecessor in office as head of state. Chief Abiola had then declared himself as head of state, which action led to his arrest and detention pending trial. He eventually died in detention in 1998 without the conclusion of his trial.

Legislature and Judiciary

So that the life, liberty and property of the subject would not be in the hands of arbitrary judges, whose decisions would be regulated only by their own opinions and not by any fundamental principles of law, from which legislators may depart but 'which judges are bound to observe' (Appadorai, p. 517),

(1)   The legislature must not have power to elect judges and
(2)   No member of the legislature should be eligible for a judicial office.

In order to maintain the supremacy of the constitution and check its violation, the judiciary, whether in a unitary state or in a federal state, should have the power to declare unconstitutional a law passed by the legislature or any other law-making body. But the judiciary should not have the power to regulate the procedures of the legislature or to prevent or stop the legislature from passing a law. The judiciary should also have the power to try any. legislator for misconduct. Finally, as a guarantee against the abuse (e.g. misconduct, receiving of presents) of judicial powers by judges, a member of the Judicial Council should be recallable by a simple majority of the constituency that elected him/her for misconduct.

29

ELECTIONS AND ELECTORAL SYSTEMS IN UNIVERSAL DEMOCRACY

This chapter discusses the elections and electoral systems that are consistent with true representative political democracy.

Elections

There are at most two types of elections in any period of rule, according to the principle of Separation of Elections:

(1) A General Universal Representation Election (GURE), to represent all the individual members of the electorate that care to vote and on the basis of which all Legislative seats and posts and Executive or Judicial Council posts at every level of government are allocated to political parties and cultural constituencies; and

(2) Merit Elections (ME), comprising:
(a) General Merit Elections (GME), by which the individual members of the Judicial Council and of the non-partisan Executive bodies are chosen, and
(b) Party Merit Elections (PME), by which the individual partisan members of the Legislature and of the Executive are chosen.
Selection by lot may replace the merit elections, where desired.

The General Universal Representation Election (GURE)

There is only one in any period of rule. It is essential for the principle of Universal Representation of Voters, which states that every voting citizen should have (partisan and cultural) representation in government through his/her personally-made choice. The purpose is

187

therefore to represent every one of the voters, in the partisan and cultural senses, in every branch or arm of government and at every level of government through this single election.

Candidates

By the principles of Limited Separation of Representation and of Group Representatives for Voters, the candidates are expressly political organisations and implicitly cultural constituencies, but not individuals. This means that, unless the alternative cultural groups are wholly geographically based, the voters may have to give an indication of their cultural groups on the ballot paper. For example, in a country/polity where the main cultural cleavage is ethnic groups, which may be regarded as territorially based, the geographical areas of a country where they predominate will be clearly demarcated once and for all and the votes of each of such areas separately aggregated after the General Universal Representation Election (GURE).

Each region, state/province/canton, local government area, or ward of a country (see the principle of Free Grouping of Citizens) qualifies as an example of such an area. This may imply movement of voters to their areas of origin to vote if they so wish, but such a movement is unnecessary because people should identify with their places of abode and because the net difference is usually negligible, so that the end does not justify the means. However, for a literate society, if desired (though unnecessary), the voters may indicate their ethnicity/geopolitical areas on the ballot papers in a way that it can be easily picked out for processing, e.g. by the computer.

As earlier discussed (Composition of a Political Party), a political organisation that wants to canvass for the people's votes must meet the following specification. It must comprise persons from all the cultural constituencies defined in the polity's constitution, since any political post may be allocated to any cultural constituency. Moreover, since any post may be allocated to any political party, and since every post may carry some requirements relating to age, gender, education, profession, etc, a political organisation must not only comprise members of all the cultural constituencies but also contain the members of each of them in sufficient number and quality to enable it hold any political post. In other words, there must be in the organisation at least some members from each cultural group who have the requisite qualifications for each post that may be allocated to the constituency.

All the primary ethnic groups qualify to be separately represented at a level of government if they are each viable to provide qualified aspirants for any political post at the level of government. As discussed under the principle of Free Grouping of Citizens, if necessary, lowest-level or primary cultural/ethnic constituencies may be combined into larger groupings – i.e. secondary and tertiary cultural/ethnic constituencies – to make them viable to provide qualified aspirants for posts in all the arms or branches of a level of government or for posts in particular branches of a level of government.

For example, primary cultural/ethnic constituencies like clans or tribes may be used for the central government's legislative Lower House posts (i.e seats and offices), which relate more to the grass roots, and then combined by language into larger secondary cultural/ethnic constituencies for legislative Upper House seats and offices and into tertiary ethnic constituencies for executive and judicial posts, which are more nationalistic.

This implies using at least two levels of cultural/ethnic groupings for a level of government. This is what obtains even in bicameral legislatures in existing parliamentary and presidential systems, where a constituency for producing an Upper House seat is a combination of a number of lower-level constituencies which produce Lower House seats.

Electoral System

Since the purpose of this election is to represent all the voters, the single member (S.M.) electoral systems – i.e. the single plurality system, the majority system, and the double ballot system – are all inapplicable to the election since they all lead to the representation of some but not all the voters as discussed under the principle of Universal Representation of Voters. Therefore, the electoral system is the Proportional Representation (P.R.) system in its various application forms described in this book. By the principles of

Limited Separation of Representation and Free Grouping of Citizens, the whole electorate (i.e. country, state or local government area as the case may be) will not be treated as a single unit but as comprising one or more levels of distinct cultural constituencies, whose votes are separately aggregated, with the appropriate political posts allocated to the cultural constituencies and to the political parties in consonance with the principles of Universal Representation of Voters, Proportional Representation of Voters, Proportional Rotation of a Scarce Political Post Type, and Co-ordinated Proportional Allocation of Multiple Unequal Scarce Posts.

The Proportional Representation system with list, in which candidates occupy political posts in the order in which their names occur in the electoral list, is inapplicable to this election because of the following reasons. First, there must be partisan and/or cultural allocation of political posts and people must be elected into the particular political posts on their personal merits. Secondly, a successful candidate has to compete for a post with others of the same cultural/ethnic constituency and, if the post is a partisan one, within a political party. Thirdly, a particular group of candidates may be required, e.g. medical doctors or engineers or females etc., and lastly the set of political posts that a political party or any of its subgroups will have cannot be known before the General Universal Representation Election is held.

Rather than use a list, there will be an allocation of the political posts in each branch or arm of government (at a level of government), first to the cultural constituencies stated in the polity's constitution for the branch of government and then, if partisan posts, to the political parties in accordance with the principle of Universal Representation of Voters.

The political posts will be allocated *after voting* and on the basis of the political parties' and/or cultural constituencies' voting strengths and not before voting on the basis of their population, in accordance with the principle of Appropriation of Political Rights. The allocation of political posts – judicial posts, legislative seats and offices and executive posts – will be in accordance with the principles of Proportional Representation of Voters, Proportional Rotation of a Scarce Political Post Type and Co-ordinated Proportional Allocation of Multiple Unequal Scarce Posts.

The supposed disadvantages of a system of proportional representation have been summarised as follows (Report of the Nigerian Political Bureau, March 1987, section 8.048, p.139):

> In the first instance, this form of electoral system removes the representative far away from his electorate. The personal relationship between the electors and the elected which is a cardinal ingredient of representativeness is destroyed. Instead, it is the political party or group that comes between the electorate and its representative. Proportional Representation gives room to proliferation of political parties. The greatest weakness of this electoral system is that it often leads to coalition governments. Such governments are often weak.

These assumed disadvantages are hereby debunked.

The argument that a system of proportional representation 'removes the representative far away from his electorate' has arisen because presently there is a misconception about so many things in the political arena (which is a purpose for writing this book) and this is just one of the things. It needs to be realised that in repre-sentative political democracy, the political party is the representative of its electors, not any individual member of the party (see the principles of Group or Corporate Representatives for Voters and Political Party Dominance), and that Proportional Representation rather than the Single-Member system is essential for the universal representation of the voting public which true representative political democracy demands.

Direct selection of an individual cannot lead to the representation of all the voters as it is only satisfactory as a method of selection on merit from a homogeneous set of candidates, as the principle of Homogeneity of Candidates shows. As selection on merit is realistic only after representation, direct selection of public officeholders by the general public/electorate is available after Proportional Representation has been used, as pointed out under General and Party Merit Elections in this chapter.

Moreover, as shown under the principle of Non-Transferability of Delegated Mandates, political parties are democratically required to make appointments in between general representation elections, as general elections are unnecessary and inconvenient for some appointments.

Furthermore, Proportional Representation is necessary because it is unrealistic to determine a choice of the public policy at the polls, as the general electorate does not have all the facts to make the choice and because no one party or single majority coalition of parties has correct answers to all the issues in the society.

The question of Proportional Representation giving room to a proliferation of political parties also does not hold water in the new dispensation contained in this book. This is because there cannot be room for a proliferation of political parties as long as a political party, to exist, needs to win sufficient votes to hold at least a political post in the branch or arm of government with the smallest number of political posts. In fact, a proliferation of political parties is possible only with partisan executive and not with universal or non-partisan executive that true representative political democracy requires. The question of a Proportional Representation system leading to unstable coalition governments is now addressed.

The Proportional Representation (P.R.) electoral system was introduced in Europe to correct rule of exclusion in the legislature. This definitely is a move towards universal and equal representation of the citizens in the legislature, though not in the executive. In the presidential system of government this measure has no direct effect on the representation of the citizens in the Executive arm of government, where the rule of exclusion still operates. However, with parliamentary systems the measure in most cases leads to a coalition of parties in the executive in order to obtain a majority of the representatives of the people to sustain in parliament the policies of the executive.

Coalition governments are generally unstable or weak, as stated above. The instability is erroneously attributed to the Proportional Representation system, which is consequently unpopular with new states. However, analysis, confirmed by available facts, shows that the instability is due to three structural defects in the parliamentary system rather than to the use of proportional representation per se.

The first cause is the parliamentary system's faulty notion that an opposition outside the cabinet is essential for a good government and that the public or general will is the will of a fixed majority of the people. The latter notion gives rise to the tying of the life of the executive (i.e. cabinet) to the ability of the executive (i.e cabinet) necessarily formed by a majority coalition of parties to control a majority in the legislature. Whereas in reality, the general will is the will of the series of combinations or alignments of parties that represent the majority of the people as issues change. This is the essence of the principle of Shifting Majority Will. No such instability will occur in a presidential system (e.g. U.S.A.) with a legislature elected by Proportional Representation.

Secondly, observation of the operation of coalition governments shows that they are usually based upon a 'senior partner – junior partner' relationship instead of being founded on the concept of equality of the voters represented. This would make the participating parties to hold public office in their own rights as in Switzerland and without which the horse-trading for which coalition is notorious will continue. In the new political order advocated in this book political posts, both in quantity and in quality, are allocated to different political parties on the basis of their voting strengths. They therefore participate in the executive in their own rights and so there is no question of any of them abdicating office for the others or holding inferior or superior political offices vis-à-vis or at the expense of the others.

Lastly, there is the rule of exclusion in the executive which leaves a minority coalition in the legislature (i.e. the opposition group) with which dissatisfied members of the ruling majority coalition can team up in order to defeat the executive in a controversial debate. If all voters are represented in the executive, i.e. there is All-Party executive as implied by the principle of All-Branch Representation of Voters and consequently conflict is resolved within the cabinet by shifting majority vote, as in Switzerland and lately South Africa, then there will be no need for the government to fall if the legislature rejects a bill from the executive. The executive would simply drop the bill or carry out the amendment proposed by the legislature.

And there will be no need for a censor vote or vote of confidence or no confidence by the legislature against the executive.

In view of all the above, it is not Proportional Representation but the undemocratic environment in which Proportional Representation is operated that is responsible for all the disadvantages erroneously associated with the use of the Proportional Representation electoral system. The Proportional Representation electoral method belongs to the Universal Representation/Rule system; therefore the Majority Representation/Rule system is inconsistent with it. That is the issue. If the Proportional Representation system is used in an environment of Universal Representation of Voters, as this book shows, full success is assured.

The number of qualified political parties

Assuming that the political posts in each branch or arm of government are allocated on the basis of the results of one general representation election, a political organisation, in order to exist separately as a political party, must win sufficient votes to hold at least a political post in the Executive Council (see the Universal System of Government), which is the branch of government with the smallest number of partisan political posts, as it is this branch or arm of government that requires the largest number of votes per partisan political post according to the principle of Proportional Representation of Voters.

This means that if a political organisation does not win enough votes to hold a political post in the Executive Council, then it cannot exist on its own as a political party at that level of government. In order that no voter will be without a partisan representative, such a political organisation must team up with another political party that has sufficient votes to exist separately or with other similar small political organisations (if any) to form a political party if their total (pooled) votes are sufficient to do so.

Such a political organisation shall have the right to team up with any political party or other such political organisation(s) of its choice. A political party that is viable at the central government level but not at a lower government level must team up with another political party of its choice that is viable at the lower government level.

Cultural and Partisan Distribution of Political Posts

After establishing the branches/sub-branches at each level of government and the number of political posts in each branch/sub-branch with its applicable set of cultural constituencies, the stage is set for the allocation of the political posts. Three different methods of allocation of the political posts to cultural/ethnic constituencies and political parties are considered in this book. These are:

(a) Parallel Method.
(b) Partisan-cum-Cultural Method.
(c) Cultural-cum-Partisan Method.

Each of these methods is discussed below.

Parallel Method

This is the method of allocation of political posts where the partisan and cultural allocations at a level of government are done independently of each other. In each case the total political posts of a branch or sub-branch or arm are involved. For the partisan allocation, if non-scarce, the posts (excluding non-partisan posts, if any) in a branch or sub-branch or arm of government are shared proportionally among political parties, using the partisan distribution of the polity's current total votes in the General Universal Representation Election (GURE) of the current period of rule.

The process is repeated for each branch/sub-branch of government. The same partisan distribution of votes is applicable from branch of government to branch of government. If the political posts in any branch/sub-branch of government are of different types and/or individually scarce, then they are ranked in descending order of importance and allocated to the political parties by the method of

Co-ordinated Proportional Representation by Multiple Unequal Scarce Posts (COPREMUSPO), but using the partisan distribution of current (not cumulative) total votes.

This makes the allocation process to be equitable while still preserving the spirit of competition among the political parties, because in the spirit of a game or competition the allocations of a political party should, in quantity and in quality, be proportional to its showing or voting strength at the current General Universal Representation Election (GURE). Any political organisation that does not have at least a political post in each of the branch/sub-branch of government, particularly the Executive Council, cannot exist separately as a political party for the period of rule and would have to join with another political party/organisation(s), as earlier discussed.

For the cultural allocation, all the political posts (both partisan and non-partisan) in a branch or sub-branch of government are shared proportionally among all the cultural/ethnic constituencies that are applicable to the political posts. The cultural/ethnic distribution of the polity's *current* total votes in the General Universal Representation Election (GURE) is used if all the posts concerned are neither collectively nor individually scarce for the constituencies. However, the cultural/ethnic distribution of the polity's *cumulative* total votes to date in the General Universal Representation Election (GURE) is used if the posts are collectively and/or individually scarce for the constituencies.

The process is repeated for each branch/sub-branch of government, using the cultural distribution of the polity's total votes applicable for the constituencies concerned.

Cumulative votes are used with the method of Co-ordinated Proportional Rotation of Multiple Unequal Scarce Posts (COPROMUSPO) in the cultural allocation of scarce posts, unlike in the partisan allocation of scarce posts, because equity devoid of competition is intended among the cultural constituencies, as each scarce post thus gets rotated equitably among them over the periods of rule.

With the two independent partisan and cultural allocations completed for the political posts in every branch/sub-branch of government, the political parties and/or cultural/ethnic constituencies from which the occupier of any of the political posts is to come are definitely known. Arrangements can then be made for the necessary cultural and/or party merit elections to choose the best of the aspirants on personal merits for the posts.

The Parallel Method has three main obvious advantages. Firstly, the cultural allocation of political posts independently of their partisan allocation underlines the importance of the representation of the cultural structure of the polity instead of the ephemeral partisan affiliation of the cultural groups, which is as divisive as it is ephemeral and so does not encourage the emergence of national political parties and hence national unity in a polity of major cultural diversity.

By allocating political posts to cultural constituencies independently of the political parties, and thereby de-emphasising the partisan affiliation of cultural groups, the role of political parties, rather than the individual political office occupiers, as the primary partisan political representatives of the people is ironically borne out.

Secondly, because the cultural allocation of posts is not made on partisan basis, the allocation is equitable and unnecessary duplication of allocation to some cultural groups that is otherwise possible, is avoided.

Thirdly, the electoral process is simplified in that the cultural or partisan distribution of the polity's total votes is much easier to obtain than the cultural distribution of every party's total votes, or than the partisan distribution of every cultural constituency's total votes. For example, the cultural distribution of the polity's total votes can be readily obtained by simply separately aggregating the votes of the areas of the polity corresponding to its cultural divisions. However, to obtain the partisan distribution of every cultural constituency's total votes, the votes of each cultural constituency will have to be additionally sorted on the basis of the political parties.

A seeming disadvantage of this allocation method but really a blessing in disguise is that there is no correlation between the partisan affiliation of the cultural constituencies (as expressed in the partisan distribution of their votes) and the pattern of their representation in government. The political officeholder from a cultural constituency, e.g. a legislator or an executive office occupier, may not necessarily come from a political party for which the majority of the constituency voted.

A lot of education may be required to make the people to understand and accept this laudable phenomenon, which is the true meaning of the principle of Separation of Representation and the only way to disengage the people from ethnic politics and produce truly nationalistic political parties and a nation. What is more nationalistic than for a southern president to come from a predominantly northern political party and vice versa, as it happened in Nigeria's Fourth Republic when Chief Olusegun Obasanjo from the South Western part of Nigeria became the Nigerian president on the majority vote of the Northern and Eastern parts of Nigeria and the minority vote of the South West, which voted massively for the opposing party.

It is high time the people divorced cultural representation from partisan representation and learnt to vote for political parties purely for what they really are – i.e. as alternative bodies of policy on the controversial issues in the society – and not for any other considerations, such as ethnicity, for which they are separately represented.

Partisan-cum-Cultural Method
This is the method of allocation of political posts where there is first a partisan allocation of the partisan political posts of a branch/sub-branch of a polity and then followed by a cultural allocation of each political party's allocated posts as well as of the non-partisan executive and judicial political posts. For the partisan allocation of posts, the procedure is the same as that described for partisan allocation of posts under the Parallel Method.

After the partisan allocation of the overall posts, then each political party's allocated political posts are shared to cultural constituencies. The sharing of a political party's allocated posts at a level of government to cultural constituencies may be done branch of government by branch of government, in which case there would be no need for inter-branch rotation of scarce posts.

But, if desired, especially where the posts are either collectively or individually scarce for the cultural constituencies, the partisan allocations for more than one branch of government may be combined where the same set of cultural constituencies are applicable for the different branches of government. (This sharing of combined posts would be preferred in this method to enable as many cultural constituencies as possible to be represented in a period of rule.)

In this case, all such partisan political posts irrespective of which branch they belong to, would be ranked in their descending order of importance, after which (inter-branch) co-ordinated rotation of the posts (using COPROMUSPO) would be done, to enable the different types of posts to be equitably allocated to the cultural constituencies over time. The cultural allocation of a party's allocated political posts would be done using the cultural distribution of the party's total votes in the General Universal Representation Election (GURE), current if the posts are collectively and individually not scarce for the cultural constituencies but cumulative if the posts are either collectively or individually scarce for the cultural constituencies.

This method (partisan-cum-cultural method) has the following advantages. Firstly, because the partisan allocation of political posts is done branch/sub-branch of government by branch/sub-branch of government and on the basis of current (not cumulative) partisan distribution of the polity's total votes, the method, like the Parallel Method, directly and precisely determines the number of political parties for a period of rule.

Any political association or group of political associations that cannot get at least a partisan political post in each of the branches/ sub-branches or arms of government considered in a period of rule, particularly the Executive Council, which has the smallest number of partisan posts, cannot exist as a political party in that period of rule. Secondly, there seems to be some correlation between the partisan affiliation of the cultural constituencies and their representation in government, since the cultural allocation of each party's allocated posts is done on the basis of the cultural distribution of the political party's votes.

This cannot even be called an advantage because it is the root cause of ethnic politics. However, there are grave disadvantages. A major disadvantage of the method is that the cultural constituencies are treated as the secondary basis of allocation of political posts, the main basis being the political parties.

This may not be readily accepted by the cultural constituencies, which regard themselves as the main units of reckoning in the polity for the allocation of political posts. Moreover, the splitting of a cultural/ethnic constituency's votes among several political parties can sometimes have adverse effects on the overall political representation of the constituency, and so makes the method inequitable (see Table 8).

Furthermore, the cultural/ethnic allocations of the partisan and non-partisan political posts to which the same set of cultural/ethnic constituencies applies cannot be done together because the one requires the cultural distribution of partisan votes while the other requires the cultural distribution of the whole polity's votes. Yet another disadvantage is that the tendency would be for the cultural allocation of partisan political posts to be handled at the party level instead of at the level of the polity's central electoral body or bodies.

Finally, the method is contrary to the spirit of the principle of Limited Separation of Representation that partisan and cultural representations of voters are separable and should be so treated. For these disadvantages, the method is not recommended.

Cultural-cum-Partisan Method

This is the method of allocation of political posts where there is first a cultural allocation of all the posts of a branch/sub-branch of a polity, followed by a partisan allocation of each cultural constituency's allocated partisan posts. All the posts (partisan and non-partisan) in a branch/sub-branch of a level of government applicable to a level of cultural constituencies are shared among the cultural/ethnic constituencies proportionally, using the cultural/ethnic distribution of the polity's *current* votes in the General Universal Representation Election if the posts are neither collectively nor individually scarce for the ethnic/cultural constituencies; or using COPROMUSPO with the cultural/ethnic distribution of the polity's *cumulative* votes to date in the General Universal Representation Election if the posts are collectively and/or individually scarce for the cultural/ethnic constituencies.

Then every cultural/ethnic constituency's allocated partisan or pseudo-partisan political posts in the branch/sub-branch are respectively proportionally allocated to the duly elected political parties on the basis of the partisan distribution of the cultural/ethnic constituency's *current* (not cumulative) votes in the General Universal Representation Election.

Any political organisation that does not win enough votes to have at least a post in each of the branches/sub-branches, particularly the polity's Executive Council, cannot exist separately. It would have to join with another political party that has enough votes or with another similar political organisation or organisations with which it will be able to have enough votes to exist as a separate political party. This coming together of political organisations is necessary in order that no voter would be without representation in an arm of government in any period.

It is noteworthy that, in this method, there is no partisan rotation of a constituency's political posts over periods of rule firstly because that would mean double rotation of posts since there is already cultural rotation of the posts over periods of rule and secondly because in the spirit of a game or competition the allocations of a political party should, in quantity and in quality, be proportional to its cultural showing or voting strength at the *current* General Universal Representation Election. However the method of Co-ordinated Proportional Representation by Multiple Unequal Scarce Posts (COPREMUSPO) may still be used for the partisan allocation since the partisan distribution of the relevant constituency's *current* (rather than cumulative) votes in the General Universal Representation Election is used. Moreover, if not otherwise disallowed, the entire partisan posts from the various branches and sub-branches applicable to a set of cultural constituencies may be combined and the cultural-cum-partisan allocations done together.

The cultural-cum-partisan method has numerous disadvantages. Firstly, the partisan allocation process has to be done for every cultural/ethnic constituency that has been allocated Executive Council post(s) before the qualified political parties for the current period of rule can be known. Secondly, it is an inequitable method because it can over-allocate posts to some political parties at the expense of some other political organisations that may thereby lose the status of becoming a political party in its own right. Thirdly, it breeds ethnic politics, as national posts are allocated to political parties on cultural/ethnic basis.

Comparison of the Allocation Methods

Table 8 gives the results of the three methods applied to the same situation.

The parallel method brings out the fact that a political party's members come from policy-heterogeneous cultural/ethnic constituencies. Therefore any one of them selected into office on the platform of any political party is a cultural agent not only of his party members but also of the entirety of his policy-heterogeneous cultural/ethnic constituency. This is nationalism and not parochialism. On the other hand, the other two methods ensure that the individual officeholders come from the cultural constituencies where their political parties have the majority votes.

This is parochialism and ethnic politics, which we should discourage if we want to build a nation out of many 'nationalities'. Moreover, the other two methods are not fully equitable. For example, the cultural-cum-partisan method allocates no political post to GNPP on the Executive Council, meaning that the political association cannot exist separately as a political party for that period of rule, whereas equitably, it is entitled to one political post (Table 8) as the parallel method and equity show.

TABLE 8

The three political posts allocation methods applied to ten hypothetical (Federal) Executive Council posts in Universal Democracy, using the results of the Nigeria's 1979 Presidential Election.

Ethnic/ Cultural Constituency (States)	Total votes cast	%	Executive Council political posts for political parties and cultural constituencies.				
			GNPP	NPN	NPP	PRP	UPN
1. Anambra	1,209.038	7.1767			P6 P3		P6
2. Bauchi	998,683	5.9821		P8 *P8* P5			
3. Bendel	669,511	3.9742					
4. Benue	538,879	3.1987					
5. Borno	710,968	4.2202	P7				
6. Cross River	661,103	3.0242					
7. Gongola	639,138	3.7939					
8. Imo	1,153,355	6.8462	*P7*		*P7* P10		
9. Kaduna	1,382,712	8.2076		P2			*P2*
10. Kano	1,220,763	7.2463		*P5* P8		P5 *P4*	
11. Kwara	354,605	2.1049					
12. Lagos	828,414	4.9174					P9 *P9*
13. Niger	383,347	2.2755					
14. Ogun	744,668	4.4204			*P10*		P10 P9
15. Ondo	1,369,849	8.1313			*P3*		P3P2
16. Oyo	1,396,547	8.2898		*P1*			P1 P6
17. Plateau	548,405	3.2553					
18. Rivers	687,951	4.0836					
19. Sokoto	1,348,697	8.0057		P4 P1		P4	
Total Votes	16,846,633	100	1,686,489	5,688,857	2,822,523	1,732,113	4,916,651
Percentage (%)		100	10.0108	33.7685	16.7542	10.2817	29.1848
No. of posts (Equitable)			1	3	2	1	3
No. of posts (Parallel Method)			*1*	*3*	*2*	*1*	*3*
No. of posts (Partisan Cum Cultural)			1	3	2	1	3
No. of posts (Cultural Cum Partisan)			-	3	2	1	4

KEY: Italic - PARALLEL METHOD
Underline - PARTISAN CUM CULTURAL METHOD
Bold - CULTURAL CUM PARTISAN METHOD

NOTES:

(i) Except in the parallel method, the partisan representation and the cultural representation of the voters are joined, because they follow the pattern of voting of the people, thus breeding ethnic politics; but in the parallel method, they are separable because political parties may often have to fill their political posts from their non traditional constituencies where they have the thinnest votes, pointing towards nationalism or non-ethnic politics.

(ii)   The Cultural-cum-Partisan method allocates no post to GNPP, which deserves one post, and allocates four posts to UPN, which does not deserve more than three posts. This makes it an inequitable method. It also ignores the spirit of competition among the political organisations, allocating the highest post type, P1, to UPN, which does not have .the highest number of votes. The Partisan-cum-Cultural method correctly gives the post to NPN but inequitably gives it to Sokoto State. Only the Parallel method equitably allocates P1 to NPN and to Oyo State which have the highest votes.

(iii) The Partisan-cum-Cultural method allocates two posts, P8 and P4, to Kano, which justly deserves only one post, and so covers only nine constituencies in this period of rule, instead of ten, as confirmed by the other two methods. So it is inequitable.

On the other hand, it allocates four positions to UPN on the Executive Council whereas UPN equitably deserves only three positions as the Parallel Method shows. Thus the Parallel Method is equitable and nationalistic and promotes nationalism whereas the other two methods are inequitable and promote parochialism and nepotism and ethnic politics.

One implication of the partisan-cum-cultural method or the cultural-cum-partisan method of allocation of political posts is that the political officeholder in cultural matters looks after the interests of only the members or followers of his/her political party, since the political post that he/she holds is allocated on the basis of either the cultural distribution of his/her political party's votes (partisan-cum-cultural method) or the partisan distribution of his/her cultural constituency's votes.

This means that in either of these two methods, the political officeholder in cultural matters is expected to look after the interests of his partisan members of his cultural constituency and not of the entire policy heterogeneous cultural constituency. Thus in the existing majority rule systems, many people usually fail to get help from the partisan political officeholders of their cultural constituency unless they are party card carriers. On the other hand, in the Parallel Method of allocation of political posts, where the cultural allocation is not done on the basis of the partisan distribution of votes nor the partisan allocation done on the basis of the cultural distribution of votes, the political officeholder is structurally encouraged in cultural matters to look after the cultural interests of the entire policy heterogeneous cultural/ethnic constituency, and not merely the cultural interests of his partisan component of the cultural/ethnic constituency.

In other words, as far as cultural matters are concerned, the whole cultural/ethnic group to which he/she belongs is his/her constituency and he/she must not be partisan in such matters. Thus the partisan political officeholder's constituency is politically heterogeneous but culturally/ethnically homogeneous. This is the parallel-allocation method situation. It is the true representative political democracy situation, in accordance with the principles of Free Grouping of Citizens and Limited Separation of Representation.

The culture cleavages and political interests of the people are separable and must be so represented. It is erroneous to join culture and policies together as one, like Siamese twins. This is what is done when political posts are allocated on the basis of either the partisan distribution of cultural votes (i.e. using the cultural-cum-partisan method) or the cultural distribution of partisan votes (i.e. using the partisan-cum-cultural method). A truly cultural group is, as far as reason goes, a culturally homogeneous group. But its members may differ on political or partisan grounds. So it is culturally homogeneous but politically heterogeneous.

Politics or partisanship should however not tear it apart. Its members must still remain a culturally homogeneous group. Take the case of a family. The husband and wife may belong to different political camps, but they will remain husband and wife, under the same roof, sleep together on the same bed and each will still trust the other to protect their family interests anywhere anytime as necessary.

In the same way, politics should not be allowed to reinforce culture cleavages in the society. Therefore, the way political offices are allocated and filled should make it possible for the cultural agents of the people to come from any of the political parties that they have voted for, not necessarily from the one for which a majority of them have voted. For instance, President Olusegun Obasanjo of Nigeria's Fourth Republic, being Yoruba, was a cultural/ethnic agent of the entire Yoruba of South Western Nigeria and yet had the votes of only a minority of the Yoruba voters (less than a quarter) at the presidential election that brought him to power in 1999. True representative political democracy should be such that any member of a cultural constituency whether from a majority or minority political party in the constituency should be able to speak for or represent the cultural constituency.

The situation whereby the partisan political officeholder from a cultural constituency comes only from the political party for which a majority of the members have voted causes politics to reinforce culture cleavage and is a root cause of ethnic politics. The separation of cultural and partisan representation of the voters solves this problem; it is entrenched by the Parallel Method of allocating political posts to ethnic/cultural constituencies and to political parties.

The Merit Elections

These are brought about by the principle of Homogeneity of Candidates and entrenched by the principle of Separation of Elections. The purpose is to elect the individual members of government – the legislators, Judicial Council members and executive office occupiers – on their personal merits for the posts held and by majority vote. There may be as many elections as there are political posts to be filled but elections to fill more than one political post or even all the posts may take place simultaneously.

There may be any number of candidates for a political post but by the principle of Homogeneity of Candidates, all the candidates for a political post must be from the cultural/ethnic constituency and, if applicable, political party to which the post has been allocated. Moreover, all the candidates should be free citizens qualified to vote in a general representation election and must satisfy the requirements of the political post to be occupied relating to age, sex, educational qualification, profession, experience and the like, if any.

The electoral system is the single-member (S.M.) majority system because the election is to appoint an individual directly into a specific political post that has been allocated to a particular political party and/or cultural constituency. The majority variant of the S.M. system should be used to ensure that the winner is selected by an absolute (not a plural) majority of the selectors. An absolute majority vote is required in the sense that the eventual occupier of the post should score more than 50% of the total votes cast whether or not there are more than two candidates.

Where there are more than two aspirants to a post, and none of them has an absolute majority of the votes cast in the first ballot, there must be a second ballot (i.e. double balloting system) at which the two topmost aspirants (i.e. those with the highest votes at the first ballot) will be the only candidates. An election where undemocratic means are used to limit the number of candidates in any way, even to two in order to force an absolute majority, is neither free nor fair and so should be rejected.

A constituency may not be a primary constituency but rather a secondary or tertiary constituency, i.e. has component primary or secondary constituencies as sub-constituencies, and the aspirants for a post may come from such different sub-constituencies. Nevertheless, in such a case, it would be wrong to treat each of the component primary or secondary sub-constituencies as single-member sub-constituencies to return a candidate each to compete for the single post at stake in the constituency because alternative sub-constituencies are universally represented and do not compete for a post. The principle is that each constituency to which a post is allocated must vote together as a culturally homogeneous unit to elect the occupier of the post or to nominate two candidates for it.

Therefore if a non-primary constituency is such that the best of the candidates cannot be satisfactorily elected by the constituency voting together as a culturally homogeneous unit, then the constituency is too large and so the whole system of alternative non-primary cultural constituencies should be redefined into smaller or more culturally/ethnically monolithic or homogeneous secondary or tertiary constituencies. Thus the candidates for a political post allocated to a non-primary cultural constituency need not come from the same component primary or secondary sub-constituency, as the government at the non-primary constituency level exists to adopt such a method in sharing its political posts among its component primary or secondary constituencies.

As the intention in merit selection by majority vote is to choose by a majority of votes the best of the candidates for a post and not to represent the voters, each voter must cast a vote for every one of the seats or political posts to be filled in the constituency in which he is voting.

This means that, for example, in primaries where two candidates are to be nominated from among more than two aspirants for a political post, it is sufficient for a selector to have only one vote because only one elective post is involved.

However, if the quantity of a political post is more than one, e.g. two or more legislative seats, then the political post to be filled is more than one and so two candidates will be nominated for each of such seats and each selector will have a vote for every two of such nominated candidates, i.e. for every one of such seats. Where a voter has more than one vote, it must be ensured that he/she spreads the votes over the required number of posts and not concentrate them on only one or fewer posts.

Party Merit Elections

By the principle of Non-Transferability of Delegated Mandates, the candidates are political party members. Every partisan political post will be filled by the absolute majority vote of a partisan electorate. The electorate must be partisan firstly because the post is partisan, allocated to a political party. If the electorate were non-partisan, it would have to fill the posts allocated to different political parties. That means that a voter will have to vote for candidates from more than one political party and that might confuse him.

Secondly, the general electorate has chosen the political parties as its de-facto partisan political representatives, to act for it in all partisan political matters, which include the filling on merit of the respective partisan political posts allocated to them. The political party is the citizen's partisan political representative. It is responsible to its voters (the people) for the actions of its members in government.

The party, not its individual party members in government, is responsible to the citizen voters. For bearing the responsibility for its agents (members) in government, the party must solely appoint its members in government. The alternative is undemocratic and illogical. In the presidential or parliamentary system, the president or prime minister is appointed by and responsible to the people and he appoints his ministers and other executive officeholders, who are responsible to him and not to the people.

As pointed out under the principle of Non-Transferability of Delegated Mandates, it is democratic and logical for a political party, a corporate representative of the people, to hold political office through its agents appointed by itself from among itself, whereas it is undemocratic and illogical for a president or prime minister, an individual, solely to appoint non-representatives of the people, into elective political office, i.e. to hold political office through non-representatives of the people, as it is the case in the majority rule systems.

Each partisan cultural/ethnic constituency may vote separately as a unit to elect an occupier or to nominate two candidates for each political post allocated to it. Generally, in order to avoid complexity, the occupier of every partisan post allocated to a cultural/ethnic constituency should be elected by the partisan cultural/ethnic constituency voting as a unit, using double balloting if there are more than two aspirants to a post and none scores an absolute majority of the votes cast at the first ballot.

However, if there is the fear that the method may produce a cultural/ethnic fundamentalist as the occupier of a partisan elective/political post, especially the more important posts like the Executive Council posts, or if it is desired to give such posts a more national outlook at the expense of increased complexity, then the whole of a political party must vote as a single unit to elect the occupier of such a partisan elective/political post, using double balloting if there are more than two aspirants to a post and none scores an absolute majority of the votes cast at the first ballot.

Alternatively, in such a case, where there are more than two aspirants to a post, it is recommended, for the sake of reducing complexity, that there should be primaries, in which the partisan cultural/ethnic constituency to which the post is allocated will vote as a unit and the two topmost aspirants (i.e. those with the highest votes at the election) will emerge as the nominees and hence as the two candidates for the final joint electorate election of the party to select the occupier of the post. If three rather than two topmost aspirants emerge in the primaries, then there should be double balloting (i.e. a second ballot) in the primaries, at which the two or three aspirants that tied in the first ballot will be the only candidates.

For legislative seats, the party members from the cultural/ethnic constituency to which a seat is allocated may solely elect the occupier by majority vote. This means that there may not be primaries in that case and there may be double balloting if no candidate has absolute majority in the first ballot. In the selections, each voter will have as many votes as the number of posts to be filled and will spread the votes over the posts.

General Merit Elections

For judicial and non-partisan (executive) political posts, there is no partisan allocation but only cultural/ethnic allocation of posts. Thus, the occupier of each judicial or non-partisan political post will be elected in either of the following two ways.

(1) By the absolute majority vote of the concerned cultural constituency or of the central/national electorate of the non-partisan learned or professional body concerned with the political post, voting as one constituency. In this case, there will be primaries, in which the (concerned learned or professional body's) members from the cultural/ethnic constituency to which the political post is allocated will vote as a unit and the two aspirants with the highest votes at the election will emerge as the two nominees for the post.

The non-partisan body's central/national electorate or the entire members of the concerned cultural constituency will eventually elect one of the two candidates into the post. If three rather than two topmost aspirants emerge in the primaries because the second and the third aspirants (say) have equal votes then there should be double balloting (i.e. second ballot) in the primaries, at which the second and third aspirants in the first ballot will vie and the winner will join the first aspirant as the two nominees. If there are only two aspirants, then there will be no election at the primaries.

(2) By the absolute majority vote of the concerned non-partisan learned or professional body's members or the entire members from the cultural/ethnic constituency to which the · political post is allocated. There will be double (or triple, if necessary) balloting if there are more than two candidates to a post and none of them has an absolute majority of the votes cast in the first ballot.

Being based on the component cultural constituencies of a polity, the second method is simpler and enables the candidates to be known in a more genuine way all through than the first method. However, the first method makes the eventual post occupier appear more nationalistic than the second method does. Moreover, the first method is a must where the general electorate, e.g. the Executive Council, needs to have a say in the selection process. This may be the case with the appointment of non-partisan executive bodies as well as occupiers of pseudo-political posts, if the polity so desires. Because of the principle of Separation of Powers, the Executive Council has no say in the selection of members of the Judicial Council.

In conclusion, it should be borne in mind that all elections, whether the General Universal Representation Election (GURE) or the General Merit Elections (GME) and the Party Merit Elections (PME), must be conducted in their entirety by the polity's appropriate electoral commissions at the level of government concerned, in accordance with the principle of Free and Fair Elections. It should also be borne in mind that any elected political officeholder, whether partisan or not, is recallable, for untoward behaviours or actions, by a simple majority of the constituency that elected him/her if a demand is made by a small percentage of the voters, the desirable percentage being determined by each polity in appropriate cases and entrenched in its constitution.

It should also be added that the merit elections – both general and party merit elections – may in their entirety be replaced by the casting of lots for the qualified aspirants for a political office, partisan or otherwise, who could serve for short periods (e.g. a year), as done in Athenian democracy described earlier in this book. In this way, the huge expenses and malpractices associated with elections to select individual political officeholders could be avoided, and the polity would be better for it. This means that there will then be *only* one election in the polity – the General Universal Representation Election (GURE). The Lot method is very democratic, being based on the equal right of every qualified aspirant for a political post to hold it. Moreover, the method does away with any subjectivity that the merit selection process may involve and cheaply affords more interested and qualified citizens the opportunity to participate in person in government.

It should be further added that, since the General Universal Representation Election (GURE) is meant to define the cultural/ethnic/geographical and partisan (or opinion) complexions of the polity, and since all voters would be represented, balloting in the election needs not be secret but voters may line up behind their preferred political parties and be counted openly. In this way, rigging and electoral fraud can be greatly reduced, if not totally eliminated. When this voting pattern is then followed (later) by the selection of the individual officeholders by lot, a polity may be said to have a satisfactory electoral system.

PART FOUR

Summary

30

THE UNIVERSAL SYSTEM OF GOVERNMENT

This chapter attempts, as an example, to draw together in a form the principles, institutions and structures of Universal Democracy that have been discussed in this book. It discusses the Executive, the Legislature and the Judicial Council. The Executive comprises the following elected bodies: the Executive Council and the General Political .Executive including the non-partisan executive bodies. Pertinent features of the new system are highlighted and various strategies for progressive transition to it from the existing political rule systems are discussed.

The Executive Council

The executive authority of a polity rests with a plural executive, a cabinet, rather than with a single executive. Like in the presidential system, the Council has a president (rather than a prime minister). He is the chairman of the Executive Council and exercises the usual powers of a chairman. He may also have some specific duties assigned to him by the polity's constitution. Unlike in the presidential system or even the parliamentary system, however, he does not select the other members of the Council, who are his colleagues and not merely his agents or advisers. They are appointed or elected in the same way as he. He is only first among equals.

215

The Executive Council's functions would involve the following:

(a) The final determination of the policy to be submitted to the legislature, including the introduction, explanation and defence of government measures on the floor of the legislature by members of the Council.

(b) The supreme control of the executive in accordance with the policy prescribed by the legislature, including the determination of how the executive authority vested in the Council in respect of appointments, foreign affairs etc. will be exercised.

(c) The continuous co-ordination, delimitation and control of the work of the several departments of the polity.

The Executive Council is a multicultural, all-party executive. The positions on the Council are filled by the process of allocation and selection as follows.

(a) The positions are first allocated to the cultural constituencies named in the polity's constitution for the Executive Council positions. The method of the allocation is the Co-ordinated Proportional Rotation of Multiple Unequal Scarce Posts (COPROMUSPO), since the Council positions may be collectively or individually scarce for the cultural constituencies. The method is simple and easily handled by the present day computers. The basis of the allocation is the equivalent cultural distribution of the cumulative total votes to date, in the polity's General Universal Representation Election (GURE).

(b) The positions are also allocated to the political associations that take part in the current representation election. The method of the allocation is the Co-ordinated Proportional Representation by Multiple Unequal Scarce Posts (COPREMUSPO), since the Council positions may be collectively or individually scarce for the political associations. Here, the basis of the allocation is the partisan distribution among the political organisations of the polity's current, not cumulative, total votes in the General Universal Representation Election (GURE) for the current period of rule.

Any political organisation that does not win enough votes for a position on the Council cannot exist separately as a political party in the polity for the period of rule. It has to join with another political party that has enough votes or with another similar organisation(s) with which it would be able to have enough votes to exist as a separate political party. This coming together of political organisations is necessary in order that every voter would have partisan representation in the Council in every period of rule, as required by the principle of Universal Representation of Voters.

(c) Then the occupier of each position is selected by lot or a Party Merit Election — i.e. a process of nomination and election as follows. (i) For each position two nominees are competitively elected, by the partisan cultural electorate to which the position is allocated, from among all the aspirants from the same electorate. These are the two aspirants with the highest number of votes. Each voter will have only one vote for each post. If there is only one aspirant, there must be a yes or no vote and the yes votes must be in the majority for the aspirant to become the only nominee. (ii) Then the general electorate of the political party concerned will by majority vote elect one of the two nominees as the occupier of the position. If there is only one nominee, he automatically becomes the occupier of the position. No undemocratic means whatever should be used to limit the number of candidates or aspirant in any way, as that would not make the election to be free and fair.

Even though a plural body, the Executive Council is a unit as regards the sovereign of the polity – the general electorate – and as regards the legislature. Undoubtedly each member of the Council is there on his/her cultural constituency's and political party's platform and would work to see his/her party's policies adopted by the government. Nevertheless, he/she is bound by the principle of Subordination of Lower Will to Higher Will, i.e. the principle of Collective Responsibility.

The Executive Council takes its decisions by either consensus or majority vote. Once a decision is taken, all members must abide by it and work to achieve it, even though it was against a member's will or against his party's at the beginning. The decision is the Council's and all its members must uphold it. Thus, the Council operates on the principle of Collective Responsibility and there is a united and indivisible responsibility. Executive acts are the acts of the Council as a body, not of the president or of any member personally.

> For all that passes in the Executive Council, each member of it who does not resign is absolutely and irretrievably responsible and has no right afterwards to say that he agreed in one case to a compromise, while in another he was persuaded by his colleagues. ·
> (Life of Robert, Marquis of Salisbury, Vol. II, p. 219-220, cited by Jennings).

This makes partisan homogeneity of the executive to be unnecessary but requires members of the Executive (Council) to be true democrats and not fundamentalists.

Therefore only true democrats must be elected into government. This is the essence of democracy. The Executive Council shall have the power to remove by its absolute majority (with party voting) any of its members that refuses to execute its policy and does not resign. Such a member will be replaced by his/her party in a party merit election as discussed above.

The Executive Council carries out the will of the legislature, whose responsibility it is to make laws for the polity. The responsibility of the executive to the legislature will be enforced as follows. In Britain, for example, the cabinet resigns if a bill introduced by it is defeated in Parliament, or if a bill introduced by a private member is passed by Parliament against its opposition. However, in the Universal System, like in Switzerland, members of the executive will not be expected to resign because a bill introduced by them, however important it may be, has failed of passage in the legislature. They will simply drop the matter, or remodel the bill to meet the criticism that has caused its defeat.

Where necessary and demanded by up to two-third absolute majority of them (with party voting), they may exercise an executive veto on the decision of the legislature as the President of the United States of America may do. However, two-thirds absolute majority (with party voting) of the legislature can defeat the veto.

The Executive Council is the sub-branch of government with the least number of partisan members. Therefore on its size depends ·the number of political parties that exist in the polity, if there must be universal partisan representation of the people in the Executive Council as the principle of All-Branch Representation of Voters requires. Its size will vary from polity/country to polity/country, but it should be small enough to enable the Executive Council to act quickly and efficiently.

It should, however, be large enough to admit a reasonable number of political parties and cultural constituencies. This will enable all the applicable (i.e. highest - level) cultural constituencies, which should be as few as possible and each as large as possible, to be represented on the Council within a reasonable number of periods of rule (two to three) if impossible in every period of rule. A number between ten and twenty, both inclusive, is recommended for the size of the Council.

The figure ten corresponds to a political party scoring about 10% of the total vote (in the General Universal Representation Election (GURE) to choose the political parties) in order to exist while the figure twenty corresponds to about 5% of the total vote. The assumption in this recommendation is therefore that no political organisation with much less than 5% of the total vote should exist separately as a political party. Nor should a political organisation be required to score more than 10% of the total vote in order to exist as a political party. Each country will decide the size of its Executive Council along the line indicated above.

However, there is nothing sacrosanct about the figures ten to twenty; other figures may be used. As an example, Switzerland has a Federal Executive Council (similar to the Executive Council being recommended here) whose membership is seven. In the context of this book, this figure requires a political organisation to score about 14% of the total vote in order to exist as a political party. However, a figure outside the suggested range may be a pointer that either the size of the Executive Council is too small or the constituencies need regrouping - i. e. another constituency level need be chosen. The size of the Executive Council may vary from period of rule to period of rule, but within the suggested range, if need be to accommodate all or as many of the cultural constituencies concerned as possible in a period of rule. But this should be done discreetly so that it will not go out of hand.

The General Political Executive

The Executive Council should be distinguished from the General Political Executive. The General Political Executive comprises all the political or elected members of the executive, who are not members of the Executive Council and who are therefore pseudo-political. It includes political members of government commissions, agencies and parastatals, partisan or non-partisan, who are in charge of one portfolio of government or another. The General Political Executive also includes members of the non-partisan executive bodies.

On the other hand, the Executive Council comprises the members of the executive in whom collectively as a body the executive authority of the polity is vested. The Executive Council members are those members of the Executive who in addition to being in charge of particular portfolios of government determine the general policy of the government in all the departments and control administration.

Thus all members of the Executive Council may be ministers although not all ministers (e.g. junior ministers) may be members of the Executive Council. The term Executive is taken to refer to both the Executive Council and the General Political Executive combined.

All General Political Executive positions will be allocated to cultural constituencies and, if any be partisan, also to political parties, as for the Executive Council positions. The cultural constituencies for the membership of the General Political Executive may be at least one level lower than those for the Executive Council. As earlier mentioned, the members of the Executive Council will be nominated by the respective cultural/ethnic electorates of the political parties concerned and elected by the general electorate of the parties concerned.

Similarly, the partisan members of the General Political Executive, which is pseudo-political, will be nominated by lot or the respective cultural/ethnic electorates of the parties concerned.

However, they will be elected by lot or the Executive Council, to give the body the final say in the selection of those that will work with them. This does not amount to transferability of delegated mandates if two nominees are duly elected for each post by the partisan cultural/ethnic electorate concerned. Similarly, the members of the non-partisan bodies such as the Electoral Commission, for example, will be nominated by the respective cultural/ethnic constituencies to which the positions to be occupied are allocated and would be elected by the majority vote of the Executive Council to give the body the final say in the selection. There shall be no partisan allocation of non-partisan political posts, for which the qualified candidates will apply on advertisement.

In order to check electoral malpractice and to ensure sound electoral judgement, a party's general electorate may be limited to the party's already elected legislative and executive members. This procedure is considered good because of their being the party in government, because of their visibility and because of the exactness of their numbers. However, the procedure is applicable only if each of the appointees is either from among the electors or from two nominees duly elected by and from among the appropriate political party and/or cultural group to which the political post has been allocated. In this procedure, a party's already elected legislative and executive members at the lower level(s) of government may be included in the party's general electorate.

What applies at the national level is also applicable at the other levels of government.

The Legislature

The legislature may comprise one or two Houses: the Upper House and the Lower House. If the legislature is bicameral, each House shall be a branch or arm of government. The choice of a unicameral or bicameral legislature shall be made by the country concerned in consideration of the points noted in the chapter on the legislature. Each country shall also decide the number of members or seats of each House of its legislature. Primary or secondary cultural/ethnic constituencies should be used for the Lower House. The number of seats in the Lower House should be large enough to allow a universal representation of all the alternative primary or secondary cultural/ ethnic groups to be achieved in the House within two to three periods of rule, if not within every period of rule. This will enhance a sense of belonging in all the communities of the polity/country. For the Upper House, on the other hand, secondary or tertiary cultural/ ethnic constituencies should be used. The number of seats should be large enough to enable every one of the constituencies to have at least a seat in every period of rule.

This ensures universal cultural/ethnic representation of voters in the legislature in every period of rule. There would be separate cultural allocations of the seats in each House, using the method of Co-ordinated Proportional Rotation of Multiple Unequal Scarce Posts (COPROMUSPO). There will also be separate (i.e. parallel) partisan allocations of the seats in each House, using the method of COPREMUSPO, as described for the Executive Council positions. The party merit election or lot process for the individual legislators is similar to that for the Executive Council members, except that the cultural rather than the general electorate of the political party concerned may make the final selection. Legislative seats and posts will be allocated separately from executive or judicial posts to ensure compliance with the principle of Separation of Powers.

There would be legislative posts or offices such as the Speaker of the Lower House and his deputy, the President of the Senate (Upper House) and his deputy and the Chairmen of the Committees of the Houses, among others. Since these legislative posts may be occupied only by legislative seat occupiers during a period of rule, cultural and partisan allocations of legislative posts may not be done separately from those of legislative seats. Doing otherwise may result in a legislative post being allocated to a political party that has no legislator from the cultural constituency to which the political post is also allocated.

Therefore the legislative posts will be listed as part of the legislative seats in the legislative House to which they belong and ranked accordingly. This is also what is done for the Executive posts: Some people may say that this method robs the legislators the opportunity to choose their legislative leaders, as it is currently the practice in many majority representation systems. The reply to this is that whoever occupies a legislative post affects the interests of the citizens as a whole not of just the legislators only.

Therefore, it is the whole people, through the partisan and cultural distributions of their votes, not just only the legislators, that should determine who occupies such a position. This will also help to avoid the situation in many majority representation systems where legislators often change their leaders in a frivolous way to satisfy their whims and caprices. A legislative House shall have the power to remove by its absolute majority (with party voting) any of its officers for misconduct. He/she will thereby lose his/her seat also. He/she will be replaced from his/her constituency and from his/her party in the same way that he/she has been elected.,

The Judicial Council

There shall be a Judicial Council that is vested with the power to appoint judges and see to their welfare and promotion. Its size will vary from country/polity to country/polity but will hardly exceed ten. There would be cultural/ethnic allocation of positions on the Judicial Council. The same cultural/ethnic constituencies used for Executive Council posts shall be applicable, for simplicity. The cultural allocation should be done independently of that for another branch or arm of government and by the method of Co-ordinated Proportional Rotation of Multiple Unequal Scarce Posts (COPROMUSPO), to enable the cultural allocation of the judicial political posts to be monitored. Cumulative votes rather than current votes are used for the allocations, since the posts are collectively or individually scarce for the cultural constituencies. There shall be no partisan allocation of positions on the Judicial Council because it is a non-partisan body selected on the personal merits of the candidates.

The candidates should be people who have never been directly or indirectly involved in partisan politics. They should also be members of the polity's appropriate learned society or professional body in the constituencies to which the positions are allocated for the current period of rule. They will apply on advertisement. The members would be chosen by lot or elected by the polity's relevant cultural constituencies' general electorate or by their appropriate learned society's or professional body's general electorate, with each cultural/ ethnic branch/component voting separately to elect its allocated member(s). Each voter shall have as many votes as the number of persons to be elected in his/her constituency. There will be double balloting if there are more than two candidates to a post and none of them has an absolute majority of the votes cast at the first ballot.

Initiative, Recall and Referendum

Citizen(s) outside the legislature shall have the right of *initiative* to introduce in the legislature private bills on any matter of public interest. It shall be compulsory for any such bill that is not passed into law to be submitted to the people, the general electorate, (in a referendum) for approval or rejection. This right shall be entrenched in the polity's constitution. Such a bill shall not go directly to the electorate in the first instance in order not to undermine the authority of the legislature.

Any elected political officeholder, whether partisan or not, shall be *recallable*, for misconduct or untoward behaviours or actions, by a simple majority of the constituency that elected him/her if a demand is made by a small percentage or number of the voters, the desirable percentage or number being determined by each polity in appropriate cases and entrenched in its constitution.

Any unwise or unpopular law against which a demand is made by a small percentage of the voters, shall be submitted to the general electorate in a *referendum* for acceptance or rejection. If rejected, the law shall cease to be a law forthwith. The desirable small percentage shall be determined by each polity and entrenched in its constitution.

The three democratic devices help to ensure that the fundamental human rights of the people such as freedom, equality, justice, etc. are not unduly subverted by the people's representatives or agents in government. As safeguards of popular sovereignty, they are part and parcel of Universal Democracy that would be invoked sparingly only when occasion really warrants. They should obviate the need for the people to resort to strikes, rebellion, revolution or civil war often to resolve issues with their representative government.

General Features

The Universal System just described has the following distinguishing features.

(a) *It is a Representative Plural Executive:* It is a fully universal representative form of government, in the sense that executive political posts, like judicial political posts and legislative seats and offices, are shared among political parties and/or cultural/geographical groups as Universal Democracy requires. Thus, they are not subject to eliminative competition among the political parties and among the cultural groups as in the case of the majority representation systems.

The political Executive, like the legislature and the Judicial Council, has a non-partisan character. This is because it is not based upon party or cultural majority in the legislative bodies, as its members are elected from all the different party groups and from all the different cultural groups. In this way, the legislature and the executive are in both the partisan and cultural senses truly representative of the politically and culturally heterogeneous society. Therefore, no partisan group or significant cultural group could be left out of government in any period of rule or reasonable number of periods of rule. The desirability and feasibility of this feature are exemplified by the fact that President Olusegun Obasanjo of Nigeria's 3-party 4th Republic appointed members of the other two political parties as ministers in his Peoples Democratic Party (PDP) government to give it a national outlook.

(b) *It is Equitable:* The partisan and cultural allocations of executive political posts, like those of legislative and judicial political posts, are equitably done. Unlike in parliamentary and presidential systems based on majority representation, political posts are not just allocated to cultural constituencies by population before voting. Neither are they subjected to partisan and/or cultural/geographical competition nor are they just limited to any majority party or just arbitrarily allocated to some sections of the polity, on the basis of some spurious zoning formulae adopted by the party in power.

Citizens do not vote for just a so-called legislative representative and a chief executive with the vice, as in the presidential system. They also do not vote for just a member of Parliament, as in the parliamentary system. Instead, as individuals in distinct cultural/ethnic constituencies, the citizens cast their votes for political parties in a general election termed the General Universal Representation Election (GURE). The votes are aggregated according to the constitutionally defined cultural, ethnic or geo-political areas. Then the political posts or offices are proportionally allocated to the cultural/ethnic constituencies on the basis of their voting strengths in the election, current if the posts are not scarce but cumulative to date if the posts are scarce.

Finally, the political posts or offices are separately proportionally allocated to the political parties on the basis of the distribution of the polity's current votes among the political parties. In this way, citizens automatically determine by the cultural/ethnic and partisan distributions of their votes what posts – executive, judicial or legislative – go to which cultural/ethnic constituency and/or which political party.

The proportional cultural/ethnic and partisan allocations of all political posts or offices on the basis of votes rather than population ensure that there is inclusive and not eliminative competition among political parties for partisan posts. Moreover, they engender equitable political participation among the alternative cultural/ethnic groups and would forever remove the cry of political marginality among the groups. Furthermore, they remove the need to organise the people into constituencies of equal or nearly equal population or land areas as is necessarily done in the existing majority representation systems.

They also obviate the need for periodic boundary adjustments to legislative constituencies, as it is the case with majority representation systems where allocation of legislative seats to cultural constituencies is based upon population. (This practice has been shown to be undemocratic, being inconsistent with the principle of Appropriation of Political Rights.) The principle of Proportional Representation of Voters so properly applied more than adequately replaces the undemocratic concept of equality of the alternative groups or units commonly used especially for a second legislative chamber in the existing political systems and which often gives rise to a proliferation of units such as local government areas as Nigeria is currently experiencing in its 4th Republic. The citizen voter is the unit of reckoning all the time.

(c) *It Can Be Rotational:* The cultural allocations of the scarce executive political posts, like scarce legislative and judicial political posts, are done equitably by the method of Co-ordinated Proportional Rotation of Multiple Unequal Scarce Posts (COPROMUSPO). This method, which uses cumulative votes to date, ensures that political posts (including legislative seats) which are scarce and so unable to go round the appropriate cultural/ethnic constituencies in a period of rule will necessarily and proportionally do so over the periods of rule.

The method, along with the twin cultural/ethnic and partisan allocations of scarce political posts, ensures that the members of the executive, like legislators and Judicial Council members, are drawn (and proportionally too) from the different cultural/ethnic constituencies. They are not drawn from just a majority political party or from just a majority cultural group or from just a majority section of the polity as does happen in the parliamentary and presidential systems. Thus, the chief executive may come from any cultural group or section of the polity, minority or majority; so also may any of the ministers and other political office occupiers, whether in the legislature, judiciary or executive.

In fact, no cultural constituency or section of the polity has a monopoly of any office. All the scarce political offices, be they judicial, legislative or executive, will, over periods of rule, proportionally go round all the cultural constituencies, no matter which political parties they vote for. The order of rotation of political posts among the cultural constituencies is not arbitrary. Rather, it is mathematically proportional to the cumulative voting strengths of the cultural constituencies, subject only to rounding off errors due to the discrete nature of political posts.

The frequency with which a cultural constituency or section of the polity holds any scarce office relative to another cultural constituency or section of the polity is also not arbitrary. Rather, it is mathematically, and so equitably, according to the cultural constituencies' relative cumulative voting strengths to date in the General Universal Representation Election (GURE). Thus the equality of legislative, judicial and executive representation of all voters, irrespective of their partisan or cultural affiliations, minority or majority, is guaranteed. No cultural/ethnic group will be marginalised. Therefore, no special protection is required for any group, for all groups are equally treated, the individual voter being the unit of reckoning.

Partisan allocation of multiple unequal scarce posts within a period of rule is also handled by the method of Co-ordinated Proportional Representation by Multiple Unequal Scarce Posts (COPREMUSPO), using current (not cumulative) votes. This helps to preserve the spirit of competition among the political parties while accommodating all the political parties and still making the allocation process equitable. It also helps to avoid making partisan allocations to extend beyond a period of rule. Here competition is interwoven with equitableness and justice.

(d) *It is Highly Competitive and Merit-oriented:* Like in majority representation systems, competition is used to select individual legislators and individual legislative, judicial and executive political officeholders. However, unlike in the majority representation systems, it is used properly – for purely merit selection between two candidates of the same political party and/or cultural group for a political post – legislative, judicial or executive. It is used after the partisan and cultural allocations of such political posts referred to above.

Thus, competition is separated from but complements representation. The equitable cultural and partisan political posts allocations are followed by the filling of the seats and posts not on the basis of a list as in majority rule systems when the proportional representation (P.R.) electoral system is used. Rather, the filling of the legislative seats and political posts is done on the basis of lot or competitive elections on personal merits, as required by the principle of Homogeneity of Candidates. This ensures that the occupier of a legislative seat or post or of an executive or judicial (political) office is the best of the candidates for the post on personal merits as judged by voters without partisan and cultural considerations. This is unlike in the majority representation systems where it is not the best candidate on personal merits for an office but often the candidate of the (plural) majority partisan and/or cultural group that occupies it.

Each partisan member of the Legislature or of the Executive is thus a member of the political party and of the cultural constituency to which the legislative seat or post or the executive post that he occupies is allocated for the current period of rule. His selection is not made by an individual like the president or prime minister or a small but arbitrary caucus as common in majority representation systems with attendant corrupt and proud political officeholders. Rather, it is made by lot or the majority vote of either the appropriate cultural/ethnic component, or the general electorate, of the political party to which the post is allocated. It is thus in compliance with the principle of Non-Transferability of Delegated Mandates.

Similarly, every member of the Judicial Council or of any non-partisan executive body is a member of the cultural constituency to which the non-partisan executive office or Judicial Council position is allocated. He is selected by lot or the cultural and/or the general electorate of the non-partisan learned or professional body concerned or by the entire cultural constituency. The candidates for Judicial Council or non-partisan (executive) posts will apply on advertisement as independent candidates – the only independent candidates allowed by the system.

The electoral system for the selection of a political office occupier is the Single Member (S.M.) system. There will be only two candidates for the election to ensure that the selection is made by the absolute (not simple) majority of the electors. If there are more than two aspirants for a political post, the double balloting variant of the Single Member system is used to ensure that the selection is still made by the absolute (not simple) majority of the voters. In that case, an election is first held to select the two top aspirants, i.e. those with the highest number of votes, as the two candidates for a second election. The aspirants are not short-listed in any unconstitutional or undemocratic way, in compliance with the principle of Free and Fair Elections.

Each voter in a cultural constituency, partisan or non-partisan, will have as many votes as the number of posts to be filled by the constituency. Thus both the Proportional Representation (P.R.) and the Single-Member (S.M.) electoral systems are appropriately employed with great advantages in the Universal System of Government.

Moreover, the replacement of cultural and partisan competition with cultural and partisan allocation of political posts makes electioneering less arduous and less expensive, as the candidates' constituencies are now more manageable.

(e) *It is Highly Political Party-oriented:* Political parties, not individuals, are elected as the people's partisan political representatives. There is no constraint on the number of political parties – that is, the political party system is completely free, except that to exist any political party must win enough votes to have at least a member in each of the partisan branches or arms of government – legislature and executive, particularly the Executive Council, which has the least number of partisan political post occupiers. This ensures that all voters have partisan political representation, and hence partisan representative participation, in all relevant branches of government, in accordance with the democratic concept of equality of political rights. It also helps democratically to put an upper limit on the number of political parties in the polity.

Moreover, all partisan posts are filled by lot or party merit elections. To further ensure the authority of the political parties, an individual member of the legislature or executive, including the president, may be removed for any untoward reason by the absolute majority vote of his or her party's members in Parliament and Executive, or by prescribed due processes of the law for misconduct. Any individual member of Parliament or Executive Council or Judicial Council may be removed for misconduct by an absolute majority vote of the respective body. Also any member of the General Political Executive may be removed for misconduct by an absolute majority vote of the members of the Executive Council.

However, in any case of removal, the replacement must come from the same political party and/or cultural constituency currently holding that post, because it has been allocated to them as a political right for the whole of the current period of rule. Moreover, the same original method of appointment used for the official being replaced must be used for the replacement. A political party may freely replace not more than 20% or one (whichever is higher) of its members in every branch or arm of government in a period of rule, if it so desires. The limitation of 20% or one is arbitrary and introduced in order to control any frivolity on the part of the political parties; so it can be any figure desired by the polity.

For the same reason, a political party may not change the occupier of any political post more than once, except the additional change is necessitated by death, resignation or removal for misconduct. Finally, party voting must operate on all issues in the Legislature and in the Executive, in accordance with the principles of Political Party Dominance and Subordination of Will. All the foregoing shows that the Universal system entrenches the discipline of political officeholders and is constitutionally enforceable. A political officeholder cannot resign, be removed or "carpet-cross" from his/her political party to another political party without losing his/her political office because the office belongs to the party not to him/her personally. This is unlike in the existing majority rule systems where political officeholders in some polities carpet-cross freely from one political party to another without sanction and thereby flagrantly alter the voters' mandate to the political parties, all because they are elected directly into political offices without the prior allocation of the offices to the political parties.

(f) *It Entrenches Separation of Political Powers:* The legislature, the Judicial Council and the executive derive their powers separately and directly from the votes of the electorate, as no arm or sub-arm appoints another. Therefore, they hold office for a fixed term, since the mandates of the electorate are, by the principle of Periodic Representation of Voters, given for a fixed term. Neither the executive nor the legislature nor the Judicial Council can be voted out of office by the other arms of government before the expiration of its prescribed term of office because by the principle of Separation of Political Powers, the one is distinct and separate from the other.

The system enhances policy continuity from government to government, as the operative majority on a particular issue would hardly change from government to government since all the polity's political parties are involved in the decision-making process always. There would also be governmental stability.

(g) *It Can Remove Ethnic Politics and Entrench Nationalism:* With the use of the Parallel method of allocation of political posts, the partisan representation and the cultural representation of the people are separable. Political parties may not necessarily fill their allocated political posts from the cultural constituencies where they have the majority of votes. In fact no one can know beforehand the cultural constituencies where the occupiers of a political party's political posts will come from. Thus the people are tuned to vote for policies and not for individuals, for they are never sure that a particular person would be their cultural agent in government as that agent may even come from the political party that has the least number of their votes. Thus people are oriented to vote for political parties and their policies/programmes and not for individuals, thus eliminating ethnic politics and entrenching nationalism and truly nationalistic political parties.

However, in the other two political posts allocation methods, i.e. partisan-cum-cultural and cultural-cum-partisan methods, the partisan representation and the cultural representation of the voters are joined, thus making it easier for the people to vote for individual persons rather than for policies or political parties. For example, the partisan-cum-cultural method allocates political posts on the basis of the cultural distribution of a political party's votes, so that the cultural constituency where the party has the highest votes may be sure of having the best or only political post of the political party.

Similarly the cultural-cum-partisan method allocates political posts on the basis of the partisan distribution of a cultural constituency's votes, so that the political party that scores the highest votes of the constituency may be sure of having the best or only political post for the constituency.

Thus in these two methods, the voters can predict the winners or their cultural agents in government by their pattern of voting. They therefore tend to vote for people rather than for policies, thus breeding ethnic politics and its vices including election rigging and political violence, with which all of us are too well familiar in our world today.

Table 9 is the summary of the cultural and partisan sharing of the hypothetical (Federal) Executive Council posts shown in Table 4, Table 5, Table 6 and Table 7, to which reference should be made now for a better understanding of Table 9.

The main point of note in this table is the national spread of the political posts allocated to the various political parties. Except in a few cases, the political parties are allocated posts that would be filled by their members from their non-traditional areas. A look at Appendix 1 and Appendix 2 will confirm this fact. For example, in 1979 GNPP has only one position on the (Federal) Executive Council, i.e. P7, which is filled by its member from Imo cultural constituency, where it scored 34,616 votes, which is only 2.05% of its total votes for that period of rule and also only 3.00% of the constituency's total votes. This is in comparison with GNPP's showings in Sokoto (409,424 votes, 24.28% of its total), Borno (384,278 votes, 22.79%), Gongola (217,914 votes, 12.92%) and the likes, which are the party's traditional areas or strongholds.

TABLE 9

The parallel method of partisan and ethnic/cultural allocation of political posts applied to the (Federal) Executive Council positions in Universal Democracy using the results of the Nigeria's 1997 and 1983 Presidential Elections

ETHNIC/ CULTURAL CONSTITU-ENCY	VOTES CAST 1979	VOTES CAST 1983	ALL	EXECUTIVE COUNCIL POSITIONS FOR POLITICAL PARTIES & CULTURAL CONSTITUENCIES											
				1979 GNPP	NPN	NPP	PRP	UPN	Total	1983 NPN	NPP	PRP-GNPP-NAP*	UPN	Total	Total for 1979 & 1983
ANAMBRA	1209038	11538283	2367321					P6	1			P5		1	2
BAUCHI	998683	1782122	2780805		P8				1	P3				1	2
BENDEL	669511	1099851	1769362						-	P6				1	1
BENUE	538879	652795	1191674						-					-	-
BORNO	710968	718043	1429011						-		P7			1	1
CROSS RIVER	661103	1285710	1946813					,	-	P5A				1	1
GONGOLA	639138	723956	1363094						-	P10				1	1
IMO	1153355	1588975	2742330	P7					1					-	1
KADUNA	1382712	2137398	3520110					P2	1		P3A			1	2
KANO	1220763	1193050	2413813		P5				1	P9				1	2
KWARA	354605	608422	963027						-					-	-
LAGOS	828414	1640381	2468795					P9	1				P4	1	2
NIGER	383347	430731	814078			P10			-					-	-
OGUN	744668	1261061	2005729			P10			1					-	1
ONDO	1369849	1828343	3198192			P3			1				P5A	1	2
OYO	1396547	2351000	3749547		P1				1				P2	1	2
PLATEAU	548405	652302	1200707						-					-	-
RIVERS	687951	1357715	2045666						-				P8	1	1
SOKOTO	1348697	2837786	4186483				P4		1	P5 P1				2	3
ABUJA	-	135351	135351						-					-	-
TOTAL VOTES	16846633	25443275	42289908	1686485	5688857	2822523	1732133	4916651	10	12081471	3557114	1897481	7907209	14	24
PERCENTAGE (%)				10.0108	33.7685	16.7542	10.2848	29.1848		47.4839	13.9806	7.4577	31.0778		
NUMBER OF POSTS				1	3	2	1	3	10	7	2	1	4		24

* PRP, GNPP and NAP were different political organizations at the 1983 elections but analysis shows that in Universal Democracy, neither GNPP nor NAP nor both of them combined could have a position on the Executive Council. The presumption here is that both organizations would team up with PRP to enhance its position, even though it would have a (lower) position on the council without them. Hence the name PRP-GNPP-NAP.

It is noteworthy that Imo State is NPP's second stronghold or traditional area in the period of rule where it scored 999,636 votes or 35.42% of its total votes, or 86.67% of the constituency's total votes for the period of rule.

Similarly the post P6 that is allocated to Anambra constituency, which is NPP's first stronghold or traditional area, where it scored 1,002,083 votes which is 82.88% of the constituency's total votes and 34.50% of the party's total votes, is not allocated to NPP but to UPN, which scored 9,063 votes, which is 0.75% of the constituency's votes or 0.18% of UPN's total votes. NPP itself is allocated two posts, P3 and P10, which would be filled by its members from Ondo and Ogun constituencies respectively, which constituencies are UPN's strongholds or traditional areas.

Moreover, NPN would fill its second post P5 (out of three) from Kano constituency, where PRP scored its highest votes of 932,803, which is 76.41% of the constituency's votes and 53.85% of the party's total votes; whereas PRP would fill its only post (P4) from among its members from Sokoto, where it scored merely 32,798 (which is 1.89% of its total votes and 2.43% of the constituency's votes) compared with NPN, which scored there its highest votes of 859,119, which is 15.10% of its total votes and 63.70% of the constituency's total votes.

However, the situation is not always so drastic. For example, in 1983 UPN would have four positions in the (Federal) Executive Council and all the four posts would be filled from its traditional areas or strongholds, where it scored the highest votes – viz. P2 (Ondo), P4 (Lagos), P5A (Ogun) and P8 (Oyo). Moreover, the Bauchi cultural constituency with the post P8 in 1979 and the post P3 in 1983 would surprisingly on each occasion be filled by the NPN party, which had the highest number of votes in the constituency in each period of rule.

The point of note in all the above is that the voters cannot easily predict beforehand the political party from which their cultural agent(s) in government would come. So they would tend not to vote for individuals but rather for political parties' policies, thereby eliminating ethnic politics and embracing ideologies, giving rise to nationalistic political parties, which is one desirable thing our political systems presently lack.

(h) *It Eliminates Carpet Crossing:* In the existing majority rule systems, individuals rather than political parties are elected by the cultural constituencies, i.e. the generality of the people, directly into political office. This procedure tends to make political officeholders see political office as their personal property that they can carry from one political party to another with impunity and without sanction. An example is Nigeria's 4th Republic where many senators and some members of the House of Representatives flippantly "crossed carpet" from one political party to another without losing their seats in spite of some (weak) provisions in the constitution to the contrary. Moreover, many a deputy governor openly fraternized with or declared for an opposing political party while still purporting to remain in his/her position. So also with some state governors.

On the other hand, in the universal system of government, partisan legislative seats and offices and executive positions are first allocated to the political parties as to the cultural constituencies before merit elections are used to elect individuals to occupy the seats and posts. It can be seen from this arrangement that the partisan political post that a political officeholder occupies is not his/her personal property but belongs first and foremost to a particular political party, which can hire and fire who occupies it and so it cannot be taken by the individual occupier to another political party. He/she automatically loses the political post or legislative seat that he/she occupies once he resigns from his/her party or the party removes him/her from the post or seat or expels him/her from the party. Similarly, the holder of a non-partisan political post cannot carry it into a political party because it may be held by only non-partisan or "independent" candidates; so, once he/she becomes a political party member, he/she automatically loses the post. Thus the universal system removes carpet crossing and produces faithful and disciplined politicians.

(i) *It Encourages Career Politicians and not Mercenaries*: In the existing majority rule systems, the tenure in office of the individual political officeholders like the president or governor is often limited by the constitution to one or two terms. Constitutional limitation in the tenure of office of political officeholders is of course undemocratic because a politician should be free to hold any office for as many times as the people truly want and freely and fairly elect him/her into the office. However, the restriction is brought about by the shortcomings in the electoral systems that are used. Such procedures sometime have the adverse effects of making the politicians bloated up, seeing themselves as being unable to occupy lesser positions in future. Moreover, in the case of some executive officeholders like ministers, the tenure of office is uncertain because they can be removed from office at the whims and caprices of the Chief Executive who appoints them in the first instance. Therefore some of these political officeholders may see themselves as mercenaries that are in office to make as much money as they can make in the shortest possible time while their tenure lasts because they may never pass through that way again in life. Little wonder then that some of such political officeholders are usually neck deep in corruption in the existing majority rule systems.

On the contrary, the tenure of office of political officeholders in the universal system is certain for a period of rule, being subject only to good conduct, and so not at the whims and caprices of any other political officeholder nor of his/her political party. Furthermore, although it may not be possible for a political officeholder to succeed himself/herself in the same office as a political office is allocated to different alternative cultural constituencies at every period of rule and a person may not belong to two or more cultural constituencies, nevertheless a person (if elected) could be able to occupy another post that is allocated to his/her cultural constituency in any period of rule. And there may be one or more posts for a constituency in every branch of government in any period of rule. The available position may be lesser than the one previously held, but then a serious minded politician should be willing to occupy any position any time any day, be it lesser or greater than any one that he/she previously held. It should be remembered that former Israeli Prime Minister, Benjamin Nathan Yahu, later accepted to be Foreign Minister under Prime Minister Sharon in November 2002. Therefore, a good, serious and dedicated political officeholder needs not fear that he/she would be out of office in any period of rule, as there would always be another political office for him to hold. Thus the universal system, unlike the existing majority rule systems, has the in-built mechanism to encourage political officeholders to be good and dedicated career politicians rather than mercenary politicians, who would loot and vandalize the people's treasury, as we witness in many existing majority rule systems today.

It is noteworthy that United States of America's former Democrat President Bill Clinton has called for a change to American Constitution's 22nd Amendment, which prevents a person from being elected president more than twice. *The Guardian* of Nigeria (Friday, 31 May 2003, page 11) quoted him as saying: "I think since people are living much longer . . . the 22nd Amendment should probably be modified to say two consecutive terms instead of two terms for a lifetime." The Amendment was passed after Franklin D. Roosevelt was elected to a record fourth presidential term in office. Such constitutional provisions are not required in the Universal system and yet rulers would be unable to succeed themselves as it happened in the time of president Roosevelt and is still happening now in some other parts of the world, for example Togo, where President Nasingbe Eyadema has been elected for a further term in office after a continuous rule of thirty-six years.

(j) *The Order of Elections is Not Open to Manipulations:* In the existing majority rule systems of government, not only may there be several types of elections but the orders of the elections are open to unwholesome manipulations to achieve dubious victory, especially for the party in power. For example, Nigeria's Second Republic was a presidential system of government. There were the local government elections, the state assembly elections, the state gubernatorial elections, the Federal House of Representatives elections, the Senate elections, and the presidential elections - six types of elections on the whole. These exclude the party primary elections to select the various party candidates for each of the six types of elections. The 1979 elections followed the order listed above, but in the 1983 elections the order of the elections was reversed. The presidential election took place first, before the Senate and House of Representatives elections. The party in power claimed to win the elections with a landslide. It claimed that once the people knew which party would form the next central government, they decided to vote massively for that party in the subsequent elections. This phenomenon the party in power tagged the "band-wagon" effect. The other parties claimed otherwise. They alleged that reversing the order of elections was a ploy by the party in power to rig the elections in its favour and that the "band-wagon" claim was a ruse. A big unrest followed the 1983 elections, which eventually led to the military take-over of power barely three months later. Even in Nigeria's Fourth Republic, the order of elections is one of the things that has tended to tear the legislature and the executive apart. The legislature favoured all the elections to take place in one day, but the executive favoured staggered elections with the presidential election coming first. This made the president to withhold assent to the 2002 Electoral Bill, seeking an amendment to it by the legislature before his signature. The legislature at first purportedly overruled the president's veto by two-thirds majority of those legislators present and voting.

Eventually the compromise was reached to hold the six types of elections as follows: the Federal House of Representatives and Senate elections on 12 April 2003, the Presidential and Gubernatorial elections on 19 April 2003, the state assembly elections on 3 May 2003, and the local government elections (tentatively) on 21 June 2003. There were thirty political parties but only twenty fielded presidential candidates. As expected, the party in power won the first two elections on April 12 with a landslide, and the "band-wagon" effect followed thereafter. At the time of publication of this book, the local government elections were yet to hold but low voter turnout was reported in the elections of May, as the people were already getting tired of "too many" elections. The expenditure on the elections was colossal.

In contrast to the existing majority rule systems, the order of the elections in the universal system is fixed. There are only two types of election: a general representation election, termed in this book as the General Universal Representation Election (GURE), meant for the partisan and cultural representation of all the voters in each relevant arm and level of government; and the Merit Elections (ME) meant for the elections of the individual partisan and non-partisan (i.e. independent) political officeholders. The representation election comes before the merit elections and the two types of election may not take place on the same day. The representation election must precede the merit elections because the individual political offices must first be allocated to the political parties and/or to the cultural constituencies on the basis of the results of the representation election before the merit elections can be conducted to fill the political posts from the respective political parties and/or cultural constituencies to which they have been allocated. Thus the order of the elections in the universal system is fixed and not subject to unhealthy manipulations by unscrupulous politicians.

It should be noted that a single representation election is sufficient for all branches of government as well as for all the levels or tiers of government, since the results of the single General Universal Representation Election can be sorted to meet the requirements of the various branches and levels of government. Thus the universal system does not require separate representation elections for the Executive and the legislature nor for the federal, state (or canton), and local governments. A single representation election would serve all these purposes in the universal system. Therefore "band-wagon" effects would be non-existent and election finance very low.

(k) *It facilitates a peaceful change of government:* In the existing majority rule systems, a change of government often starts with party primary elections and some categories of people in government often have to resign their employment months before the change-over in order to be able to contest the elections, which are usually contests between individuals from different political parties and different cultural groups. The elections are therefore both representation and (purportedly) merit contests in one fell swoop without distinction. They are therefore often attended with all kinds of disorder and unrest of the highest degree.

On the other hand in the universal system, the representation election is separate from and comes before the merit elections. The representation election involves only cultural constituencies and political organizations, and so does not involve the election of individuals into political offices. Moreover, the election is used for the allocation of partisan and non-partisan political offices to the political parties and/or cultural constituencies. There is no elimination of any cultural group or political party but rather all of them are equitably accommodated. Therefore, the basis for tension is not there and hence peaceful election results. Moreover, the merit elections would not start until all the cultural groups and political parties have known the political posts that are allocated to them. Therefore, individuals do not have to give up their employment or resign their posts early in the changeover process, since they are not directly involved in the representation election. Moreover, for the merit elections they have a clear idea of the posts and offices at stake and are therefore in a better position to decide whether to contest and therefore resign their appointments or not. Also the period between the representation election and the merit elections can be made long enough to accommodate the resignation notice. Furthermore, political tension is removed or minimized, since the merit elections take place within political parties and within cultural constituencies rather than across the political parties and across the cultural constituencies.

(l) *The Principles are Constitutionally Enforceable:* All the principles and features of the universal system are constitutionally enforceable and so would be enshrined in the polity's constitution. They are also applicable to the national government as well as to the state (or canton) and local governments. They will therefore render unnecessary all the arbitrary and spurious zoning formulae and strategies that various political parties in power often develop on their own to share political offices among the cultural or geo-political groups of the people.

(m) *Progressive Transition from Majority Rule Systems is Possible:* The universal system of government described above does many things differently from the currently existing systems of government. However, perhaps because of the "inertia attached to current practice" or for any other reason, some countries might consider it to be too big a step to take in one fell swoop. For instance, "Old prejudices die hard. We have been doing this thing like this before and so we will continue to do it like that," is a common excuse for resisting desirable changes. Therefore, some countries might prefer a gradual or progressive approach for transition from the existing majority rule systems to the universal system.

The question then arises: can · the existing systems of government be gradually replaced by the features of the universal system in order to improve the existing systems: and perhaps come to the new eventually? The author believes that this is possible. A close study of the universal system will reveal that the system is more a proper reordering and resetting of existing political institutions than a total development of entirely new ones. The existing systems have many square pegs in round holes and many round pegs in square holes. By using the appropriate principles of Universal Democracy, many necessary pegs may be reordered and put in the right holes, in order to solve particular problems, independently of the other pegs that are still wrongly placed. Therefore the principles of universal system of government can be used to solve the problems of the existing systems of government progressively.

For example, if a polity operates the presidential system of government, the principle of Homogeneity of Candidates coupled with the principle of Free and Fair Elections will guarantee the best presidential election possible under the presidential system. The principle of Homogeneity of Candidates requires that there should be partisan and cultural homogeneity of the individual candidates for a partisan political office or only cultural homogeneity for a non-partisan political office. Although the office of the president is a partisan post, nevertheless the presidential system of government has a partisan single executive and so there cannot be partisan homogeneity among the candidates for the presidential election. Therefore, only cultural homogeneity of candidates is possible and consequently hundred per cent success cannot be guaranteed. For the cultural homogeneity of candidates, a general representation election is required to precede the presidential election.

Any of the legislative elections in the presidential system - either the Senate or House of Representatives election - can serve the purpose because they are adulterated representation elections. The post of the president and other desirable political posts will be allocated to the relevant alternative cultural constituencies among which the post(s) should be rotated over the years, based on the cumulative popular vote of the chosen representation election, as the universal system requires.

Then each of the contesting political parties will choose its candidate for the post of the president (and if required for the post of the vice-president) from the same cultural constituency(ies) to which the post(s) is/(are) allocated for the current period of rule. In this way all the candidates for the post of the president will be from the same cultural constituency and all the candidates for the post of the vice-president will also be from the same cultural constituency (but different from that for the president), and cultural homogeneity of the presidential candidates will thus be achieved. Provided that the constituencies are truly culturally homogeneous, voters would be able to vote for the presidential candidates purely on the basis of their policies and programmes, devoid of any cultural considerations. Not only does this procedure result in people voting for candidates' policies and programmes, the absence of cultural conflict would also greatly help to douse any tension caused by whatever election irregularities that may occur.

The elected candidate (with his/her vice, if any) would be able to serve for only a term at a time, as the posts of president and vice president would necessarily and equitably be allocated to other cultural constituencies at the next period of rule. In this way, presidential elections would be conducted as peacefully as possible with the presidential system of government. It is the author's considered opinion that the people of a country should consider free grouping and universal cultural representation in all branches or arms of government as the minimum requirements for their mutual inter-relationships.

The following are further examples. If a polity prefers to continue with the presidential system of government and so has a president (or state governor) instead of having an Executive Council at the top, the presidential system can be suitably modified to reap some of the benefits of the universal system. For example, the presidential election can serve also as the General Universal Representation Election (GURE) and so there would be no parliamentary/legislative elections. It should be noted that most of the tables in this book use the results of Nigeria's presidential elections. There would be partisan and cultural allocations of legislative seats and offices but no partisan allocation of the executive posts since only one political party will form the executive; but there would still be universal cultural allocation of the executive posts to enable the president (or governor) to continue to fill the posts equitably among the cultural constituencies forming the polity. The usual practice in the existing systems is for the president (or governor) to fill the posts arbitrarily or on the basis of an arbitrary zoning formula adopted by the party in power and which is not constitutionally enforceable. On the other hand, the universal system uses a formula that is not only well-established on the popular vote and so equitable but also nationalistic and so constitutionally enforceable. This solves the problem of cultural marginality that is very common in the existing majority rule systems and which is usually the basic cause of political turmoil in such systems, as already observed under the principle of Universal Representation of Voters. The president may then personally appoint the individual executive political officeholders from the appropriate cultural constituencies as the presidential system permits or if desired they may be selected by lot or party merit elections in accordance with the universal system.

If it is desired to retain the single member (SM) electoral system in electing the parliamentarians in accordance with the majority rule systems but zone the legislative political offices (not the seats) to the cultural constituencies in accordance with the principles of the universal system, then the parliamentary elections would be used as the General Universal Representation Election (GURE) and the political offices would be allocated to the cultural constituencies accordingly. However a note of warning must be sounded here that restrictions that some offices such as the speaker of the lower house or the president of the upper house should come from the majority party or party in power may not hold because the party in power may not have legislators from the cultural constituency to which such a political post is allocated, unless the allocation would be restricted to the cultural constituencies where the party in power has legislators, which of course is undemocratic.

If it is desired to solve the problem of legislators carpet crossing from one political party to another without sanction, or to prevent the use of independent candidates for legislative seats and offices, which are partisan posts, then legislators may not be elected directly by the cultural constituencies using the SM electoral system but rather the legislative seats must first be allocated to the political parties as to the cultural constituencies before the individual legislators are selected by lot or party merit elections as required by the universal system.

Moreover, if it is desired to ensure a responsible executive, check the "second-term" or perpetual self-succession bids of presidents, governors and local government chairmen and thereby create career politicians rather than the mercenary political officeholders that the existing majority rule systems tend to produce, then the executive positions, like the legislative positions, must first be allocated to the political parties as to the cultural constituencies before lot or merit elections are used to select individuals to occupy the posts. In this way it may not be possible for a person to succeed himself/herself in the same office as that office will most likely be allocated to different cultural constituencies at every period of rule and a person may not belong to two or more cultural constituencies. However, a person could be able, if elected, to occupy another post that is allocated to his/her cultural constituency in the current period of rule. Thus there is no need for a constitutional but undemocratic provision to limit the number of terms a person can hold a particular political office, as self succession in any office is hardly possible in the Universal system.

Finally, if a country wants the Universal system of government but prefers a partisan executive with it in the meantime, then that half-way house can be used. The only modification required to the description of the system given above is that the positions on the Executive Council are not allocated to the political associations that take part in the General Universal Representation Election (GURE) since only one party will form the Executive. Rather, the political party that wins the largest number of votes in the election is asked to form the Executive Council, that is to say that all the Executive Council positions are allocated en masse to the political party with the highest number of votes, irrespective of whether the number of votes is up to half of the total number of votes cast at the election or not.

The Executive Council positions are then filled by lot or Party Merit Elections as earlier described under the system, if a partisan plural (rather than single) executive is desired. However, if a weak partisan plural executive (like that of Britain) or a partisan single executive (like that of the United States of America) is desired, then only the Prime Minister (as in Britain) or the President with or without his/her vice (as in the U.S.A.) will be selected by lot or party merit elections in accordance with the universal system and the Prime Minister or the President will then appoint his/her ministers as the parliamentary or presidential system allows, but from the respective cultural constituencies to which the offices have been allocated. As earlier pointed out, it must be added, however, that it is undemocratic for a Prime Minister or President to make political appointments as this is in contravention of the principle of Non-Transferability of Delegated Mandates.

EPILOGUE

Former American President, Abraham Lincoln, defined political democracy as "government of the people, by the people, for the people". The *Concise Oxford Dictionary* (1982 edition) also defines political democracy as "government by all the people, direct or representative". The main problem with (representative) political democracy today is how to define or obtain a model or representation of all the people that is realistic enough to truly be the "government of all the people, by all the people, for all the people". This book has attempted the solution of this problem.

The kernel of the book is that all free citizens who are entitled and care to vote at a general (universal representation) election are entitled to universal and equitable cultural/ethnic/geographical representation, and hence to universal cultural/ethnic/geographical representative participation, in every arm or branch of the government of the country/polity. In addition, they are entitled to universal and equitable partisan representation, and hence universal and equitable partisan representative participation, in every relevant arm or branch of government. Moreover, the devices of the initiative, recall and referendum, wisely applied, are needed to safeguard the people's sovereignty and ensure their fundamental human rights. The winner-takes-all representation system, whereby the so-called majority voters get represented and the so-called minority voters are denied representative participation in government, is inconsistent with representative political democracy and so undemocratic and should be abandoned forthwith. It cannot truly pass for the government of all the people, by all the people, for all the people. It is the main cause of the turmoil in many countries of the world today.

The book discusses the democratic concepts, principles, structures and institutions to make the universal and equitable partisan and/or cultural representative participation in every arm of government possible for all voters. The author urges countries/

247

polities of the world, including his own beloved country, Nigeria, to embrace the democratic measures by making appropriate changes to their constitutions without delay, in order to usher in the new era of peaceful and cooperative living within and among the nations of the world that the book is destined to bring. Amen.

APPENDIX 1
Nigeria's 1979 Presidential Election Results

States	VOTES CAST		VOTES CAST FOR POLITICAL PARTIES				
	Number	Proportion of all	GNPP	NPN	NPP	PRP	UPN
ANAMBRA	1,209,038	0.071767338	20,228	163,164	1,002,083	14,500	9,063
BAUCHI	998,683	0.059280866	154,218	623,989	47,314	143,202	29,960
BENDEL	669,511	0.039741532	8,242	242,320	57,629	4,939	356,381
BENUE	538,879	0.031987341	42,993	411,648	63,097	7,277	13,864
BORNO	710,968	0.04220238	384,278	246,778	9,642	46,385	23,885
CROSS RIVER	661,103	0.039242441	100,105	425,815	50,671	6,737	77,775
GONGOLA	639,138	0.03793862	217,914	227,057	27,856	27,750	138,561
IMO	1,153,355	0.068462048	34,616	101,516	999,636	10,252	7,335
KADUNA	1,382,712	0.08207646	190,936	596,302	65,321	437,771	92,382
KANO	1,220,763	0.072463322	18,482	243,423	11,082	932,803	14,973
KWARA	354,605	0.021049013	20,251	190,142	1,830	2,376	140,006
LAGOS	828,414	0.049173862	3,943	59,515	79,320	3,874	681,762
NIGER	383,347	0.027755111	63,273	287,072	45,292	14,555	14,155
OGUN	744,668	0.044202779	3,974	46,358	2,343	2,338	689,655
ONDO	1,369,849	0.081312925	3,561	57,361	11,752	2,509	1,294,666
OYO	1,396,547	0.082897692	8,029	177,999	7,732	4,804	1,197,983
PLATEAU	548,405	0.032552796	37,400	190,458	269,666	21,852	29,029
RIVERS	687,951	0.04086112	15,025	499,840	98,754	3,312	71,114
SOKOTO	1,348,697	0.080057362	409,424	859,119	12,504	32,798	34,852
ALL	16,846,633	1	1,686,489	5,688,857	2,822,523	1,732,113	4,916,651
Percentage (%)		100	10.0108	33.7685	16.7542	10.2817	29.1848

APPENDIX 2
Nigeria's 1983 Presidential Election Results

STATES	VOTES CAST		VOTES CAST FOR POLITICAL PARTIES					
	Number	Proportion of all	GNPP	NAP	NPN	NPP	PRP	UPN
ANAMBRA	1,538,283	0.0455241	36,165	27,511	385,297	669,348	16,103	23,859
BAUCHI	1,782,122	0.0700429	37,203	18,979	1,507,144	65,258	54,564	98,974
BENDEL	1,099,851	0.0432275	11,723	8,653	452,776	53,306	7,358	566,035
BENUE	652,795	0.0256568	19,897	10,573	384,045	152,209	6,381	79,690
BORNO	718,043	0.0282213	179,265	15,698	348,974	26,972	26,996	120,138
CROSS RIVER	1,285,710	0.0505324	16,582	10,967	696,592	46,418	8,229	506,922
GONGOLA	723,956	0.0284537	28,407	12,985	316,643	170,535	12,891	182,495
IMO	1,588,975	0.0624516	52,364	32,694	398,463	1,064,436	18,370	22,648
KADUNA	2,137,398	0.0840064	80,862	37,369	1,266,894	225,919	300,476	225,878
KANO	1,193,050	0.0468905	35,252	14,207	383,998	274,102	436,997	48,494
KWARA	608,422	0.0239128	7,670	6,056	299,654	16,215	3,693	275,134
LAGOS	1,640,381	0.064472	11,748	8,636	126,165	119,455	6,570	1,367,807
NIGER	430,731	0.016929	12,984	8,182	272,086	112,971	8,736	15,772
OGUN	1,261,061	0.0499636	6,874	2,862	43,821	5,022	4,449	1,198,033
ONDO	1,828,343	0.0718595	11,629	10,566	366,217	20,340	7,052	1,412,539
OYO	2,351,000	0.0924016	15,732	9,891	885,125	34,852	9,174	1,396,226
PLATEAU	652,302	0.0256375	18,612	10,490	292,606	280,803	11,581	38,210
RIVERS	1,357,715	0.0533624	12,981	15,061	921,664	151,558	4,626	251,825
SOKOTO	2,837,786	0.1115338	46,752	22,152	2,605,935	63,238	24,280	75,428
ABUJA	135,351	0.0053197	1,103	977	127,372	4,156	641	1,102
ALL	25,443,275	1	643,805	284,509	12,081,471	3,557,114	969,167	7,907,209
Percentage (%)		100	2.5034	1.1182	47.4839	13.9806	3.8091	31.0778

NOTE: The author was not unaware of allegations against the incumbent party in power (NPN) of widespread rigging of the 1983 elections, culminating in the military take-over of power. The author considers that even extreme cases are good examples for the system under consideration.

REFERENCES

1. ANON, *The Times of London*, (1970), 17 August, London.
2. ANON, French Revolutionaries (1767), *Declaration of the Rights of a Man*.
3. ANON, *Daily Times of Nigeria*, (1992), Wednesday 2, December, p.5.
4. ANON, Macmillan Students' Encyclopedia of Sociology.
5. APPADORAI A. (1975), *The Substance of Politics*, Eleventh Edition, Madras: Oxford University Press, p. 583.
6. ARISTOTLE: *The Politics*, London: Penquin Books. 1981 Edition and Translation.
7. BERNARD, M.C. (1865), *An Introduction to the Study of Experimental Medicine*, English Translation (1949), Paris: Henry Schuman, Inc.
8. BLACKSTONE, R. *(1949)*, *Virginia Woolf*, London: Hogarth.
9. BODIN, JEAN: Sovereignty.
10. BROOKS, HARVEY: *The Government and Politics of Switzerland*.
11. BRYCES, J. *Modern Democracy*, Vol. F, Chap. xxxii to xxxvii
12. BURKE, EDMUND (1779), Speech to the Electors of Bristol on 3 November 1774. *The Works of Edmund Burke*, Vol. II, 'The World's Classics', pp. 159-66.
13. CROWDER, MICHAEL, *The Story of Nigeria*, Faber and Faber, London, 1978 Edition.
14. DAVIES, J.T. (1973), *The Scientific Approach*, 2nd Edition, London: Academic Press Inc. (London) Ltd. p. 185.
15. DUVERGER, MOURICE (1954), *Political Parties*, New York: John Wiley and Sons Inc.
16. FREEMAN, E.A. (1873), *Comparative Politics*, Lecture II. Macmillan.
17. GARNER, J.W. (1932), *Political Science and Government*, Chap. xix, America: American Book Company, p. 677.
18. GETTELL, R.C. (1933), Political Science, Chapt. X Ginn.
19. GRANT, A.J., *Greece in Age of Pericles*
20. HAMILTON, A., JAY J.J. AND MADISON, J., *The Federalist*, Dent. Everyman Library.
21. HARRIS, PETER (1986), *Foundation of Political Science*, Second Edition, London: Hutchinson & Co. (Publishers) Ltd., pp. 246-247.
22. JACOBSEN, G.A. AND LIPMAN, M.H., *Political Science,* Second Edition, New York, London: Barnes & Noble Books.
23. JENNINGS, W. IVOR (1951), *Cabinet Government*, Second Edition, Cambridge, p. 217.

24. KURFI, AMADU (1983), *The Nigerian General Elections 1958 and 1979 and Aftermath,* Lagos: Macmillan Nigerian Publishers Ltd.

25. LASKI, H.J. (1967), *A Grammar of Politics,* Fifth Edition, p. 27, London: George.

26. MONTESQUIEU, C.L., *The Spirit of Laws,* Second Edition, Hafher.

27. New Age Encyclopaedia (1981), Lexicon Publications, Inc., Vol. 5.

28. NNOLI OKWUDIBA, (1986), *Introduction to Politics,* Nigeria: Longman (Nig.) PLC., p. 234

29. NWAKWO, U. (1988), *Strategy for Political Stability,* Lagos: Oliver Ibekwe & Associates Ltd.

30. ODUMEGWU-OJUKWU, EMEKA (1989), *Because I am Involved,* Ibadan - Spectrum Books Ltd.

31. OKADIGBO, CHUBA (1987), *Power and Leadership in Nigeria,* Nigeria: Fourth Dimension Publishing Co. Ltd., p.1.

32. *Oxford Advanced Learner's Dictionary of Current English,* 1974- Edition.

33. POPPER KARL R. (1945), *The Open Society and its Enemies, Vol. 2, First Edition (Fourth Edition, 1962) London: George Routledge.*

34. POPPER, KARL R. (1963), *Conjectures and Refutations,* London: Routledge and Kegan Paul.

35. POTTER, ALLEN M; FORTHERINGHAM, P; KELLAS, J.G. (1981), *American Government and Politics,* Third Edition, Faber and Faber Limited, London.

36. RODEE, C.C. ANDERSON, T.J. CHRISTOL, C.Q. GREEN, T.H. (1983), Introduction to Political Science, International Student Edition p. 559.

37. SCHUMPETER (1950), *Capitalism, Socialism and Democracy,* New York: Harpers Row.

38. SHEHU, MUSA, *Social Cohesion and National Integration, Daily Times* of Nigeria, April 23 1983, Nigeria, p. 12.

39. SYKES, J.B. (1982), *The Concise Oxford Dictionary of Current English,* Oxford University.

40. THE BIBLE SOCIETY, *Good News Bible,* Collins, 1976 Edition.

41. THE HOLY BIBLE, King James Version.

INDEX

www.ingramcontent.com/pod-product-compliance
Lightning Source LLC
Chambersburg PA
CBHW061005280326
41935CB00009B/847